QUANTUM LEARNING

& INSTRUCTIONAL LEADERSHIP

in Practice

Dedicated to

Olivia Le Tellier,
My companion for time and eternity, and
Yvonne Signe Randall Le Tellier,
My mom and good friend.

Quantum Learning

& Instructional Leadership

in Practice

John Parks Le Tellier

CORWIN PRESS
A SAGE Publications Company
Thousand Oaks, CA 91320

For information:

Corwin Press
A Sage Publications Company
2455 Teller Road
Thousand Oaks, California 91320
www.corwinpress.com

Sage Publications Ltd.
1 Oliver's Yard
55 City Road
London EC1Y 1SP
United Kingdom

Sage Publications India Pvt. Ltd.
B-42, Panchsheel Enclave
Post Box 4109
New Delhi 110 017 India

Printed in the United States of America

Library of Congress Cataloging-in-Publication Data

Le Tellier, John Parks.
Quantum learning & instructional leadership in practice / John Parks Le Tellier.
    p. cm.
Other title: Quantum learning and instructional leadership in practice
Includes bibliographical references and index.
ISBN 1-4129-3989-5 or 978-1-412939-89-8 (cloth)
ISBN 1-4129-3990-9 or 978-1-412939-90-4 (pbk.)
    1. Learning. 2. Teaching. 3. Educational leadership. I. Title.
II. Title: Quantum learning and instructional leadership in practice.
LB1060.L3829 2007
371.102—dc22

                                                    2006014233

This book is printed on acid-free paper.

06 07 08 09 10 9 8 7 6 5 4 3 2 1

Acquisitions Editor:	Elizabeth Brenkus
Editorial Assistant:	Desirée Enayati
Production Editor:	Denise Santoyo
Copy Editor:	Karen Taylor
Typesetter:	C&M Digitals (P) Ltd.
Indexer:	Jean Casalegno
Cover Designer:	Monique Hahn

Contents

Preface

The development of this extensive repertoire of teacher and leadership strategies has an unusual and interesting history. Bobbi DePorter, one of the founders and president of a company called Quantum Learning Network, set in motion a sequence of events more than twenty years ago that has had a profound impact on thousands of teachers and students around the world. My own experience is closely linked to these events and this history, and it has helped prepare me to recognize the power of this curriculum to maximize the potential of classroom teachers and school administrators. We discovered a recipe for improving performance in the educational organization, a recipe that blends effective classroom practice with motivation and leadership.

In 1978, a psychiatrist from Bulgaria named Dr. Georgi Lozanov gave a lecture in Europe relating his research about what we now call accelerating learning. Dr. Lozanov's conclusions were astounding and set in motion events that changed many of our basic beliefs about effective teaching methodology.

Dr. Lozanov demonstrated that he could accelerate a student's ability to learn and retain information. When he presented his findings at the conference in Europe, he shocked many of his listeners with the results from his research with students. Following the conference, the Soviet-backed Bulgarian government took special interest in his work and immediately placed Dr. Lozanov under house arrest to prevent him from sharing his research. Dr. Georgi Lozanov remained under house arrest for more than a decade. He continued his research, but the sharing of his results was carefully controlled and monitored by the Bulgarian government.

It was shortly after Dr. Lozanov gave his lecture in Europe that Bobbi DePorter became aware of his work. Bobbi had already founded a school called the Burklyn Business School. It was an innovative program, and Bobbi was interested in learning strategies that would help students at the school. She wanted to know if it was possible to accelerate the encoding of long-term memory. She established contact with Dr. Lozanov and invited him to come to the United States for a vacation.

Surprisingly, the Bulgarian government allowed Dr. Lozanov to make the visit. They impounded his research, held his family, and tattooed a symbol on his right hand near his thumb, so he could be easily identified. They sent a bodyguard to accompany him and ensure his return.

Dr. Lozanov stayed for three weeks in Bobbi DePorter's home. During this visit, Dr. Lozanov worked with a group of volunteer students to demonstrate what he had learned. Dr. Lazanov introduced the students to a language they had never experienced and demonstrated how they could accelerate their learning.

Following his visit, Dr. Lozanov returned to Bulgaria and continued his research and his communication with Bobbi DePorter. He wanted to escape from Bulgaria with his family. Bobbi and several other individuals raised money to help him escape, and he and his family were finally able to do so. They moved around Europe for a time, secretly going from location to location. Money was funneled to them through a contact in Europe, and their whereabouts were kept hidden. Dr. Lozanov and his family eventually settled in Austria.

Two years after the visit, Bobbi and others interested in Lozanov's work developed the first SuperCamp. The original SuperCamps were academic, motivational, and life skills programs for high school students, but they were later expanded to include programs for elementary, middle school, and college students. They are rigorous ten-day programs designed to teach learning and life skills and build learner confidence.

SuperCamp program locations have included Stanford University, Wake Forest, University of Wisconsin, Claremont College, Colorado College, and Hampshire College, as well as England, Singapore, Hong Kong, Malaysia, Switzerland, Australia, Mexico, China, and Taiwan. Over 40,000 students have graduated from the programs. Follow-up studies of the effects of the program on these students have revealed some impressive results.

The SuperCamp programs have been like a learning laboratory that have been ongoing for more than twenty years. It has been a constant search for "what works." As the programs matured, it became apparent that many of its aspects would be effective for classroom teachers and school leaders. Many powerful Teaching strategies have been identified, and, as a result, the Quantum Learning for Teachers Training and the Quantum Learning and Leadership Program for School Administrators were developed.

ABOUT TERMINOLOGY USED IN THIS BOOK

We refer to many of the strategies identified over the years as "moves." The word "move" is used to indicate a specific action taken by a teacher or school leader. Moves are not theories; they are actions. Examples include changing instructional position, using anchor music, creating an empowered classroom climate, reinforcing content, and increasing as well as sustaining motivation in school organizations. Teacher moves are the concrete actions used by teachers to educate students. Leadership moves are actions used by teachers and school administrators to upgrade performance and motivation in the classroom or school organization.

WHO SHOULD READ THIS BOOK

The book is valuable for teachers in all teaching arenas including elementary, middle school, high school, college, and graduate–level programs. Teachers will find a rich repertoire of effective strategies that can be easily implemented to improve teaching effectiveness. They will also discover powerful ideas and strategies for improving motivation in students and for strengthening character. They will discover how to implement and support leadership in the classroom. Perhaps, most important, teachers will experience renewed energy and passion for their profession, and will experience an increase in their own motivation.

The book is also written for school principals and other educational administrators who work directly with teachers in the role of an educational leader. They will discover a powerful new way to view leadership, and the book will serve as a valuable resource of specific actions designed to upgrade the effectiveness of the educational organization. Specific strategies for improving sustainable motivation and energy throughout the organization will be discovered in every chapter. The book will serve as a handbook for teacher improvement strategies that can enhance the effectiveness of any professional educator. It will also serve as a valuable resource for those who work directly with parents.

Both the teacher and the principal will learn the important new breakthroughs in neuroscience and cognitive science that are directly related to effective learning methodology. They will learn the science behind accelerating the encoding of memory in the human brain and will gain important brain-based insights that explain the foundation of many of the teacher and leadership moves presented in the book. This material can also act as a guide by showing what students should know about how their brain works and how they can increase learning capacity by using good brain-based strategy.

HOW THIS BOOK IS ORGANIZED

The book is organized into six chapters. Chapter 1 sets the stage for the other five chapters and develops a working definition of leadership. The topic of leadership throughout the organization is explored, and the theme of durable motivation is introduced. Durable motivation is a term used in the book to indicate motivation that is sustainable over long periods. The remaining five chapters focus on four educational connections. Those include the context connection, the cognitive connection, the character connection, and the classroom connection.

Chapter 2 introduces the theme of context with a primary focus on context for the professional educator. Systems thinking, the definitions for the main event of education, and specific strategies for staying resourceful are presented.

Chapter 3 covers the cognitive connection by updating the teacher and principal on important brain discoveries that are directly related to teaching and leadership. This information is an essential part of the book because it provides the background for understanding the science behind the teacher and leadership moves included in the chapters that follow. The material in Chapter 3 is referenced throughout the remainder of the book.

Chapter 4 is a return to the context connection, but this time with a focus on creating an empowering context for students. Specific moves for establishing an effective classroom climate are explored. This chapter includes effective strategies such as creating a focus on effort, the use of inclusive language, the effective use of music in the classroom, establishing equal-value relationships, and creating a classroom or school "home court advantage."

Chapter 5 covers the character connection with an introduction to the concepts of cognitive anchors and the importance and power of overarching principles. The chapter is a treasure trove of stories and examples that can be used with students. The material is organized around the "gold coin of respect" and the "four gems of excellence," which include integrity, ownership, positive mental attitude, and perseverance. The chapter also contains a positive self-coaching script for students.

Chapter 6 provides an extensive coverage of effective classroom strategy as the classroom connection unfolds. A powerful strategy for the brain-based presentation of content, called the "connected quartet," is explored. An effective protocol for reinforcement is presented with many effective teacher moves. The ALERT model for helping students focus their working memories is developed and is followed by an extensive list of effective state management teacher moves. The chapter is followed by a resource section with diagrams of the brain; a brain preferences survey to measure style, modality, and brain dominance; and a powerful tool and strategy for teaching effective expository reading methodology to students.

Chapters 2 through 6 each contain a section titled "Catalogue of Educational Moves." The purpose of this catalog is threefold. First, it will function as a valuable tool to help the reader identify the specific teacher and leadership moves presented in the chapter and will also function as a review of the chapter content. These catalogs will serve as a valuable resource in the future for identifying moves for implementation into classroom practice and enhancing leadership.

Chapters 2 through 6 also each include a section called "Leadership Notes." The purpose of these sections is to advise the reader about how specific moves can be used as leadership initiatives. These sections are for the teacher and the principal, and they create an important focus on leadership and motivation, allowing the reader to better assess the potential of certain moves as leadership initiatives.

Acknowledgments

I express thanks to Bobbi DePorter, Joe Chapon, Jenny Severson, Sue Pepe, Carol Fetzer, Joanna Hibbard, and Jenny Gomez for their support and encouragement. I also extend special thanks to Steve Miller, Steve Hall, Sharon Rybak, and Pete Carter, who read portions of the manuscript and gave me valuable feedback. I express gratitude to my editors at Corwin Press, with special thanks to Elizabeth Brenkus who first recognized the potential of this project and gave me valuable encouragement. I also express thanks to my brilliant and patient copy editor, Karen Taylor.

Corwin Press gratefully acknowledges the contributions of the following individuals:

William Fitzhugh, Fifth Grade Teacher
Reisterstown Elementary School, Reisterstown, MD

Jane B. Huffman, Associate Professor
Educational Administration, University of North Texas, Denton, TX

Steve Hutton, Educational Consultant
Villa Hills, KY

Kenneth Killian, Assistant Professor
School of Education, Vanguard University of Southern California, Costa
   Mesa, CA

Johnnie Roebuck, Coordinator and Professor
Problems for Educational Leadership, Henderson State University,
   Arkadelphia, AR

Richard Yee, Principal
Oster Elementary School, San Jose, CA

Ted A. Zigler, Assistant Professor
Educational Leadership Program, University of Cincinnati, OH

About the Author

John Le Tellier is an international trainer and educational consultant helping teachers, school administrators, and parents understand the process of learning and the recipe for enriched learning environments. He has helped thousands of educators and parents understand the fascinating connections between learning and the brain, giving them insights into specific strategies that can be used to enhance and accelerate the encoding of long-term memory. Le Tellier has trained educators in over 250 schools in the United States and at numerous international locations. He is a frequent presenter at national and state educational conferences speaking on educational methodology and leadership.

Le Tellier was the founder and former director of the Colorado Neuro-Learning Center in Denver, Colorado, where he worked with students who had sustained brain injuries. Through this work, he made discoveries that enhanced his extensive knowledge in motivational psychology and neuroscience. He is also a former principal and teacher, and he has spent hundreds of hours in private practice as a counselor working with students and their parents to enhance academic performance.

He resides in Idaho Springs, Colorado.

1

Leadership and Motivation

The purpose of this chapter is to establish the important foundational principles and definitions used as a basis for the discussions that follow in other chapters. We begin by examining a definition of leadership, and then create distinctions between leadership and administration. We then examine the concept of leadership throughout the organization and discover important principles related to durable motivation, which is motivation that can be sustained over time.

LEADERSHIP

Let's define leadership as actions that result in the improvement of organizations through positive modeling, positive motivation, and the implementation of specific initiatives. This definition is applied to both the school organization and the classroom organization.

The school organization has a principal or headmaster as its primary leader, and a classroom organization has a teacher as its primary leader. A leader is someone who models, motivates, and initiates acts of leadership. The leader leads. The leader pulls the organization to higher ground. This is different from pushing. Pushing can also motivate, but it is based on the avoidance of negative consequences.

For example, suppose a school has a strict policy about teachers being on time to work. Records are carefully kept, and, if a teacher is late three times or more, pay is docked for each subsequent late day. A teacher may be motivated to be on time to avoid this consequence, and, in this circumstance, we could say that the consequence pushes the teacher to be on time. This is not leadership, however, and this is not what is meant by "positive motivation" in our definition. Let's examine this issue.

Pushing has an important place in the success of an organization. The purpose here is not to minimize the importance of establishing consequences for guiding behavior in the educational setting, but to simply define leadership as something different and show that greater strength in leadership will diminish the need for dependency on the avoidance of negative consequences and will bring new energy and vitality to the organization.

Thinking about the difference between influence and control might be helpful. Leadership is about having a positive influence on the individual members of the organization. Pushing has more to do with control. The leader thinks more in terms of having *influence with* the members of the organization instead of having *control over* the members of the organization. This positive influence is what is meant by the term positive motivation.

Educational leadership is different from other kinds of leadership. It is complex, and many of the "acts of leadership" necessary for effectiveness are unique to the educational arena. Our focus on leadership is not about the "traits model" of leadership or the "leaders are born" philosophy. Effective leadership can be learned (Lambert, 1998). Effective leadership does require strong character and competency, but the effective leader must also initiate effective leadership moves. Once implemented, these moves become known as "acts of leadership." We will explore powerful leadership moves or acts of leadership as well as the extensive repertoire of effective teacher moves related to establishing durable motivation throughout the educational organization.

Administration and Leadership

It is helpful to make a distinction between administration and leadership, whether at the school level or in the classroom. Being a good administrator is a valuable asset to an educational leader. A good administrator or manager is effective at keeping the systems that operate in an educational organization working efficiently. Good administrators keep things running smoothly. They pay attention to the details of the operation. They keep communication lines wide open and anticipate and solve problems.

A school principal or teacher can be an excellent administrator and not be a strong leader. The school or classroom may operate very efficiently. An educational leader, on the other hand, moves the entire organization or classroom to higher ground. These leaders motivate and energize individuals in the organization or classroom to higher levels of performance. They improve the quality of life. Indeed, they make the organization or classroom come alive.

Leadership has some important dependency on good administration. Usually, good administration is essential for educational leadership to flourish. The more effective the administration, the better positioned the principal or teacher is to take the role of an educational leader. If the administrative systems are not running smoothly, the principal or teacher will have little time to devote to effective school leadership.

There are many strong school leaders who are not naturally good at administration. In fact, this is not uncommon. Some have difficulty focusing on the details of administration. Many principals who find themselves in this situation are wise enough, however, to recognize the importance of good school administration and have compensated for their own weakness by assembling a strong administrative team. These principals hold in high esteem a good school secretary and other support staff. They take extra precautions to make sure communication flows well by meeting with their team regularly. Once the administrative systems are working effectively, they focus more attention on acts of leadership without minimizing the importance of administration.

At the school level, these administrators work hard on the art of delegation. Those principals who did not compensate for their lack of administrative ability are still plagued with administrative challenges and have not had an opportunity to develop their leadership potential.

A similar situation exists in the classroom. A teacher must continually examine and upgrade the administrative system that is operative in the classroom. When this system is working well, it positions the teacher to be more effective with leadership.

The Ladder of Leadership

An analogy might be helpful for viewing the relationship between administration and leadership. Imagine a large platform that can be raised 10 feet above ground level or lowered 10 feet below ground level. Let this platform represent levels of effective administration. Imagine that the higher the platform, the more effective the administration in the school organization or the classroom. The lower the platform, the less effective the level of administration.

Picture a 10-foot ladder being safely secured to the platform. This ladder represents higher and higher levels of leadership. Now put the educational leader on the platform. If the platform is at or below ground level, the leader may climb the ladder of leadership, but the efforts may not be effective or even noticed because the level of effective administration is low. Raising the level or platform of effective administration enables the school leader to climb to greater heights with leadership.

Figure 1.1   The Ladder of Leadership Rests on the Platform of Administration

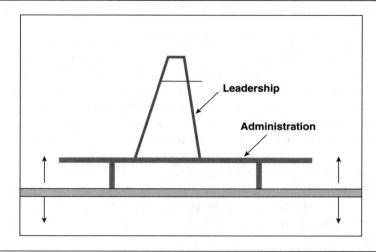

A school leader who climbs this ladder takes the entire organization along. Effective administration is not dependent on strong leadership, but effective leadership has some dependency on good administration. Some leaders have 20-foot ladders! They command a great repertoire of effective leadership moves.

We will use the term "school leader" to describe an administrator acting as a leader and the term "classroom leader" to describe the teacher who acts as a leader. The term "educational leader" will be used as a general term including both groups.

Classroom Acts of Leadership

To determine whether a particular move is a teacher move or an act of leadership, we need to examine how the move is used and implemented. For example, if a teacher introduces a character concept to students, models it, motivates students to use it, and reinforces it so that it becomes an important initiative in the classroom, we would classify this as an act of leadership.

On the other hand, a teacher might use a certain communication technique to enhance student learning. If it works well and is successful, we would call this an effective teacher move rather than an act of leadership. This move is a strategy that a teacher uses to improve teaching. If we were observing, we might say, "That was an effective teacher move." We might share it with other teachers as a move they may want to add to their own repertoire to enhance their effectiveness.

Suppose this teacher starts thinking about this communication strategy and decides it would be valuable for students. The teacher explains the strategy to students and has them practice the skill. The teacher continues to reinforce this communication strategy and motivates students by modeling and coaching. Students are motivated to use this strategy on a regular basis. This teacher has enhanced the communication ability of students, and this strategy has become a classroom initiative. Now, the teacher has changed classroom communication by modeling the strategy and getting students motivated to follow the teacher's example. This teacher is a classroom leader, and this classroom initiative is an act of leadership. It has shifted beyond "teacher move" to the arena of leadership.

Perhaps we walk into a different classroom and discover a teacher engaging in an opening tradition with students. This teacher has students focused and ready to learn in less than one minute. We continue to observe a number of strategies that maintain student focus. We conclude that this teacher employs some very effective teacher moves that maximize student attention.

Later, we observe this same teacher in a discussion with a student about something that occurred at recess. This educator is very respectful to the student and reflects back what the student is communicating. To our surprise, we observe the student engaging in the same behavior. Later, we observe two other students settling a dispute and witness similar behavior. Upon inquiry, we learn that this teacher has been modeling and teaching a particular listening strategy with students. The teacher has successfully motivated students to use this move. This teacher is engaged in classroom leadership and the implementation of this move is an act of leadership: an *action that results in the improvement of the organization through positive modeling, positive motivation, and the implementation of a specific initiative.*

In another classroom, we are immediately taken by the enthusiasm and excitement of the teacher. There is a great sense of joy and wonder about learning. The climate is positive and upbeat. We notice that the teacher's positive mental attitude and excitement has encouraged the students to high levels of motivation and attention. Are we witnessing teacher moves or acts of leadership?

We are probably seeing both. Certainly enthusiasm, excitement, and a positive mental attitude are powerful teacher moves. They are moves that teachers can learn to employ on a regular basis to enhance learning. These moves can easily slip into the arena of leadership. If, by modeling these behaviors and encouraging students to have a positive mental attitude, a teacher motivates students to begin to change their own behavior, then this teacher has stood before them as an effective leader. Because modeling is so powerful, it can become an initiative for students to imitate just by the fact they are experiencing it.

A teacher's influence as a leader will be greatly enhanced if this teacher has rapport with students and a relationship based on respect. The teacher will be positioned to empower students, and modeling will be an effective classroom initiative as students are motivated to follow the teacher's example.

Schoolwide Initiatives

Let's consider another possibility. What if a teacher is using a strategy as an effective teacher move, but does not introduce it to her students. In an observation, the principal notices this move and asks the teacher about the strategy. The principal is impressed by the effectiveness of this particular move and feels it would be advantageous for the entire staff. At a faculty meeting, the principal and teacher share the strategy and model it. The principal sets in motion the necessary steps to motivate staff to make this a schoolwide initiative. The move is modeled and reinforced. It may even be advanced to the student and parent arenas. It eventually becomes part of the culture of this particular school. The strategy has shifted from "teacher move" to the arena of school leadership. It is part of the culture because of an act of leadership by the principal.

Perhaps we notice that students at every grade in a particular high school are using an effective expository reading strategy. All teachers, students, and parents know this strategy, and it is consistently employed. We immediately recognize this as a schoolwide initiative and can be sure that it is in place due to an act of leadership at the school level.

Positive Modeling

From our definition, we can see that an educational leader functions as a model for others to follow. This is true of the classroom leader and the school leader. According to *Webster's*, "a model is a standard of excellence to be imitated." Being this model of excellence is one of the essential roles for an educational leader, and it requires that the leader establish a good reputation. In other words, the leader must be viewed as having strong character and as being competent. Acts of leadership build the leader's reputation regarding competency and strength of character, and modeling has a direct link to motivation.

MOTIVATION AND SELF-DISCIPLINE

Motivation, as can be seen from our definition, is a critical ingredient for leadership. Motivation works in an inverse relationship with self-discipline. Consider the following definition for self-discipline: *Self-discipline is doing what needs to be done, when it needs to be done, when you don't want to do it.*

When we are motivated to do something, we do not have to call on self-discipline to get it done. Self-discipline is not needed if we want to do something. But when motivation is low, then we must rely on our self-discipline to accomplish the task. Many of our students do not have high levels of self-discipline. Developing self-discipline can take a long time for many students. Stated simply, when motivation is high, self-discipline can be low; when motivation is low, self-discipline must be high. This inverse relationship between motivation and self-discipline (and the fact that students are generally just beginning to develop self-discipline) makes moves that result in higher levels of motivation especially important in education.

Self-discipline and motivation are necessary for success in life. None of us could have become educators without both operating. We work all our lives to develop higher levels of self-discipline. Life is much more enjoyable and our contributions often greater when we are able to use motivation instead of self-discipline. The educational leader is always aware of this important dynamic and employs motivation to upgrade the efficiency of the school or classroom organization.

DURABLE MOTIVATION

Leadership cannot be separated from motivation, and effective leadership is about durable motivation. This is motivation that is sustainable. It is motivation that is carefully orchestrated. It is not about giving a pep talk or an inspirational speech. It is systemic, and requires that the educational leader set in motion many variables that establish higher levels of motivation in the classroom or entire school organization or, indeed, the entire school community. It involves establishing motivation as a general disposition (Brophy, 2004).

Motivation is action oriented. It must be associated with an action such as accomplishing a task, learning something new, or rehearsing a skill. In order for motivation to be associated with the completion of an action, there must be desire. Desire is the first step in the motivational sequence. The next step is hope. Hope is a belief that it is possible to actually accomplish the task. When this hope is added to desire, we can then add action.

Desire → Hope → Action

Desire is strongly influenced by two important variables. These include *direction* and the individual's *value perception*. Both of these factors can be influenced by effective leadership moves. Direction refers to an individual's concept of where she or he is headed and includes those things that this individual would like to accomplish. If people are presented with a direction that is not of interest to them, they will not be motivated. A person's value perception is related to the value that individual places on completing the action. This value perception can greatly affect the level of motivation. If people do not perceive any value in completing an action, motivation will not occur.

Hope is also strongly influenced by two important variables. These include *self-efficacy* and *support*. Self-efficacy is the individual's perception about what he or she is capable of accomplishing. What achievements are possible? If people feel the task is not possible, motivation will not be present (Brophy, 2004). Individuals with high self-efficacy are not so dependent on others, but explore their own ideas and have a greater tendency to act on them (Caine & Caine, 1997). Support is also an important factor in fostering and sustaining hope. This is especially true if self-efficacy is low. Support includes encouragement, coaching, and modeling.

Because desire and hope are critical components of motivation, they are important considerations for durable motivation and leadership. Looking at this from the aspect of the variables that influence desire and hope, we can arrive at the following chart.

Let's keep these four variables in mind and notice how particular moves and acts of leadership are related to this model.

Figure 1.2   The Four Ingredients of Durable Motivation

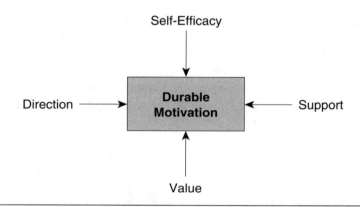

THE LIGHT OF LEADERSHIP

The model of leadership presented here has a strong theme of distributed leadership. This concept of leadership, which sees leadership as a group activity working through and within relationships throughout the entire organization, has been a prevalent focus in education for more than forty years. Distributed leadership already exists in the educational organization, and it can be good or bad. It can be found in classrooms, in the hallways, in lunchrooms, and throughout the entire school community (Hargreaves & Fink, 2006). To be successful, it must be guided and sustained with positive initiatives and definite purpose.

Strong leadership is about the orchestration of many variables in the organization. This orchestration creates what we might think of as the light of leadership. Enthusiasm, confidence, energy, and motivation initiated by the leader moves through the organization like light. It strengthens and encourages others to higher performance. It is positive, renewing, and encouraging of growth. As it moves, it ignites other sources of positive leadership that add their own light until it shines in every corner of the organization. It strengthens and improves the quality of life and brings new vitality to the classroom and school.

FOUR EDUCATION CONNECTIONS

Bobbi DePorter and I, and many other individuals associated with Quantum Learning, have spent our lives searching for effective teaching and leadership moves. This book is about enabling teachers and administrators to expand their own personal repertoire of effective moves. This book is about putting our heads together to explore these moves one by one. It would be most effective to sit together in a room and share these discoveries. Then you would be able to feel our passion and experience our excitement. Because this is not possible, I will do my best to help you glimpse the power of these moves. I am absolutely convinced they will enhance your success as an educator.

The catalog of moves in this book is extensive. It would be naive to think that every move is right for every educator. The idea is to be a bold, but discriminating, shopper. Locate those moves that will be of most value for you in your particular educational situation and setting.

We will divide our study into four school and classroom connections.

- The **context connection**
- The **cognitive connection**
- The **character connection**
- The **classroom connection**

The effective school and classroom leader will be a leader in each of these four connections. We will begin by exploring the context connection.

RESOURCES

Brophy, J. (2004). *Motivating students to learn.* Mahwah, NJ: Lawrence Erlbaum.

Ginsberg, M., & Wlodkowski, R. (2000). *Creating highly motivating classrooms for all students: A schoolwide approach to powerful teaching with diverse learners.* San Francisco: Jossey-Bass.

Hargreaves, A., & Fink, D. (2006). *Sustainable leadership.* San Francisco: Jossey-Bass.

Marzano, J., Waters, T., & McNulty, B. (2004). *School leadership that works: From research to results.* Alexandria, VA: Association for Supervision and Curriculum Development.

2

The Context Connection

Context for Teachers and Administrators

CONTEXT

Setting and maintaining proper context is like preparing soil before planting a garden and tending the garden during the growing season. When educators invest in these essential steps, the seeds of educational best practice and leadership can flourish and produce a bountiful harvest. Without proper context, both the teacher and the administrator may experience reduced capacity to empower students or staff to achieve at high levels of performance. Even the best seeds planted in poor ground and poorly maintained may wither and die or, at best, produce a scanty crop.

Our exploration of context will be done in two parts. This chapter focuses on the context we set for ourselves as educators. It deals with moves we can make individually to stay resourceful. In Chapter 5, we explore the context we create for students.

How do we stay resourceful and excited about our profession in a climate where the winds of criticism are howling around us? How do we stay energized when the demand placed on us as educators continues to increase? How can we lengthen our stride when we already feel we are stretching as far as we can? How do we avoid confusion with so many voices shouting their own brand of essential educational agendas?

STAYING RESOURCEFUL

Can we maintain our positive mental attitude and our educational focus? Can joy and wonder for learning and excitement about teaching still be a hallmark of our instruction? Yes. But these are difficult times for teachers and administrators, and there is little we can accomplish by doing nothing. We must be proactive. We must guard and strengthen ourselves. We must consistently take the steps necessary to keep ourselves resourceful.

I do a significant amount of woodcutting with my chain saw every year. I learned a long time ago the importance of taking time to keep it sharp. It takes me about 10 minutes to sharpen the chain. When I was a novice, I did not want to take 10 minutes every hour to sit down with my file and do this chore.

As I became more experienced, I discovered that I could cut a considerably greater amount of wood if I was diligent with the sharpening task. The same is true for us as educators. If we do not take steps to stay resourceful, we will feel our enthusiasm and excitement begin to diminish. We might even go into a survival mode where getting through another day becomes our focus. We must be proactive about staying resourceful.

Our enthusiasm, excitement, and positive mental attitude are like a battery that needs recharging on a regular basis. If we do not take these recharging steps by being proactive about staying resourceful, it slowly begins to lose its power. Because it does not happen all at once, it can be difficult to notice the loss until, one day, we wonder what happened. We might let it diminish so far that we come to the point in our career where we ask ourselves, "Why am I doing this?" or "What happened to me?"

Remember our discussion in Chapter 1 about motivation and self-discipline. We defined self-discipline as doing what needs to be done, when it needs to be done, when you don't want to do it. If we lose our motivation, we must depend on self-discipline most of the time. This dependence reduces the quality of our lives and begins to take a toll. If we can take steps to stay motivated, we can look forward to our contribution in this profession on a daily basis. We will smile more and be far more productive. This would constitute a significant personal victory.

SYSTEMIC AND PERSONAL VICTORIES

There are two categories of victories needed to get exceptional results in a classroom or school. These include systemic and personal victories. Let's explore this idea with the intent of creating a distinction between these two types of victories.

Let's begin by aligning our thinking on what we mean when we use the word "system." A system is parts put together into a whole designed to accomplish a purpose. There are many different kinds of systems.

Computer systems, school systems, classroom management systems, instruction systems, or business systems are all examples of systems.

The Bicycle Race

A bicycle makes a great example of a system. A bicycle is made up of many parts assembled together into a whole. These parts include sprockets, a chain, gears, tires, spokes, a frame, a seat, handlebars, etc. All of these individual parts are put together to create a system we call a bicycle.

Suppose you get a call from a friend who asks, "Would you like to ride in a bicycle race?"

You say, "I don't think so."

But what if your friend is persistent, saying things like, "Oh, it's for a good cause. It's going to be fun. There will be lots of people we know and plenty of food."

Pretend your friend talks you into this. You are thinking, "Run a little race, eat a little food, see some friends, and all for a good cause."

You go to the garage and get out your bicycle. This bicycle has been in your family for a while. It is in good shape. It was brand new in 1989, has three forward speeds, and they all work. The tires are good, the seat is good, and the paint still shines in a couple places. You jump on this bicycle and take it for a spin. Yep, you recognize this bicycle. This is your bike all right.

On Saturday morning, you go to the bicycle race. Right away, you notice that something is wrong. The other bicycles do not look like your bicycle. They are what we call "high tech." Some of them have 27 forward speeds carefully set in the correct ratios for racing. And these people! There is something wrong with them. They are intense. Some of them even have stripes on their clothing. You are just standing there thinking, "What happened to have a little fun, run a little race, eat a little food, and see some friends?"

Right at this moment, something very unusual happens. An idea just pops into your head. As you are standing there looking around, you think, "I don't care! I don't care about their fancy bicycles and the stripes on their clothing. I am going to win this race. I am going to put so much effort into this that I will win the race."

Will you win the race? Not a chance! You will not win this race. Why not? Because the system you use is not powerful enough to win the race. Even with all the effort you will put into this attempt, you will not win this race.

It will take three things to win this race: a powerful system, good effort, and skill. These three working together will create the possibility of a win. We need a powerful system and strong effort and enough skill to operate the system effectively.

There are educators who are putting in very strong effort but who may not be winning the race. They may be losing the race, but not for lack of effort. Do you operate a powerful system in your classroom or school? Is it powerful enough to win the race? Are there some things you can do to upgrade your system? Are there some parts that need to be replaced? Perhaps there are some things that should be added. Is it time for a tune-up?

Suppose you are standing there deciding you are going to win the bicycle race, and your friend comes up and takes a look at your bicycle.

"You can't run a race with that bicycle," your friend exclaims. "Here, use one of my bicycles."

Now this is a bicycle that is made for racing. It has 27 speeds carefully set and tuned for racing. You can pick it up with your pinkie finger. This is a real racing bicycle.

Now will you win the race? It is perhaps in the realm of possibility. It's a maybe. You would certainly have to know how to operate this new system, and you might need time to gain the requisite skill.

Two Kinds of Error

There are two kinds of possible error associated with this example. They include systemic error and personal error. If you start out giving excellent effort but your chain breaks, that would be an example of systemic error. It means your system broke down. It could be something much more subtle. Maybe your gears are not tuned properly, and there is a split second delay in the shifting process. It breaks your rhythm and creates less efficiency. This is also an example of systemic error.

What if you look around at the other people and decide you do not stand a chance of winning this race even though you have an excellent system. What if self-efficacy is low and you place little value on winning the race? Or what if you have no motivation and only use self-discipline in participating because you said you would? As a result of this thinking, you give only a marginal effort. This would be an example of personal error. What if you do not follow the protocol for shifting your gears because you lack the necessary skill, or what if you get distracted? These are also examples of personal error. Skill is a personal development issue, and a lack of skill is considered personal error. We may have a great system, but perhaps we have not yet developed the skill to operate it effectively.

Both kinds of error can be present in a school or classroom. We should be careful not to confuse systemic error with personal error. When things are not working up to our standards, we should analyze the situation to determine what kind of error is involved by asking, "Is this situation a result of personal error, systemic error, or a combination of both?" By accurately separating the two kinds of error, we are much better positioned to find effective solutions for upgrading effectiveness.

Two Kinds of Victories

Now, let's turn this thinking around and look at it from the other side. We already know there are two kinds of error. They are called systemic error and personal error. There are also two kinds of victories. These include systemic victories and personal victories. It takes both kinds of victories to win the race. Both kinds of victories are also needed in the school and classroom. Holding proper context for ourselves is an essential move for getting personal victories. A good place to start is with our understanding of the importance of our profession.

IMPORTANCE OF TEACHING

Let's begin with this statement: *Teaching is the most important profession in the world.* Perhaps some may think this statement is too bold or even arrogant. To this I would respond that no arrogance is intended, but the statement is true.

If you do not believe this statement is true with all your heart and soul, then what profession do you think is more important? What if you said to a surgeon that teaching is the most important profession on earth. He might turn to you and with some agitation in his voice reply, "Let me explain what I do for a living! I save lives. I do it day in and day out! I save lives!" To this statement you would calmly respond, "Your teachers must be proud of you!"

It is true, isn't it? Teaching and education are the foundation of our society and the basis for individual and societal improvement and increased quality of life. The very first move we should make is to firmly plant this idea in our thinking and protect it like a precious gem. We must maintain this context. Once we have done this, the next move is to stay clear about our purpose or the main event of education.

THE MAIN EVENT

In 1927, a young man stood on the shore of Lake Michigan. He looked out at the icy waters and reviewed the decision he had made. It was his intent to swim out as far as he could and drown. He had decided to end his life and the pain he felt. He had been expelled from Harvard twice. He had failed in business after several attempts and had just lost his little daughter, Alexandra, to spinal meningitis. He felt the option of death was more tolerable than the pain he felt.

As he stood there, a thought formed in his mind. "What if I continued to live and just dedicated my life to helping others and making the world a better place? What if I gave my life away instead of throwing it away?"

This thought riveted his attention and changed his direction forever. He resolved to let this idea guide the rest of his days on earth. He made a decision to spend the rest of his life making contributions that would improve life throughout the world.

His name was Buckminster Fuller. He became an architect, an inventor, and a philosopher, and he was considered by many to be one of the greatest minds of the twentieth century. He came up with the idea that the whole is greater than the sum of its parts and called it synergy. He invented the geodesic dome, which was used to build the Epcot Center. It is the only known structure that becomes stronger the bigger it gets. He created an energy grid system for the distribution of electricity throughout the world to relieve suffering. It is still being used as a model. He wrote 20 books and held 27 patents. He received 47 honorary doctorate degrees for his extensive contributions.

The Bee and the Flower

Let's borrow some ideas from Buckminster Fuller. First, picture a flower in full bloom growing majestically in a field. Now imagine a bee buzzing in a straight course toward the flower. Think about the relationship between this bee and flower. Consider the question, "What is the main event or main purpose between a bee and a flower?" Many educators might state that the main event in this relationship is pollination.

Buckminster Fuller would not agree that the main event between the bee and the flower is pollination. He would say the goal, or what we are calling the main event, is for the bee to get nectar. The bee really has only one purpose, and that is to get nectar. It gives no thought at all to the process of pollination. Pollination is a side effect that occurs as the bee goes about its goal to get nectar. Fuller had a special term for these side effects. He called them *precessional effects.* Pollination is a precessional effect, and let's label the process of the bee getting nectar the *main event.*

Figure 2.1   The Main Event and Precessional Effects

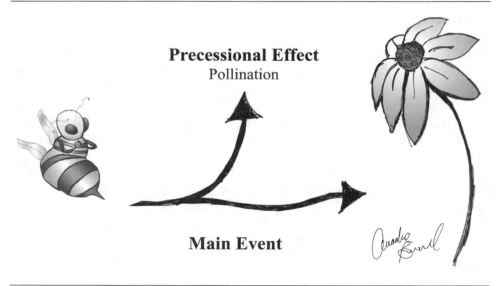

Credit: Anadine Burrell, 2006.

The Soccer Game

Suppose you are standing on the sidelines of a soccer game watching third and fourth graders play in a tournament for a soccer league. You notice that many of the parents standing on the sidelines are taking the game quite seriously. Your attention is drawn to a father who keeps yelling instructions and criticisms to his son. The father seems agitated that the team is losing the game and concerned that his child is not playing well.

As you stand there, you begin to wonder about the purpose of having these children engage in this activity. Why did these parents enroll their children in this league? What should be the purpose or main event for enrolling a child in a soccer league?

Many reasons might come to mind as an appropriate main event. Perhaps it was because parents wanted their child to learn cooperation skills or to be engaged in physical activity. Perhaps they wanted them to experience the sport and have a chance to socialize with other students. Maybe they wanted their child to have fun or learn about sportsmanship. Perhaps parents felt the coach would help build their child's confidence. One or more of these reasons, plus many others, might constitute a viable main event. If the members of the team do build their confidence and learn soccer and cooperation skills, they may win some games. This would be a precessional effect.

Is it possible to focus on the wrong objective as the main event? What might happen if we substitute winning the game as the main event? What might happen to sportsmanship? Who would get to play? How might a primary focus on winning affect the self-esteem of some of these children? How might it affect the parents' communication with their children? How might it affect the coaching of the team? Another way to state these questions is to ask, "How might having the wrong objective or being unclear about the objective or main event affect the context under which we operate?"

Main Event of Education

Let's examine a different important question. Is having high scores on standardized assessments the main event of education? Some might be confused by this question. Perhaps it would be better to ask, "*Should* scoring high on standardized tests be the main event of education?"

I have discovered in working with teachers and school principals throughout the United States and Canada that the vote is a resounding and emphatic "NO." We certainly would like our students to score high on tests and should do everything we can to prepare them to do well, but scoring high should be a precessional effect. If scoring high on standardized assessments is a precessional effect, then the question immediately presents itself, "What should be the main event of education?"

When I ask educators this question, I usually get a number of excellent suggestions. These frequently include such things as helping students become lifelong learners or building strong character and citizenship. Other responses frequently include helping students gain the knowledge they will need to be successful, teaching them how to get along with other people, or how to build enough skill so they can be productive members of our society. Let's look at a different kind of response to this question.

LAW OF SOURCE AND RESOURCE

We can use the "law of source and resource" to help us define the main event of education. The law of source and resource can be stated as follows:

If you *build* the source, you *build* the resource.

If you *protect* the source, you *protect* the resource.

If you *diminish* the source, you *diminish* the resource.

If you *destroy* the source, you *destroy* the resource.

Money Example

The use of a money example can bring quick understanding of this law. Pretend you have one million dollars. For the sake of this example, the one million dollars is tax free. Suppose you decide to put this money to work. You engage an investment counselor who assembles a portfolio designed to maximize your financial returns. For the sake of making the example easy, let's make the pleasant assumption that you earn 10 percent on your investments.

If you earn 10 percent per year on the one million dollars, you will receive $100,000. Let's call the one million dollars the *source*, and the benefits you get from it or the money you earn the *resource*. The resource is the reward or benefit generated by the source. Now let's examine the law again.

If you *build* the source, you *build* the resource. If you get another $500,000, you would have 1.5 million dollars as a source. This means you now receive $150,000 per year.

Let's go back to the one million dollar example. After receiving your money, suppose you decide to purchase an airplane or yacht and take $300,000 from the original million. This will leave you $700,000. Now, you will earn $70,000 per year. If you *diminish* the source, you *diminish* the resource.

All of Life

The law of source and resource operates in all of life. Why do we organize training for our staff? Why do we continue to study and learn and attend workshops? Why are you reading this book? So you can build the source. What source? You are the source. Why do we continue to build our repertoire of effective teaching and leadership moves? So greater resources will be available. So we can use these valuable resources to maximize our success in our professional arena.

Why are our students in school? They are in school to build the source. Why? So resources will accrue. They gain content knowledge by adding to their existing intellectual capital. They build communication skills, confidence, self-discipline, and effective problem-solving and thinking skills. Many will become lifelong learners. These gains are like adding money to the original million dollars.

What are the resources your students might expect for investing all this time in building the source? They will learn independence and be able to function in our culture and society. They will be able to communicate with other educated people and experience the joy of making a positive contribution. They will earn a good living and have healthy relationships. They will be good citizens and avoid the penalties of the law. They may enjoy better health, and they will certainly enjoy the benefits of reading, writing, and thinking. They may enjoy the benefits of effective problem solving and decision making. Their confidence and self-discipline may allow them to enjoy the benefits of positive thinking and the joy of accomplishment.

The law of source and resource operates in the professional arena, the business arena, and the social arena. If you build the source, you build the resource. A friendship, for example, is a source. It can be built, protected, diminished, or destroyed. Many valuable resources come from a friendship, and the stronger the source the more benefits we receive.

THE LAW AND THE MAIN EVENT

Let's go back to our original discussion of main events and precessional effects and use the law of source and resource as the main event of education. We might say it like this: *"The main event of education is to build the source so greater resources will result."* The source we are talking about here is the student. Seeing this as the main event of education can help clarify some of our thinking and assist us in staying focused on our primary objective even in the midst of so much educational clamoring.

Building the source includes all aspects of improvement including content knowledge, character, confidence, health, self-discipline, communication, relationship skills, citizenship, problem solving, thinking skills, time and task management, practical life skills, and many others. Building the source includes everything that will lead to greater resources or benefits for that student.

Our job is to change lives by building on the potential of our students. We are building content knowledge and character. We are upgrading skills in the academic and social arena. We are building the source, so greater resources will be available. By upgrading these individual sources, we are upgrading society as a source and improving the quality of life for all. What a profession this is! I am proud to be a part of it.

TWO IMPORTANT CONNECTIONS

We have identified two important context connections. The first one can be stated, "Teaching is the most important profession in the world, and I am proud to be part of it." We should keep this true statement present in our thinking. Making a poster of it and placing it where we will read it frequently would be proactive and helpful.

The second connection has to do with defining and staying focused on our general purpose. This connection can be stated, "The main event of education is to build the source." Our understanding of this connection is based on an understanding of the law of source and resource, which operates in all of life. Application of this law demands our recognition that we must build and protect ourselves as a source if we expect to have the resources to build our students. We also learned that there are two kinds of victories needed to win in the educational arena. These include systemic and personal victories. Personal victories can be strengthened by understanding the nature of giving in our profession.

A GIVING PROFESSION

How much should we give? This is a difficult question, and many dedicated educators who failed to keep a healthy balance between giving and protecting themselves as a source have left the profession. We should not attempt to run faster than we have strength for. We should make a valuable but reasonable contribution.

How many teachers would say that they could meet all the needs of all their students? This would be a bold claim indeed! It is not reasonable. We have to use ourselves as a source wisely and in a way so we can have the greatest impact. When is enough, enough? How can we use ourselves as a source wisely? When do we begin to diminish the source? Remember, if you diminish the source, you diminish the resources. If you destroy the source, you destroy the resource.

Most educators put in more time on their job than they are legally contracted to give. I think this statement did not come as a revelation to you. Educators give extra time to their students or in planning and preparing high quality instruction. Time is spent with students who are struggling with particular issues or personal problems. There is a special term we can use to describe this giving of extra time, energy, and resources. It is called *"educational charity."*

Educational Charity

So there you are working on a lesson plan in the evening or over a weekend. Or we find you working with a student who asked you for help after the time you had planned to leave the school. Perhaps you are standing in the hall during your valuable and inadequate planning time coaching a student who is suffering from failures in the social arena. Or there you are as a principal working late because your entire day was chopped up with meetings or unscheduled situations that needed your attention. Educational charity is something we have always given in this profession. Educational charity is a choice. It is a choice educators often make. It is a wonderful thing and provides another reason to be proud of our profession.

Remembering that educational charity is a choice is an important move for strengthening our personal context. When we forget to view it in this way, our context can quickly shift and become negative. We may begin to lose sight of one of the beautiful things about our profession. We may begin to feel that the job is demanding too much, and our positive mental attitude may take some serious hits. We may even begin to feel some bitterness about our giving and feel as if we are not in control! There is a precious personal reward received when we quietly and freely give of ourselves for the benefit of others. This giving carries with it a sense of satisfaction and the rewards that attend kindness. We must not allow this reward to slip away.

Educational Grace

Something else is common in our profession, something that is similar to educational charity, but goes beyond it. The word charity is not strong enough to describe it. This something is called *"educational grace."* A helpful way to understand the meaning of grace is to consider an example. Let's examine an incident that occurred during and immediately following the Civil War.

A mother watched as her husband and all three of her sons left home to fight in the conflict. She stayed behind to keep up their place with the help of neighbors and friends. She felt a deep and worrisome concern for the welfare of her family. She watched them leave through the tears she could not hold back.

She learned in the months that followed that her husband and her two oldest sons had been killed in battle. She could not locate her youngest son, who did not come home after the war. After following every lead she could discover, she learned he was in prison, having been accused and later convicted of treason. He was waiting to be executed. Her heart cried out in anguish. The burden of this news was almost more than she could bear. She felt helpless and lost. At first, she could think of nothing to do to help her son. Then an idea came to her that moved her to action.

(Continued)

(Continued)

> She traveled to meet the one man she felt could help her 23-year-old son. Through sheer persistence, she was successful in getting an audience with President Abraham Lincoln. When she entered the office of the President, she was scared, but hopeful. She was confident that this was her only chance to help her son.
>
> She did not make excuses for her boy. She did not say that her son was only 23 years old and did not know any better. She did not claim he was innocent or that the situation was unfair. No, she did not say any of these things. She did one thing. She begged for mercy.
>
> She explained the sacrifice her family had made. She explained that she had lost her husband and her two oldest sons in the war, and this boy was the only family she had left. She pleaded with President Lincoln to let her take her son home. Abraham Lincoln pardoned the boy, and he went home with his mother.
>
> Source: Conference talk (1992), Parker Colorado State Conference, Parker, Colorado.

We cannot say that the young man deserved the pardon. He received a free gift. It was an act of mercy. He received something he had not earned or even deserved. He received something he *could not* earn. He received favor and good will, freely given. He received grace. It was a gift. This is what we mean by educational grace.

Many are the educators who have stretched out the hand of friendship and concern to a student who did not deserve it. The student may be rude, uncooperative, or angry. Perhaps these students do not appreciate the help they receive or the efforts of the educator. And yet the educator reaches out to them and sticks with them. The students receive favor and good will, freely given. They receive a gift: something they did not earn.

Perhaps this educator saw something in this student that the student could not see. Maybe the teacher knew that the student was struggling with failure or low confidence. Perhaps this educator had moves in his or her repertoire that were sure to help, even though the student was not particularly receptive. Sometimes it is a parent who does not deserve the help of an educator, but the teacher or administrator gives it for the student's sake. This act, too, is educational grace. Charity is not a strong enough word to describe it.

If you have been giving such things, I hope you feel a deep down sense of satisfaction, even if you failed to get the results you wanted. Perhaps your gift was not received. You were the giver of a gift, and you should retain the quiet strength that comes from giving. Educational grace is a choice. It is yet another beautiful thing about our profession, and holding this context is helpful for maintaining a positive personal perspective.

Maintaining such a perspective is a personal victory. We should always keep the giving nature of our profession present in our thinking.

Remembering that educational charity and grace are choices is an important aspect of our context. We should always recognize that we are in control of these choices, or we will minimize the precious rewards associated with them. Combining thoughts about the importance of our profession, the main event of education, and educational charity and grace will help support us in maintaining a more positive perspective.

POSITIVE SELF-COACHING

The idea of taking control of our context or perspective is an important one. It means we begin to take charge of our own thoughts. It also assumes the idea that there are proper thoughts that build the source as well as thoughts that diminish the source. Just how important are our thoughts?

As a Man Thinketh

In 1910, James Allen published his classic essay titled "As a Man Thinketh." In this essay, he writes, "As the plant springs from, and could not be without, the seed, so every act of a man springs from the hidden seeds of thought, and could not have appeared without them." He then expressed the idea in this poem:

> Mind is the Master power that molds and makes,
>
> And Man is Mind, and evermore he takes
>
> The tool of Thought, and, shaping what he wills,
>
> Brings forth a thousand joys, a thousand ills:
>
> He thinks in secret, and it comes to pass:
>
> Environment is but his looking-glass.[1]

It was also in this essay that he penned his famous lines, "He who has conquered doubt and fear has conquered failure. His every thought is allied with power, and all difficulties are bravely met and wisely overcome."

These words by James Allen emphasize the importance of monitoring and taking charge of our thinking. We can choose to be proactive. We should not leave our thoughts to chance and allow our thinking to drift with the circumstances of the day. We should set our sail and move ourselves in our own chosen direction.

Set Your Sail

I remember years ago standing atop an earthen dam that formed a reservoir. There were many small sailboats and windsurfers taking advantage of a beautiful morning. The sails were colorful, and I was quite taken by the sight.

As I stood observing, I noticed that these little vessels were all moving in different directions. I also knew that the wind was sweeping across the water in one direction. I marveled at how each craft was using the same wind to set its own direction. It reminded me of a verse in a poem by Ella Wheeler Wilcox:

> One ship drives east and another drives west
> With the selfsame winds that blow.
> 'Tis the set of the sail
> And not the gales
> Which tells us the way to go.[2]

Our thinking sets our sail and determines the way we will go. It is true for us, and it is true for our students. We can choose to take proactive steps to improve and maintain our positive mental attitude. We can choose to use proper thinking to guide us. One effective and proactive step we can take is to become our own best coach.

Become Your Coach

Do you talk to yourself? You sure do. Constantly. We can learn to guide this self-talk to be sure it is productive and moving us in a proper direction. Doing this can make a very significant difference in our outlook or perspective, and can help us conquer our doubts, fears, and negative outlooks. Coaching ourselves to excellence through positive self-talk can greatly enhance our ability to get the personal victories we need in our professional arena.

Positive self-coaching is a powerful tool. It is not new. It has been used extensively in the training protocols of Olympic athletes for years, as well as for improving performance in music and the arts. It is used by high performance human beings.

Effective teachers and administrators are high performance human beings. They stand as models of excellence to be imitated by the rising generation. Their performance is more important than that of an Olympic athlete or of other high performers in music or the arts. Educators can include positive self-coaching as part of their ongoing training and fitness program. We can use it to build and protect the source, and to help insure continuous personal victories. We can use it to help set our sail.

Self-Coaching Script

The concept is quite simple: Replace weak thoughts with positive, proper thoughts. The idea of replacement is important here. It would not be effective for us to attempt to just quit thinking negative thoughts. The only way we can upgrade our thinking is by replacement. You cannot just leave a void. It cannot be done.

The process begins with the creation of a self-coaching script. Below is a sample script for a teacher, which can easily be modified for a school administrator. The script is only a sample and may be too long for some individuals. Your own script might be only two or three paragraphs. You can combine suggestions from the script with other areas for improvement that are important to you but are not included in the script. Use the script to stimulate your thinking and wording. Developing and using your own script will position you to model this process for students who may desperately need your help to change their own contexts or outlooks.

Sample Script

Today is a great day. I feel great. I am full of life, energy, and enthusiasm. I can choose to have a great day, and I choose to have a great day today.

I am positive, confident, and in control. I like who I am, and I like my style. I am intelligent, competent, and caring. I would rather be me than anyone else in the world.

I am an excellent teacher. I am effective and efficient. I am talented and able to get the best my students have to give. My instructional effectiveness is high, and I am an expert at maintaining the interest and attention of my students. My classroom management is excellent, and my students are cooperative. My students see me as a model for success and high achievement. They know I respect them, and they respect me.

My standards for my students are high, demanding, but reasonable. I am an expert at staying motivated and motivating my students to do their best. I create a strong focus on effort and give continuous acknowledgement for the progress of my students. My positive mental attitude has a strong positive influence on my students. I am an effective educational leader.

I easily maintain valuable relationships that build strong rapport with my students. My students feel safe and supported in my classroom and in my presence. I create a strong sense of belonging for each of my students. My students trust me and feel my genuine care and concern for their success.

I maintain excellent relationships with the parents of my students and enjoy strong support. Parents admire my ability to bring out the best in their children and appreciate the competency I demonstrate in my teaching. Parents appreciate my positive, proactive approach to problem solving and the implementation of academic interventions.

I am a positive force for cooperation and high professional standards. I treat all staff members with dignity and respect. I foster opportunities for collaboration, and I am a valuable resource for helping and encouraging other staff members.

I am proud to be a professional educator and part of the most important profession in the world. I love what I do. I change lives and set students up for success in life. I am a high performance human being. I take care of myself and stay resourceful. I maintain balance in my life. The joy and wonder for learning I create in my classroom is a hallmark of my instruction. I orchestrate success for myself and for each of my students.

Using Your Script

When you revise this script or create your own, be sure to write the characteristics you are describing as if they were already fact. So if you are working to get more balance in your life, you would write, "I maintain balance in my life." School administrators can easily modify the above script to fit their particular situations. Remember, the script should help us move in the direction of self-improvement; it should set our sail. It should also help recharge our battery. It is fine to describe traits that are already well developed as an acknowledgement and confirmation.

The next step is to use the script on a daily basis. A good plan is to read it first thing in the morning and right before you retire at night. It is more effective to read it aloud.

One excellent plan for self-coaching is to tape-record your script and listen to it on a regular basis. Perhaps you could listen in your car on the way to work and on your way home. This is one way I have used my own self-coaching script.

It may not be long before you will have your script committed to memory. For me, this just happened naturally, but you could also make a concerted attempt to memorize it and then repeat it twice daily.

I maintain a more positive mental attitude because of this proactive move. It has been a valuable support when situations and life got particularly challenging. It has trained me to see the positive in situations and in people and to stay better focused on goals set for my own self-improvement. It has been an important source of energy for recharging my battery. It has helped me not only to maintain proper context for effective teaching and leadership but also to gain important personal victories.

Positive self-coaching is a tool that helps us stay focused on the rewards of success instead of the penalties of failure. We should stay focused on success so our thoughts will move us in that direction.

The Rewards of Success

Imagine you are going to give a speech to several hundred people. It is a very important event with many teachers and administrators in the audience. You begin two weeks before the event to prepare your speech. In your preparation, you begin to picture all the things that could go wrong. You picture yourself getting totally mixed up and forgetting what to say. You look at your audience and see concern and discomfort reflected back. You continue to attempt your message, but you know it is not working. You feel fear and panic wash over you. It finally gets so bad that you become ill and make an apology. You walk off the stage. It is still two weeks before the event, and you are already not feeling so well.

This scenario is a little dramatic, but how effective would these fears be as preparation for an important event? What if a professional athlete or concertmaster prepared this way? How might it affect performance? This is an example of focusing on the penalties of failure. Often, one consequence of focusing on the penalties of failure is failure.

On the other hand, what if you prepare properly for this event? You picture yourself in front of the audience. You are calm except for the excitement you feel about the great speech you have prepared. You are confident and in control. You picture yourself giving your speech with clarity and a passion for your message. Your audience is responsive and focused on your every word. Your thinking is clear and your expression engaging. As the speech ends, you receive a standing ovation and feel the joy of excellence and accomplishment. Many come to congratulate you on a job well done. This is an example of focusing on the rewards of success. Often a benefit of focusing on the rewards of success is success. It's still two weeks before the event.

Positive self-coaching helps us get into the habit of staying focused on the rewards of success. Using it helps promote a positive mental attitude and moves us in the direction of a proper focus for our thinking. Because of the demands of our profession and the constant requirement to solve problems, an educator can gradually begin to lose proper perspective or context. We must be proactive in protecting the proper thinking of a high performance human being.

Catalogue of Educational Moves

1. Recognize the importance of setting and maintaining a strong context connection on a personal level.

2. Keep the idea that you are part of the *most important profession in the world* always present in your thinking. Post this thought where you will see it regularly.

3. Remember the advantage of motivation over self-discipline and consistently look for ways to increase your motivation.

4. Keep the perspective that both *systemic* and *personal* victories are necessary to maximize your potential as an educator.

5. Use the concept of *systemic and personal error* to analyze situations that require improvement. Be careful not to confuse personal error with systemic error, as this will cause you to take personally things that are external. Stay open to getting help from others whom you trust to analyze systemic and personal error.

6. Keep the *main event* of education clearly in mind as defined by the *law of source and resource*.

7. Keep present in your thinking the fact that the law of source and resource operates in all of life and for you personally. If you build the source, you build the resources.

(Continued)

(Continued)

8. Stay focused on the giving nature of our profession. Use the concepts of *educational charity* and *educational grace* to help define this important aspect of our profession.

9. Continually acknowledge that educational charity and grace are a choice. Internalize the satisfaction and other rewards that attend this generous giving to others.

10. Diligently seek balance in your life. Do not attempt to run faster than you are able. If you catch yourself, stop and take proactive steps to regain your balance. Seek the help of those you trust.

11. Consider yourself a *high performance human being.*

12. Keep present in your thinking the fact that all action begins with thought, and that our dominant thinking determines who we are and how we will act.

13. Use a formal regimen of *positive self-coaching* to set your sail and move toward destinations of your own choosing. Use it to build your confidence and to maximize your talents. Use it to recharge your battery and maintain your positive mental attitude. Use it as a regular part of your mental fitness program. Stay focused on the rewards of success and on your positive and personal self-coaching script.

14. Remember how rich you are. Even though you are not paid commensurate with your level of education and contribution, if you earn an average teacher salary, you are still in the top 1 percent of wealth worldwide.

15. Count your blessing on a regular basis, and name them one by one.

16. Associate with other people who display a *positive mental attitude.*

17. Read books that *recharge your battery,* support your positive mental attitude, extend your joy and wonder for teaching, build your motivation, and enhance your enthusiasm.

18. Avoid negative school politics and colleagues. These consume your precious time and energy and can erode your positive mental attitude.

19. Continue your professional learning. You are either *green and growing or you are ripe and rotting.* Stay green and growing.

20. Give your smile away on a regular basis.

21. Contribute to the positive context of your school by being a model of high professional standards.

22. Consistently exhibit a positive attitude toward work, colleagues, and students.
    - Consistently dress in an appropriate and professional manner.
    - Seek opportunities to foster cooperation and collaboration among fellow staff members.

- Treat all staff members with dignity and respect.
- Support other staff members in your conversations with students and parents.
- Be cooperative and supportive of office staff.
- Maintain the proper protocol for communicating concerns about school-related issues.
- Constructively resolve conflict with other staff members.
- Be proactive in communicating with parents.
- Be consistently to work on time.
- Report to school meetings on time.
- Exhibit high standards of language with students, parents, and staff.

LEADERSHIP NOTES

Setting positive context is an essential part of leadership and effective teaching. As pointed out in the beginning of this chapter, it is like preparing the soil and tending a garden in preparation for a bountiful crop. This chapter had *setting context for ourselves* as its focus. An educational leader is a model of excellence for others to follow. We like to be around and are more powerfully influenced by people with a positive mental attitude. There are many other aspects to building context for others, and these will be the focus of Chapter 5.

The building of positive context in a school should be a major initiative for the school leader. The moves in the preceding list provide a good starting place. A principal can introduce to staff many of the themes presented in this chapter as specific moves in creating a strong context connection in the school. A school leader can help staff stay focused on these important moves by attending to them in faculty meetings and reinforcing them in conversations and other school meetings.

Many of the moves in the list above would also apply to leadership in the classroom. For example, students who are old enough to understand about the relationship of motivation and self-discipline or who would be able to use self-coaching can benefit greatly in establishing their own positive contexts. There are also several other ideas in the list that are effective for setting positive context for students. As already stated, we will focus on this later.

Consider how the items in the list relate to creating durable motivation in the organization. Notice how each move relates to one or more of the motivational factors of direction, value, self-efficacy, and support. Obtaining higher levels of durable motivation in an organization, including a classroom, is about orchestrating many different moves and acts of leadership. We create a context where motivation can thrive.

RESOURCES

Graves, D. (2001). *The energy to teach.* Portsmouth, NH: Heinemann.

Intrator, S. (2002). *Stories of the courage to teach: Honoring the teacher's heart.* San Francisco: Jossey-Bass.

Palmer, P. (1998). *The courage to teach: Exploring the inner landscape of a teacher's life.* San Francisco: Jossey-Bass.

NOTES

1. James Allen, *As a man thinketh* (1910; repr., Marina Del Rey, CA: DeVorss & Company, 1979). Used with permission.

2. Ella Wheeler Wilcox, *Everyday thoughts in prose and verse* (1901; repr., Whitefish, MT: Kessinger Publishing Company, 2003).

3

The Cognitive
Connection

This chapter will establish the physiological foundation of many of the teacher and leadership moves presented in this book. It explains why these moves work. Our knowledge about the brain and the mechanics of how learning occurs is advancing at a rapid pace. Breakthroughs in brain scanning techniques and recent findings in the field of biochemistry are supporting this new wave of discovery. Educators should stay current on new findings that have direct application to our profession. Being knowledgeable about how the brain works and how learning occurs is an important leadership connection.

This chapter is not an in-depth study of brain anatomy, neuroscience, or biochemistry. Only information considered important to educators is presented. As educators, we must use our time wisely. We need to know the bottom line and let the specialists in science continue their work. For those who wish to go into more depth or look at specific studies, a list of references is provided at the end of the chapter.

OVERVIEW

Let's begin by getting an overview of what we will cover. We will begin by learning about general brainwave states. This information will be important for establishing proper reinforcement strategies that insure long-term retention of content. It is also important for understanding effective moves involved in holding student attention.

Following the material on brainwave states, we will consider two very important concepts from cognitive science related to comprehension of content. We will then investigate one of the most important contributions from neuroscience for understanding how learning actually occurs in the brain. Knowing the neuroscience of learning will prove significant for several reasons, including that this knowledge has implications for changing behavior and supports the importance of life-long learning.

We will then take up three additional subjects important to educational practice beginning with a discussion of memory. The educator can gain valuable insights from the latest findings from memory research. Educators should keep an eye on this area of exploration because encoding content into memory is such an important objective of our profession. After our discussion of memory, we will look at another important player in the data trading game, the emotional center of the brain. Because this center can work for or against us, we want to learn how to maximize its support for learning. Finally, we will take a brief look at some of the latest findings regarding the effect of the environment on the brain. All information presented in this chapter is related to specific teacher moves and leadership strategies covered in subsequent chapters.

The information contained in this chapter is meant to be shared with students who are old enough to understand it. Students are generally quite interested in how the brain works and how learning occurs. It is also important for students to understand why the learning strategies we are encouraging them to use actually work. This understanding will support them in their motivation to apply the strategies and will help them be more participative. For reference, diagrams of the brain are included in the Resources section at the end of the book.

BRAINWAVE STATES

Brainwaves are electrical waves and can be measured using an instrument called an electroencephalograph. To accomplish this, a cap is placed on the head with wires running to a computer. The instrument measures the electrical activity of the cerebral cortex, which is the very outer portion of the brain where higher order thinking occurs. The computer translates this information into graphic data that show the brain waves. Scientists have divided these waves into four general categories.

Delta State

The first category of waves is called *delta* brainwaves. This category of waves includes the slowest and longest of the brainwaves. When our brain is in delta state, meaning that most of our brainwaves are in this delta category, we are in deep sleep. During this delta state, the brain and body heal and prepare for another day; the chemicals and nutrients needed for metabolism are replaced, and the by-products of the day's chemical activity are carried away. When this process is complete, we can get up in the morning and feel the energy necessary for another day of activity. If this deep sleep is interrupted, we may feel less than fully refreshed.

Although the delta state is not a learning state, it is important for learning. Students who receive inadequate delta sleep may suffer a lack of the necessary energy to attend properly, their ability to learn and remember will be hampered, and they may show symptoms of a number of other problems related to learning (Sprenger, 2002). *Learning requires work.* This statement probably comes as no shock to you, but it may surprise some of your students. Getting students to understand this important concept is a teacher move I always make. I also like them to understand the concept that work can be enjoyable.

To a neuroscientist, this work is described as the electrical and chemical energy necessary to make changes in the brain. To learn we must cause certain nerve cells, or neurons, to fire. The term "neuron" is the scientific term for nerve cell. This "firing" refers to the electrical energy that must move across a neural network for learning to occur. A neural network is a group of nerve cells or neurons working together. Getting this neural activity to happen is the work needed for learning, and adequate delta sleep helps ensure that the resources are available for these processes to occur.

Theta State

As brain waves get faster and closer together, they fall into the category of *theta* waves and we enter the theta brainwave state. This is also a sleep state, but the theta state is very different from the delta state. It could be called a processing state. The brain is busy processing information from the day and storing what it thinks is important into certain memory banks (LeDoux, 2002; Restak, 2001). In this state, dreaming occurs and also rapid eye movement (REM) sleep. This state is very important for learning because of the memory functions that occur during this sleep state.

We actually want our students processing our content and their learning from the day during this state so that both will be encoded into long-term memory. To encourage this to happen, we can make very specific teacher moves based on what we know about this processing state. We will not detail these moves here, but will cover them carefully in the chapters that follow.

We have discussed two brainwave sleep states. These include

Delta   0–4 cycles/second   Deep sleep/brain heals itself

Theta   4–8 cycles/second   Processing sleep/dream and REM sleep

Scientists measure brainwaves in cycles per second, and each cycle can be thought of as a complete wave per second.

Alpha State

Let's now turn our attention to the two brainwave states of an awake brain. The first of these is called the *alpha* brainwave state. We could describe this state as relaxed, alert focus. The word relaxed as used here means free of tension, fear, anxiety, or stress. In the alpha state, we are relaxed but alert and attentive. This is a powerful learning state, and one we often try to orchestrate in the classroom. Much of the material we will examine related to classroom climate and the delivery of content will be about moving students more toward the alpha brainwave state.

You can detect each of the brainwave states that we have just discussed in your sleeping cycles. Have you been in a very deep sleep and had someone or something abruptly interrupt your sleep? You were really down deep in your sleep and tried to become alert. It may have been difficult, and you might not have felt well-rested for an hour or so after the experience. This situation could result in a headache for some people.

Normally, you would cycle up and out of delta as you enter theta state. You would then cycle into high theta state and then into low alpha. Next, you would become barely awake and change your position in bed and then cycle back down into theta and after a time back to delta. If you were processing actively in theta and then moved too high into alpha, you might experience a condition I call "busy brain." You continue to process, but want to go back to sleep. You tell your brain to knock it off, but it won't listen. This tension could go on for some time before you finally get back to sleep and start a new cycle.

In the morning, you may awake a little before your alarm and just lie there on the edge of sleep and being awake. You are so comfortable. You are right on the edge of theta and alpha. Once you are up and moving, you cycle into alpha where you become more alert and focused. It probably will not take long before you cycle up into the next awake state. This is called the *beta* brainwave state.

Beta State

Beta state could be called divided focus. Generally, this is a higher energy state, and the brain tends to shift focus from one thing to another. Beta state is your organizational state just before your day starts as a professional educator. You are thinking about what you will need to prepare for the day, who you will need to talk to, what phone calls you will need to make. Your brain is busy organizing your activity.

Beta state includes a very wide spectrum of brainwave activity, and, in its lower frequencies, it is a very useful classroom state and a common state for many different kinds of student activity. It can be seen when students are in discussions or working with other students on projects.

Higher frequencies of beta brainwave state include very agitated states and may include fight or flight reactions. These states can also be seen when a student is about to give a presentation to classmates, so high levels of fear and anxiety are present. As educators, we may work to move agitated students to a lower beta or alpha state by trying to get them to relax.

High beta states affect our ability to retrieve memory or to function well with cognitive data. This fact has frequently been referred to as downshifting. Downshifting refers to the process in the brain where the channels to the cerebral cortex (that outer portion of the brain where memory is stored) are blocked so that other centers designed for survival can get full energy and can maximize their function. One common result of this process is called test anxiety.

Students with test anxiety may sit in an exam unable to recall material they knew earlier because they cannot access it in the cerebral cortex. Their anxiety has caused the brain to downshift. Once they are out of the exam and have become relaxed, they can then remember the material. We will be looking at a number of moves to solve this and similar memory challenges.

We have now discussed all four categories of brainwave states. They include

Delta	0–4 cycles/second	Deep healing sleep
Theta	4–8 cycles/second	Processing sleep
Alpha	8–12 cycles/second	Relaxed alert focus
Beta	12–150 cycles/second	Divided focus to agitated states

We now have established what neuroscientists mean by the terms delta, theta, alpha, and beta brainwave states. We will refer back to this information as we examine the reasons behind educational best practice. Let's now examine two important concepts from cognitive science related to comprehension.

PICTURING AND COMPREHENSION

Have you ever had a student read to you or observed a student read to someone else and noticed that, although the mechanics of reading seemed good, the student had almost no comprehension of what he or she had read? Many educators have experienced this situation.

Have you ever been reading along, just buzzing through some content, and caught yourself thinking about something entirely different from the content you were reading? This is an interesting phenomenon, and it demonstrates something important about our brains. It shows that we are able to partition activity in the brain. You were able to do two things at once. You can continue with the mechanics of reading while you are think-ing about something else. The reason you were able to do this is that you were using habituated behavior.

Habituated Behavior

For some of us, driving to work in the morning may be a similar, seem-ingly unconscious, experience. You grab your keys, get in your automo-bile, and go through all the complicated maneuvers related to driving. Once at work, you hardly have a clue how you got there. You were not thinking about driving. Perhaps you were doing some planning, listening to the radio, or thinking about a variety of issues that had nothing to do with driving. Your working memory was engaged in activities other than driving, and your brain was doing more than one thing at a time.

You were using habituated behavior to handle the task of driving. To a neuroscientist, this means that the neural networks you were using for driving were well-established and efficient. The term neural network, remember, refers to brain cells working together to carry out a particular function. A neuron is designed to communicate with other nerve cells using electricity and chemistry. When we say a particular group of cells is efficient, this means you do not have to generate much electrical energy to get these networks to do their work. You just switch them to autopilot.

When you were first learning to drive, this was not the case. Autopilot had not been installed. Your neural networks for driving were not yet established. You were thinking of each little move: the blinker, the brake, steering, judging distance, the accelerator, checking the mirror, etc. Your brain was ablaze with electrical activity.

In a task like reading, habituated behavior is very helpful, but going through the motions of reading without comprehension does not accom-plish the purpose of reading. Reading has no value without understand-ing, and comprehension requires a specific cognitive activity separate from the mechanics of the reading process. In other words, while the neural net-works related to the mechanics of reading are doing their work, another set of specific neurons must also be engaged in work for comprehension to occur.

Comprehension

We sometimes refer to this work by using the word attention. The term "paying attention" means that we are causing particular sets of neural net-works to be active. In our reading example, this work must occur in addi-tion to the work required for the mechanics of reading and is a specific, identifiable cognitive activity. The term we will assign to this cognitive activity is *"picturing."* This knowledge leads us to our first critical educa-tional fact. ***There is no comprehension without picturing.***

We can begin to see the truth of this statement by examining how we learned to use symbolic language to build our auditory and sight-word vocabularies. The brain of a baby is ready and waiting to receive language even before it is born. This predisposition allows the child to begin its collection of a massive amount of intellectual capital and to have it available for communicating, thinking, and understanding its world.

It all begins when a baby starts seeing things in the environment. Babies begin to discriminate shapes, and these shapes are processed in the brain in an area called the visual cortex. The visual cortex is located in the very back of the brain. If you touch the back of your head, you will be right over the visual cortex. This is the area of the brain where sight is processed. We actually see with this part of the brain.

Suppose a baby sees an object that has four legs, a tail on one end, and a head on the other. The baby will actually see this object several times in her visual field, and the memory of this image is stored in the visual cortex. It is just an object that can move around on its own. The baby has no symbolic language to comprehend it or name it.

Later a parent makes a sound that is new to the child. The sound is "CAT." This sound goes into the ears of the child and is processed and recorded in another part of the brain called the temporal cortex located right above and in front of the ears. If you put your hands right in front of your ears, you will be right over the temporal cortex of the brain.

The sound "CAT" is repeated several times to the child when the object is in the room. At some point, the child makes a connection or association between the sound and the object. When this happens, the child has a sound in her auditory vocabulary and can experience what we call comprehension. Comprehension occurs because the sound is now attached to the picture the child has stored in his or her visual cortex at the back of the brain.

We can now check this comprehension. We could say the word "CAT" when the animal is not present. The child may look around for the actual object. If this happens, we can be certain the child has comprehension and that an association between the sound and the picture stored in the visual cortex has been formed. The child is picturing. When the child hears the sound, she or he can access the picture from memory. If babies hear a sound and cannot access a picture, they will not experience what we call comprehension.

Later, the child attaches written symbolic language to the sounds of language. This process will usually begin by learning the individual symbols we call letters and associating these shapes with their proper sounds. The child can now look at the group of symbols *CAT*, recognize the sound they make, and then access the stored picture to get comprehension. You did the same thing when you first saw the symbols "CAT" printed above.

See if you can catch yourself doing this. Read the following sentence: *The young child ran across the busy intersection.* Did you get a picture? *The dog knocked the vase off the table with its tail.* Did you get a different picture? *Her glasses fell off her nose and right into her soup.* If you comprehended these sentences, you were attaching the symbolic language above to pictures you have stored in other parts of your brain.

When you caught yourself reading but thinking about something else, you had no comprehension because you were picturing something unrelated to the content. You were activating the wrong neural networks to get comprehension, and working memory was engaged in a different activity. The term "working memory" will be discussed in greater detail later, but for now it is used to refer to what it is you are focused on. In order for students to comprehend, they must use their working memory to picture the content.

This need to picture is also true for listening. *There is no comprehension without picturing.* There is no comprehension without the particular picturing related to what is being communicated. In other words, it's not just any picturing; it is the picturing related to the content that must occur. This critical educational fact has many implications for effective teacher moves.

Connecting to Existing Schemata

Let's explore another related concept. If you have accessory naviculars, you should be proactive about getting something done. This is especially true if they are bilateral. They are not always bilateral, but they can be. Bilateral accessory naviculars can create some special problems and are worth the cost of repair. If you are experiencing the difficulties associated with bilateral accessory naviculars, I recommend you take action. Solving problems related to bilateral accessory naviculars can improve the quality of life.

How was your picturing working in the paragraph above? Did you experience some difficulty? If you did, I suggest this was because you were not familiar with the term "bilateral accessory naviculars." You were struggling to make meaning. This brief demonstration brings us to a second critical educational fact: ***Students make meaning by connecting to existing schemata.*** It is this existing schema that allows us to engage in picturing. You were unable to engage in proper picturing because you could not connect to any existing schema when trying to comprehend the phrase "bilateral accessory naviculars."

The term schema refers to our intellectual capital. In other words, your schema is the knowledge you already have, the knowledge that you bring to the table in a learning situation. It is all the information you have gathered, all the vocabulary you know, all the concepts you understand, all the math you have learned, and everything you have learned about the use of symbolic language. Contemplate this statement: *Schindler is considered a hero by many of the Jewish people.*

Did this statement have any meaning for you? It may have caused you to connect into a particular bank of schemata about World War II. Everything you know about World War II is part of this particular schema domain. There are many other ways to tap into this bank of knowledge. For example, just saying the name Hitler would likely connect to the same schema domain.

We can use your existing schemata to bring meaning to the paragraph about bilateral accessory naviculars. A navicular is a small bone in the ankle. Now you are picturing because you have "bone" and "ankle" in your store of symbolic language, and they are attached to pictures. The word accessory means extra, and the word bilateral refers to both feet. You also have schemata for these terms. If you have bilateral accessory naviculars, you have an extra navicular bone in each of your feet.

When you first encountered the bilateral accessory navicular paragraph, you may have been paying attention and attempting to comprehend or picture the correct meaning. In other words, you were giving a good effort. Your working memory was scanning your memory banks in an attempt to connect to something you already knew to allow you to picture what was being communicated. But it was unable to pull together the materials you needed for understanding. Its precious store of schemata was not adequate in this case, and it came up empty-handed or with the closest thing it could find. I then gave your working memory some proper connections by giving you words that were already in your schemata. You immediately began the process of picturing to get comprehension.

It is possible to connect into the wrong schema and think you have understanding when you do not. Students hearing you use the term *guerrilla warfare* might not know the use of the word and may hook into the only schema that is present in their intellectual capital, creating pictures of jungle gorillas in combat using the techniques and strategies you are describing and wondering why we didn't think of this sooner.

Importance of Content

Teaching students with insufficient schemata for making meaning of present content is a common educational challenge. For example, in order for fifth grade students to learn well in fifth grade, they need to have much of the third and fourth grade intellectual capital well established. If they do not, they will be greatly handicapped throughout the remainder of their educational career unless an intervention is applied to correct the deficit. Their working memories will constantly come up empty-handed.

We have all worked with students who did not have the background knowledge or intellectual capital to understand what we were trying to teach. They had insufficient schemata. We are confined by the educational fact that *students make meaning by connecting to existing schemata*. For a student to be successful, these connections must be made. We all have to build on the foundation that already exists.

This educational fact sheds light on the importance of the content we teach. Our content is critically important for future learning. Every vocabulary word, math concept, cultural understanding, or scientific fact adds to the student's schemata and is valuable for that student. The importance of building a rich supply of ready-to-use schemata cannot be overstated. This bank of schema is critical for problem solving, analysis, reasoning, and other high order executive thinking skills.

The variation in the schemata of our students places a serious burden of responsibility on the educator to continually check for student understanding. This process is referred to by Madeline Hunter as "dip sticking." Hunter is a pioneer in educational best practice and advocated the concept of frequent and informal checks for understanding (Hunter, 2004). The differences in levels of schemata begin very early in the learning career of our students. I learned this from my own experience.

I began my teaching career as a public elementary school teacher. I was assigned to teach fifth and sixth graders in a mixed grade level setting. It was a year-round school with the nine weeks on, three weeks off, nine weeks on calendar configuration. This schedule meant that a teacher tracked off for three weeks four times a year. In this particular school, there were four tracks, and when the teacher was gone on a three-week break, three-fourths of the students were still in school and one-fourth tracked off on vacation with the teacher.

This situation necessitated the use of roving teachers who would take over the class when the teacher was on break. The regular teacher was expected to prepare three weeks of plans for the students who were still in school. Of course, the students who were on break at the same time as the teacher did not receive any of the curriculum presented by the roving teacher during their break. Are you picturing? Are you also shaking your head in wonder and disbelief? It was an experimental plan that only lasted for two years. After all these years, I am still shaking my head.

As a first year teacher, I was struck with what I thought was a particularly clever idea. I decided I could work during my three-week breaks and make more money. I volunteered to track in for the kindergarten teacher while she was on her three-week break. I suppose you are shaking your head again and wondering why I did not just stay with my own students. Another teacher had already been hired for that, and her contract and schedule were set. So I taught fifth and sixth grade for nine weeks and then taught kindergarten for three weeks, and I followed this schedule throughout the year. I was impressed with my brilliance because I knew teachers did not need breaks. I made serious revisions in my thinking before my second year of teaching.

I remember being apprehensive about working with kindergarten students. But there was one thing I felt would be very positive and would make the job easier. At least they would all be in the same place as far as their intellectual capital was concerned. Those of you who have worked with very young students are already beginning to chuckle. Was I ever in for a surprise!

This assumption turned out to be a long way from reality. Some of those short, energetic people had come from language-enriched home environments and others from language-deprived environments. Indeed, by the time students enter their formal education years, they are already significantly spread out in their levels of working schemata. I remember thinking that this was not fair to the teacher, but I was not sure who should receive my complaint.

We have established two important ideas about the cognitive process of learning. The first is that *there is no comprehension without picturing,* and the second is that *students make meaning by connecting to existing schemata.* We will now look at some important discoveries in neuroscience that have direct application to classroom methodology.

BRAIN PLASTICITY

At Colorado NeuroLearning Center, I had the privilege of working with Leisha, a fifth grade girl who had sustained serious head injuries. Leisha taught me some of my most important lessons about learning and the brain.

Leisha was walking home from school with her older seventh grade brother when a pickup truck came around a corner and, in attempting to miss another car, skidded sideways. The truck hit the curb with both front and rear wheels next to where Leisha and her brother were walking. On the back of the truck was a camper that was not tied down and was being transported from one location to another. It flipped off the truck, landed upside down on top of Leisha, and crushed her between the camper and the sidewalk. Her brother, Ryan, was able to get out of the way in time, but Leisha never even saw the camper.

Ryan was hysterical. He could not see his sister, but he knew she was under the camper. Other people who saw the accident quickly worked together to tip the camper over. Leisha had extensive head injuries. She was rushed to a nearby hospital. They were able to keep her alive, and immediately attempted to find her mother.

It took Leisha's mom about an hour to get to the hospital after her daughter had been admitted. After looking at her daughter, bandaged, in a coma, and hooked up to life support, she asked the doctor what she should expect. The doctor was honest. Leisha's head injuries were extensive. He told her it was doubtful her little girl would live.

After about an hour, Leisha showed some signs of improvement. She was taken into surgery, and this further stabilized her. Leisha's mom became more hopeful the following day and again asked the doctor what he thought. She was told that it was probable that her daughter would live but that Leisha would have very limited function. She was informed that Leisha probably would not be able to speak or hear and would have limited cognitive ability.

We learn a lot about the human brain from head injury. This is especially true now with our advances in scanning technology and our ability to pinpoint with incredible accuracy where injuries or abnormalities occur in the brain. Leisha has an amazing brain.

Leisha graduated from high school. She has all A's and B's on her transcript. She was staffed out of special education in her freshman year because she did not qualify. She has many friends and her coordination is average. How can this be? If you look at scans of her brain, you would discover that large portions of her brain do not function as a result of her injury. What happened to Leisha's brain? How can her brain function as effectively as it does? At the time of her accident, the answer to this question was not clear, but now we understand what went on inside Leisha's head.

Dr. Marion Diamond's Research

The answer has come from a number of neuroscientists and biochemists doing research on the brain. One neuroscientist who has made especially valuable contributions is Dr. Marion Diamond. As part of her research at the University of California's Berkeley campus, Dr. Diamond measured the density of brain tissue and tracked the data on laboratory animals. After several years of study, she came up with the premise that *environment affects the density of brain tissue in the cerebral cortex* (Diamond & Hopson, 1998). Remember that the cerebral cortex is the very outside of the brain.

The idea that environment could affect a physical characteristic such as density was rather shocking at the time. Neurobiologists considered it a well-established fact that the brain does not grow additional brain cells, and most scientists dismissed her premise.

To test her hypothesis, Dr. Diamond set up what she called "enriched environments" for laboratory rats. You might be wondering, "What exactly is an enriched environment for a rat?" An enriched environment for a rat was a community of twelve rats in one cage. These rats were given lots of toys and things to do. The control group rats were kept in individual cages and were kept clean, healthy, and well fed.

Later, when the density of the brain tissue of the enriched environment rats was compared to that of the control group, an amazing fact was discovered. The rats in the enriched environments had cerebral cortex tissue that was denser than the control group rats. Although the findings were clear, the reason for this result was not. What could possibly explain the greater density?

Further study by Marion Diamond and her team of researchers revealed that this increased density had nothing to do with additional neurons, or brain cells. It was all about connections! This is the first key to understanding what happened in Leisha's brain. To better understand Dr. Diamond's findings, let's consider the basic structure of a neuron.

Neurons

Neurons have many different shapes and configurations based on their function. One thing they all have in common is their design for communicating with each other. Each neuron has a cell body containing a nucleus and other structures common to all the cells of the body. The cell body stores genetic material and is a production center for proteins and other molecules needed by the neuron to accomplish its unique function.

Neurons also have fibers, which branch from the cell body and act as the receivers of messages from other neurons. The branches that receive messages are called *dendrites*. The number of these projections can vary greatly, but, in many cases, they look like a tree in full blossom due to the sheer complexity of dendrites from a single cell. These individual cells with their dendrites form a complex and tightly entangled forest of communication networks. Some researchers suggest that a single complex neuron can communicate with as many as 100,000 other neurons either directly or indirectly (Greenfield, 1997; Restack, 2000). These fibers or dendrites receive electrical impulses and carry them toward the cell body. These electrical impulses received from other neurons are called *action potentials.*

Cell body	Main part of the cell/stores genetic material/performs normal cell functions.
Dendrites	Nerve fibers that receive electrical impulses from other neurons and carry them to the cell body.
Action Potentials	The name neuroscientists use to describe the small electrical impulses used by neurons to communicate with each other.

The neuron (nerve cell) can also send out impulses or action potentials to other neurons. This is accomplished by sending a signal down the *axon* of the nerve cell, another fiber that extends from the cell body and carries electrical impulses or action potentials *away* from the cell. Although the cell may have many dendrites originating at the cell body and then branching out, it has only one axon. This one axon also branches out at its end. The ends of these branches are called *axon terminals.* A single neuron having one axon may be connected to many other neurons via these numerous axon terminals located at the end of each branch. In other words, we have only one axon leaving the cell body but then branching out at the other end of the axon. With dendrites, we have many that start at the cell body and also branch out. Because of this, we say we have many dendrites but only one axon. However, both dendrites and axons branch out.

The length of an axon may be very short, allowing the cell to send messages only to other neurons in its immediate neighborhood. Some neurons prefer to talk long distance. The longest neurons extend from the brain all the way to the base of the spinal column in the lower back.

Axon   A nerve fiber extending from the cell body of a neuron that carries action potentials away from the neuron. These fibers may be short or several feet long. The end of an axon branches into additional fibers.

Axon terminals   The end of each nerve fiber at the end of an axon. Axon terminals are at the end of each axon fiber where the axon branches out at its destination. Each of these branches forms a communication link with other neurons.

New Connections

The studies of Marion Diamond and of numerous others at universities and research institutes around the world have now established that the density of neural connections involving dendrites and axons is affected by the demands placed upon the brain. This means the brain is constantly changing physically throughout life to adapt to environment (Diamond & Hopson, 1998; Restak, 2001). These findings shook the neuroscience community and revised our basic understanding about how the brain functions. They have led to valuable research designed to reveal how learning actually occurs in the brain.

The increase in density in the enriched environment rats was the result of millions of additional connections between neurons. This means that cells were actually forming more dendrite branches and axon branches as learning occurred. The same result has been demonstrated in the human brain.

Examination of the brain of a 25-year-old high school dropout who did not continue with education or reading and the brain of a 25-year-old graduate student will reveal that the brain of the graduate student has millions and millions of additional connections. This results in greater density. The more you learn the denser your brain becomes. Learning is about making neural connections and establishing neural networks. We are talking about physical changes in the brain. The very fact that you are reading this book probably indicates that you are dense!

The ability of the brain to reshape itself based on the demand placed upon it is called *plasticity*. This ability was originally suggested by the Canadian researcher Donald Hebb in 1949, and it is frequently expressed as *Neurons that Fire Together Wire Together*. This saying is known as Hebb's postulate. Dr. Hebb did not have the sophisticated scanning technology or the benefit of recent discoveries in biochemistry that we have today, so he was unable to prove his theory. He believed that when learning occurs actual physical changes also occur in the brain (Hebb, 1949). Researchers have now shown that his ideas are correct (Glanzman, Kandal, & Schacher, 1990; Martin & Kandal, 1996). It is plasticity that explains how Leisha's brain was able to adjust to her injury. Her brain actually formed new neural pathways to compensate for the damage she had sustained. Her brain physically changed to adapt to the new situation and the new demands placed upon it, an adaptation that permitted her survival and her learning.

Neural Density	Refers to the density of the cerebral cortex, the very outer covering of the brain where long-term memory is stored and where higher order thinking occurs. The more we learn the more connections we create between neurons. This results in greater tissue density in the cerebral cortex.
Plasticity	Neuroscientists use this term to describe the ability of the brain to change and reorganize itself. It refers to the building of new connections between neurons and the formation of new neural networks as learning occurs (Restak, 2001).

The brains of our students are changing as learning occurs. They physically change as schema is established, as habits form, and as character develops. These changes occur by adding neural networks, reinforcing existing networks, or by eliminating networks.

Eliminating networks does not sound like an action we want going on in our brains, but it is a reality. There are two sides to the plasticity coin, a coin that is inscribed with the words *Use it or lose it.* Neural networks that are not used are eliminated or commandeered for other functions. Neuroscientists have a very polite term for the process of losing neurons. It is called *pruning.*

Life-Long Learning

Plasticity occurs throughout life, but it is true that a young brain is more moldable than an older one (Carter, 1998). Leisha had a fifth grade brain at the time of her accident, and it was highly moldable at that stage of her life. Although a younger brain may have greater plasticity, learning should clearly be a life-long pursuit based on our understanding of what it takes to keep the brain active and healthy.

My mom is now eighty-three years old. She was very excited when she turned eighty. She told me that life begins at eighty. "You would not believe what you can get away with when you are eighty," she exclaimed. People just think, "Oh, its okay, she's eighty."

When she was 78 years old, she decided she would like to jump into the world of computers. I bought her a starter computer to see how she would like it. Last year she got rid of that one and upgraded to a more powerful model because the one I got her was not "meeting her needs and was not fast enough."

She loves to surf the net. She reads documentaries and articles on all sorts of interesting topics. She likes to stay current on world events and get in-depth reports. She constantly communicates with a network of other seasoned adults who send things of interest to one another.

She insists that her mind is improving and that her memory is getting better. I have also noticed this positive change. It should not be too surprising based on what we know about the brain. She is reinforcing neural networks and adding to her schemata. She loves to learn. She is experiencing the positive side of brain plasticity.

THE SYNAPSE

We just learned that brain cells communicate with each other using projections that include dendrites and axons. An action potential can move away from the cell down an axon to the dendrite of a receiving cell. The axon and dendrite generally are not physically connected. They are not "hard wired." There is a small gap between them, and the message from one neuron must somehow get across this gap. This intersection between an axon and a dendrite is called a *synapse*, and this is where the critical brain chemistry for learning occurs.

Neuroscientists call the cell sending the message down an axon the *presynaptic* neuron, and the cell on the other side of the synapse that owns the dendrites receiving the message the *postsynaptic* neuron. In other words, the presynaptic neuron is the sender, and the postsynaptic neuron is the receiver. The messengers that carry the signal across the synapse are chemicals called *neurotransmitters*.

Synapse	The intersection where an axon and dendrite meet.
Synaptic gap	The very small microscopic gap between an axon and a dendrite. The axon and dendrite do not quite touch. The synaptic gap is filled with extra-cellular fluid. This gap is where important brain chemistry for learning occurs.
Presynaptic neuron	The neuron sending a message down its axon to other neurons. It can be thought of as the cell in front of the synaptic gap that wants to get its message across the gap to the dendrite of another cell.
Postsynaptic neuron	The neuron that receives a message from a presynaptic neuron. It can be thought of as the cell on the other side of the synaptic gap that gets the message sent from the presynaptic neuron.

Neurotransmitters   The chemicals that work in the synaptic gap to get the signal from the presynaptic neuron to the dendrite of the postsynaptic neuron. These chemicals are stored in the axon terminal of the presynaptic cell and are released when the action potential reaches the terminal. They act as little speedboats to get the message across the gap to a docking station on the dendrite.

The message in a synapse only moves in one direction because only the axon terminals have the storage containers for the neurotransmitters and only the dendrites have the docking stations or receptors necessary to receive them. The synaptic gap is filled with fluid allowing the neurotransmitters to move across the synapse.

Sending Action Potentials

When the action potential moves away from the cell body down the axon to an axon terminal, it causes the release of the neurotransmitters being stored at the terminal. Once released, the neurotransmitters speed across the synapse and dock at receptors on the dendrite. If enough of these neurotransmitters dock on receptors, it causes a signal to be sent to the cell body of the *postsynaptic* cell, and it may fire its own action potential.

The voltage of an action potential is about 60 millivolts. A millivolt is one-thousandth of a volt. The voltages basically do not vary. It is not the voltage of the individual action potential that causes the postsynaptic cell to fire, but the frequency of the action potentials and the combination of action potentials from a number of presynaptic cells firing at the same time. All of this happens with incredible speed, which can be measured in milliseconds. The distance across a synapse is measured in angstroms. An angstrom is one ten-millionth of a millimeter.

It is the job of the dendrites to carry the messages they receive to the cell body. Just receiving an action potential from one presynaptic neuron will seldom be enough to cause the postsynaptic cell to fire an action potential down its own axon. It would normally take many presynaptic neurons transmitting their messages at the same time for the message to be continued.

Recap

Let's summarize what we have just covered. Neurons have two kinds of projections or nerve fibers: axons and dendrites. The axon carries the electrical impulse or action potentials away from the cell body, and the dendrites receive action potentials from other cells. When an action potential is sent down an axon, it comes to the axon terminals where chemicals called neurotransmitters are stored. When the action potential reaches these terminals, the neurotransmitters are released and speed across the synaptic gap to carry the message to the little docking stations or receptors located on the dendrites of the postsynaptic cell. If the postsynaptic cell receives enough messages from its many little docking stations located on its dendrites, then it may fire its own action potential.

HEBB'S POSTULATE

We are now positioned with enough knowledge of neuroscience to understand Hebb's postulate, *neurons that fire together wire together.* This idea can also give us a glimpse of how learning actually occurs in the brain. With this schema in place, we can also reference it to help us understand the biological foundations of important educational strategies.

Consider carefully what happens at the synapse. The more branches at the end of an axon of a particular presynaptic cell, the more power this neuron has to communicate and cause action potentials in postsynaptic cells. We can say that the more branches it has the more power it has because, when an action potential moves down an axon, it fires all the branches like a domino effect. Now here is something interesting, and a discovery that marks a major breakthrough in biochemistry.

When the postsynaptic cell fires, it sends back chemicals that strengthen the cell that sent it the message, the presynaptic cell. This would be like sending someone a thank you gift. Some of these chemicals are called neurotropins, and they perform an important function. If a neuron does not occasionally get a dose of these neurotropins, it may actually die (Kotulak, 1996). Thus we see the chemistry behind the phrase "use it or lose it." There is more. Much more.

Chemicals sent back to the presynaptic cell can cause it to form more branches, giving it more power in the future (Sylwester, 1995). This would be like sending a construction crew back to the presynaptic cell. There is also some evidence that these chemicals can affect the concentration of neurotransmitters and streamline the releasing of neurotransmitters. So the presynaptic cell also receives little consultants from the postsynaptic cell that improve production, causing the presynaptic cell to be even more efficient—like the ones you use when you are driving. There is more.

When the postsynaptic cell receives action potentials at particular locations, it sends out its own construction crews to build more of its own dendrites at that location (Greenfield, 1997). Neurons are constantly changing based on the communication from other neurons. This is what neuroscientists are referring to with the term plasticity. These additional dendrite branches allow for even more connections with the presynaptic cells that are regularly communicating at certain locations, thus increasing efficiency. With enough connections, a single action potential sent down an axon can have a much greater effect. There is more. There is another very specialized construction crew that only does remodeling in the postsynaptic cell.

When a postsynaptic cell fires, it sends out a remodeling crew to work on its existing dendrites. These workers are special proteins. Their job is to build more receptors or docking stations on the existing dendrites, which allows the neurotransmitters to have a much greater effect. The more receptors the neurotransmitters have available for docking, the greater the impact of the presynaptic cell and the more efficient the synapse.

Many neuroscientists believe that these changes at the synapse explain how learning occurs (LeDoux, 2002). When we learn, there is an actual physical change in our brain. We have been examining brain activity at the level of a single synapse to help us understand the process, but it is important to keep in mind that this process happens on a much grander scale. When you learn a new vocabulary word, millions of neurons fire and are involved in this process.

It is the increase in branching that caused the greater density in the cerebral cortex that Marion Diamond picked up in her research. It was the greater learning in the enriched environment rats that caused this increase in branching and in neural connection. This same process allowed Leisha to recover many of her cognitive functions. Being dense has taken on a whole new meaning! Our goal as educators should be to create greater density in our students.

Our new knowledge of neurons and of the principle of neural plasticity is helpful for understanding other important aspects of brain function including memory, recall, the effect of emotion on cognitive processes, and how the environment affects the shaping of the brain.

MEMORY

Scientists used to think that memory was stored as an entire isolated entity in a particular location in the brain. This idea has proved to be incorrect (Given, 2002; LeDoux 2002). Memories are not stored like a snapshot in one specific location. A memory has to be reconstructed each time. If you are remembering a family picnic, you must bring all the pieces of the event together. The memory of the way the stream looked where some of you were fishing is in one part of the brain. The memory of the delicious potato salad is in another place. The water fight, the drive, the smell of the food cooking on the grill and how hungry you got waiting to eat, the thrill of the tire swing, the sound of the children laughing as they played a game of tag—all these memories are stored in different neural networks depending on which of the senses sent the input to the brain.

Because of the reconstructive process of remembering, memories can change over time as the brain changes (Schacter, 2001). These changes often present a problem for those who are called to act as a witness and to testify about something that happened years before. Because of its plasticity, the brain that recorded the memories is the not same brain recalling them. Additional schemata have caused new neural networks to be established, and some networks have been pruned away for lack of use. Perhaps parts of the memory are there and other parts are gone. You might notice this when you discuss an event with someone else who was there. Perhaps they will mention things you had forgotten.

Working Memory

In order for all these individual segments of a memory to be formed into a memory of a whole event, there must be a place in the brain where these individual pieces of memory can be sent to create a composite. In other words, if you are cooking up a memory, all the ingredients must be brought together into the same pan. There are a number of places in the brain where the axons of neurons from various parts of the brain converge. The locations where these axons come together are called *convergence zones.* Let's look at an example.

Neurons that process sight are very specific in their function. Some neurons process color while others process shape or line or movement (Guenther, 1998). A small network may process lines that are at 37 degrees off the horizontal, and a different network may process lines that are at 82 degrees. These networks can be used repeatedly to process what we are seeing.

All of these individual network centers send information to convergence zones. These zones then forward the signals on to larger zones, and these in turn send their memory formations on to even bigger zones. The same process occurs with the other senses. We can easily see that there must be a master zone where all the senses send their individual memory composites so the whole can be created.

The master convergence zone is located way up front in the brain, right behind the forehead. This is the area of the brain where executive function occurs (LeDoux, 2002). It is our executive control room, where processes like reasoning and problem solving happen. It is our center for logical thinking and analysis. Axons from the smaller convergence zones terminate here. Neuroscientists believe that this is where *working memory* is stationed (Restak, 2001). In order for working memory to be effective, it must receive information from many parts of the brain at the same time, and this executive control room receives information from all over the brain.

Working memory will process what we are paying attention to at any particular moment. If we were remembering the picnic while a brain scan is being done, this area would light up with activity. If we became distracted by something, then the picnic memory would be immediately bumped out and our working memory would process something else.

The front of the brain is where mental work gets done. This work includes things like comparing, predicting, estimating, and judging. Working memory will only focus on one thing at a time (Hirst, Spelke, Reaves, Charack, & Neisser, 1980). This is an important characteristic of working memory and an important educational fact.

Working memory functions with data coming in from our senses as well as from the schema stored in our long-term memory (Carter, 2002). We are constantly using this schema to interpret what is coming into our brain from our senses. The working memory is constantly activating the schema in order to find what specifically is needed for the task it is performing. The greater the bank of the schema, the richer will be your mental processing. This is another very important educational fact.

If you are watching a football game, you are processing the action and also constantly accessing the schema you have stored in your football memory domain. This processing would be very different in the brain of someone who knows nothing about the game compared to that of a retired professional football coach. Just imagine how differently these two people will process what they are seeing. The coach will have such a rich supply of schema that he will analyze defensive and offensive strategy, see strengths and weaknesses in the two teams, and understand a vast number of variables that the novice could not begin to interpret. These differences in processing ability, which can be attributed to differences in schema, are true in all areas of mental activity, including math, science, history, literature, government, and social situations. Educators witness this every day in their classrooms. Students with a rich bank of available schemata are better able to participate in discussions, draw logical conclusions, make predictions, analyze data, and solve problems.

Recap

Let's review what we have just covered. We learned that memories are stored at many locations in the brain depending on which of our five senses of sight, smell, taste, touch, or hearing recorded the sensory input. We discovered that, to create a memory, we need convergence zones where the data can be brought together. This process starts with data arriving at small convergence zones that then send their composite data to larger zones. These data finally all come together in the master convergence zone in the executive control room located in the front of the brain right behind the forehead. Working memory is located in this control room and is able to use data sent from all the smaller convergence zones, allowing us to focus and think.

To educate students, we must engage their working memories. We cannot teach them anything without the working memory. We must capture it and hold it long enough to allow the process of creating memory to take place. Of course, we are interested in a particular type of memory called long-term memory. Actually, we have to go even further than that. We are interested not only in getting our content into long-term memory but also in having it put into the memory in such a way that it can be recalled. This raises the issue of another important control center.

In order for the executive control room to function properly and get its work done, it cooperates with another control center located more in the center of the brain. This center is called the memory control center, but it frequently goes by its technical name, which I am sure you will agree is quite odd. It is called the hippocampus. This word means "sea horse shaped," and this brain part got its name because, with a little imagination, you can see a resemblance.

The Memory Control Center

The hippocampus has a very important job in the brain. It is located toward the middle on the inside of the temporal cortex, the part of the brain located in front and above the ears. The hippocampus is the memory control center in the brain and is responsible for encoding long-term declarative memory.

The word "encoding" means putting memory into storage. Declarative memory is the kind of memory related to language or any memory that can be described using language, including actual experiences. The memory of the picnic is this kind of memory. Nondeclarative memory refers to memory that is not related to language like the actual process of riding a bicycle or other types of habituated motor behavior.

The hippocampus is responsible for storing memory related to the use of symbolic language. We do all our thinking using symbolic language. Scientists learned the important function of the hippocampus from Henry.

Henry was suffering from very severe seizure activity caused by dysfunction of the temporal lobes of his brain. One way to correct this problem, when nothing else will work, is to remove parts of the temporal lobe. Henry had this surgery performed in Albany, New York, when he was 29 years old. When they removed portions of his temporal lobes, they also removed his hippocampus. This was a serious mistake.

Without a hippocampus, Henry could no longer encode any long-term declarative memory (Cohen & Eichenbaum, 1993). Henry is in his seventies now and lives in Canada. The therapist that has been working with him for over forty years introduces herself to him each day and explains where he is. Henry has not encoded a single declarative memory since the age of 29. His memories before he was 29 are still there. He still lives in that world. He has not added a single new word to his vocabulary and does not remember anything that has happened since his surgery. He does not recognize himself in the mirror because the physical changes he has undergone have not been recorded in his memory. Henry can read the same page from a book over and over again and enjoy it each time as if it were his first reading. He has no awareness that his parents are no longer alive.

The Memory Pathway

In order for a memory to be encoded by the hippocampus, the information must first enter our working memory. From there, it can be sent to the hippocampus for immediate storage. If what we are teaching does not get into working memory, then it cannot be encoded as long-term memory. In other words, if we do not have attention, memory will not be processed.

The hippocampus itself stores a memory initially; it actually has its own memory storage banks. It primarily stores short-term memory. The hippocampus sends memory out of its storage banks to longer-term storage locations in the cerebral cortex (Carter, 1998; Greenfield, 1997). If the picnic we described earlier happened last year, the hippocampus would not light up on a scan as you recall the event. The working memory is getting the information directly from the storage locations in the cerebral cortex. Because Henry's working memory can still get information directly from these storage locations, he is able to retain his memories that were stored before his surgery, although he also lost memory that had not yet been transferred by his hippocampus.

We can see that the hippocampus and working memory have an interesting partnership. Working memory sends data to the hippocampus for storage. For a period of time, the hippocampus stores this memory in its own memory banks. Later, it ships it off to other locations. The executive control room sends data to the hippocampus using axons from neurons located in the area of working memory that terminate in the hippocampus. But there are also communication lines running the other way. In other words, neurons in the hippocampus also have neurons that terminate in the executive control room. This allows the hippocampus to send back memory still stored in its own memory banks when it is needed for working memory. Once the memories are gone from the hippocampus, the executive control room has to retrieve data from various locations in the cerebral cortex in order to form a memory.

While you are sleeping, the hippocampus is very busy encoding memory into its own storage banks as well as sending memory up to the cerebral cortex for long-term storage (Carter, 1998; Wolfe, 2001). This is what is going on during theta brainwave sleep. As educators, we are interested in getting the hippocampus to consider our content important and to get it stored so it can be easily recalled. The hippocampus will do this for you. You just have to ask it properly and show it what you want it to do. More to follow.

There is another player in this data storage game. It has great power and can be very bossy. In fact, it is so powerful that it can commandeer working memory, leaving the educator helpless to teach a student. This player is the emotional control center, which is called by the technical name *amygdala*. The word amygdala means "almond shaped," and this structure, which sits near the hippocampus, is indeed almond shaped. With this player in the game, things really get interesting.

EMOTION

We use three educational channels to teach students. Almost everything they know has been learned through these three channels—the visual channel, the auditory channel, and the kinesthetic channel. Students learn by seeing, hearing, and doing. The two primary channels are visual and auditory. Most of what they have learned in school has been received into the brain using these two channels because of their role in learning and using symbolic language.

When data from the outside world enter the brain through any one of these three educational channels, the data are first sent to a relay station called the *thalamus*. Everything from each of these three channels goes directly to this relay station. The data are then sent in two directions. One direction is called the high road by neuroscientists, and the other direction is called the low road. Let's talk about the low road first.

The Low Road

Sitting right under the relay station is the amygdala, the emotional control center. The thalamus sends all data to the amygdala for screening. The amygdala immediately processes the information coming into the brain from the three educational channels and checks it using its own private memory banks. It has an important responsibility with respect to the data and must make split-second decisions: It must check the data to determine if they should initiate a fear, anxiety, or stress response in the body (Restak, 2001).

The private storage banks of the amygdala only store certain types of memory. They store negative memories or memories related to aversive stimuli received through our sensory channels (LeDoux, 1996). The amygdala stores memory related to fear, stress, anxiety, and threat. This memory is unconscious memory and would be described as nondeclarative. Let's see how this works.

Pretend you are walking in the forest. Suddenly, out of the corner of your eye you discern a curved shape. You immediately get a response in your body. Your heart rate increases, your breathing changes, and your focus becomes riveted. This low road response came to you through the amygdala. The amygdala was monitoring all data from the sensory channels except for the sense of smell, which is wired differently.

The High Road

You look at the shape and tell yourself it is not a snake; it is only a curved stick. This reasoning comes from the high road through the cortex, and it shuts down the stress response initiated by the amygdala. This high road pathway is much slower than the route to the amygdala. This is why,

Figure 3.1   Emotion and Memory: The High and Low Roads

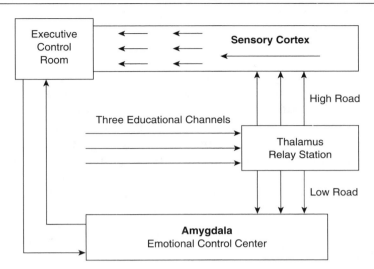

Data coming into the brain using the three educational channels (visual, auditory, and kinesthetic) travel directly to the *thalamus* where they are sent to the *sensory cortex* via neural pathways called the *high road* and to the *amygdala* via neural pathways called the *low road*. Data sent to the *sensory cortex* move to the *executive control room* located in the frontal area of the brain. The *executive control room* communicates with the *amygdala* allowing us to influence emotional response with our conscious thought. The *amygdala* can also influence our thinking and attention through neural pathways that run from the *amygdala* to the frontal areas of the brain.

when you saw a potentially dangerous shape, you reacted before you even had time to think. Let's explore the high road.

When visual, auditory, or kinesthetic data reach the relay station, or thalamus, they are also sent out to various areas in the cerebral cortex, the high road. The visual data go to the visual cortex, the auditory data to the temporal cortex, and the motor data to various motor centers in the cerebral cortex.

These various sensory inputs sent out by the thalamus on the high road are combined into convergence zones and make their way to working memory in the executive control room where reasoning and decisions can be made regarding the data. It is here that you analyze the situation and determine that there is no threat. You look at the curved shape and determine that it is just a stick. This process takes more time compared to the quick action of the amygdala, but, once it has reached its decision about the stick, the executive control room begins shutting down the response already generated by the amygdala. As a result, your heart rate begins to return to normal, and you can resume your walk.

It is true, however, that you might exercise more caution as a result of the fear response having been initiated, even though it was a false alarm. Some structures in your brain may stay on high alert to try to protect you.

This may be true even though your executive control room tells you there is nothing to worry about. This scenario has important implications for students and educators.

Emotion and Memory

When the amygdala initiates a fear, stress, anxiety, or threat response, it commandeers working memory. The effects of the amydgala's action are easy to see when the danger is imminent, but the amygdala also commandeers working memory in more subtle ways. Have you ever been worrying about something while trying to focus on something else you had to get done? You probably had your executive control room send out the message that you are not going to worry about that right now, you will worry about it later. The amygdala gets the message and says, "Well, we will see about that!" This is when the amygdala can get really bossy. The thing you are not going to worry about just keeps popping into your working memory. The amygdala has many neurons with axons that terminate in the executive control room where working memory carries out its tasks. You become very distracted as the amygdala continues to fight for working memory. This situation can make learning almost impossible.

Unreasonable Fears

The amygdala is where phobias are stored (Carter, 1998). When a person with a phobia is having a brain scan and is being engaged in his or her phobia, the amygdala lights up. Let's examine another scenario that will help summarize what we have learned and also show how a phobia might occur.

Suppose you are walking in a new neighborhood. You are very relaxed and just enjoying the beautiful morning and the well-kept yards as you stroll along. Unbeknownst to you, you are being carefully watched. A small canine creature is waiting for you. He waits for people exactly like you and for these special moments. He knows all about timing. He waits until you are at just the right spot and then charges you with all the energy contained in his small body. He catches you completely off guard.

Before your executive control center even gets the data, your amygdala has responded to protect you. You are ready for fight or flight. The chemistry in your body changed instantaneously. You have already jumped back, and your heart is racing.

The data now reach your executive control room. You quickly analyze the situation and notice the fence and the size of the dog. You determine that there is no danger and begin to use your executive function to get the amygdala to back off. You perhaps begin to experience some different feelings related to the dog other than fear, and you may even utter a few words to that effect.

Learning has taken place. The amygdala is powerful when it comes to learning. Changes have taken place in the brain and will be reinforced when you sleep. Three days later, you are walking along the same street, but you do the most unusual thing. You cross over to the other side of the street at a certain location and then cross back some distance further down the street. A cognitive scientist would say you have associated minor stimuli with a major aversive stimulus.

The major aversive stimulus was the dog and his carefully planned routine. The minor stimuli you associated with the dog included the location of the house, its shape, the fence, the yard, the color of the house, and many other things. You normally would not even notice these things, but learning took place in your brain as synapses changed and neural networks were modified. The work of plasticity has been done.

What if this scenario happened to you when you were a child? You would not have full use of your executive function because it is the last part of the brain to mature, reaching full maturity when people are about 23 years of age. So, when you were a child, a dog frightened you, but then you got over it—almost.

Now you are an adult, and you are afraid of dogs of a certain color. Your executive control room explains to you that this fear is not rational. But this is not a declarative memory issue. When you see a dog of a certain color your body just responds without any dialogue. You just get this feeling of fear and anxiety. You just get a reaction in your body and no amount of talking or thinking seems to make any difference. You have a phobia, and you have no idea where it came from. You do not even remember the incident with the dog. During a brain scan, your doctor discovers that, when you are engaged in your phobia, the amygdala lights up.

A phobia is certainly an extreme case. Most of us will never experience anything so dramatic. Perhaps a student just gets an uneasy feeling when walking into a math class. Or maybe this feeling happens when the student has a male teacher. Perhaps students are anxious when they are called on to answer questions even though they are sure they have the right answers. Maybe a student is nervous about participating in a sport or meeting new people. The student just gets this uncomfortable physical response. We might call it an unreasonable fear.

Managing Fear, Stress, and Anxiety

The proper way to get these responses to shut down is to use the executive control room to take control. This is what counseling, coaching, and encouragement are all about. It is also what therapy is about, but, certainly, therapy is for more difficult challenges. In a therapy situation where fear, stress, or anxiety is creating a serious problem, the objective is to bring the amygdala under control through use of the executive control room. In some cases, drugs may be used until word therapy can make the necessary changes.

The executive control room uses a chemical to shut down the amygdala. This natural body chemical is called serotonin. Serotonin works in the synaptic gaps in the amygdala and inhibits the action of the neurotransmitters. In other words, because of serotonin, the signal cannot get across the gap as well, and the action of the amygdala is decreased, causing the fear, stress, and anxiety responses to be shut down or moderated. Once the serotonin does its work, the axon terminals that released it take it back up, and the amygdala is normalized or reaches homeostasis.

The target of drugs like Prozac or Paxil is the amygdala. These chemicals are in a class of drugs called SSRIs, which stands for Selective Serotonin Reuptake Inhibitors. These drugs inhibit the reuptake of the serotonin by the axons, leaving it in the synaptic gaps. Because of this, the serotonin continues to inhibit the response of the amygdala by decreasing the action in the synapses. Consequently, these drugs, which are called antidepressants, help moderate feelings of fear, stress, or anxiety.

The amygdala plays an important role in the education of children, and sometimes not a very positive one. It will frequently be our goal to get the amygdala to back off so the student can use his or her working memory to learn. There are many teacher moves and leadership moves that can help with this process.

THE ADOLESCENT BRAIN

It may be helpful for us to focus briefly on the adolescent brain. The prefrontal cortex is the last part of the brain to mature and, as already noted, it may not be fully mature until about age 23. Consequently, the frontal lobe's capacity to control emotion is not fully operational during a person's adolescence. This fact is rather inconvenient during the teenage years because the prefrontal cortex is where judgment, rational thinking, and the consideration of consequences for behavior occur. It is also the part of the brain used to control or inhibit our behavior and emotional responses (Sousa, 2006).

Children with younger brains rely on the mature frontal lobe of an adult parent or teacher to help guide their behavior and deal with their emotions. But, as the child enters the teenage years, independence becomes an important issue. An adolescent sees the "use" of an adult brain as interference, nagging, and unnecessary control.

This imbalance in maturity can cause problems because the amygdala and other brain structures associated with emotion are very active during this stage of life due to chemical and hormonal changes. The lack of balance in maturity between the frontal cortex and this emotional network called the limbic system accounts for much of the frustration experienced by parents and teachers with adolescents. The imbalance results in impulsive and sometimes irrational behavior. It interferes with the proper consideration of long-term consequences for decisions and actions and results in what adults might describe as poor judgment. As the teenager's frontal cortex continues to mature, we will witness better self-control because the behavior of the adolescent is not so much at the mercy of the limbic system.

Drug Abuse

This imbalance in the adolescent brain places the teenager at high risk for drug abuse. Drug abuse is based on the power of a chemical to mimic the action of a neurotransmitter in the brain so that the brain is tricked into responding as if an actual neurotransmitter were present (Greenfield, 1997). These drugs tap into the brain's reward and pleasure pathways.

Because of the strong emotions attached to these pathways, the brain is quickly instructed by the drug. It immediately changes neural networks to let the adolescent know that this drug is something good and something it wants. The reward and pleasure centers may quickly stop responding to real-life events and people and only respond to chemicals. Because the frontal lobe is not mature, the momentary pleasure takes charge without any thought of future consequences. The frontal braking system is not in place or strong enough to influence the situation.

The use of drugs disturbs the normal balance of dopamine in the brain, a powerful and important neurotransmitter. The drug creates a much higher dopamine effect than what would be normally experienced by winning at a sport, receiving praise, or completing an important project. The brain immediately begins to rewire to demand this high. The other normal highs no longer motivate the adolescent.

Drugs like cocaine increase the firing in the synapses in certain locations in the brain resulting in greater synaptic activity. I teach my students that there is no such thing as drug abuse. I teach them that using drugs in this way should not be called drug abuse, but should be called brain abuse. All the so-called recreational drugs modify what happens in the synapses. It is all brain abuse, and sometimes this brain abuse can result in permanent changes at the synaptic level. Synapses burn out. The cells can actually fire themselves to death, which can cause a whole array of mental and memory problems. Entire networks can be lost.

The drug ecstasy is perhaps one of the most dangerous. It is neurotoxic and actually causes lesions at the terminals of neurons that produce serotonin in the brain. This drug actually destroys nerve cells in the brain responsible for memory and learning. It can take the brain up to seven years to compensate for this damage through plasticity, but the damage to the serotonin producing cells is permanent. Plasticity cannot repair this kind of damage.

The adolescent brain has a high level of plasticity. If an adolescent is engaged in sports, music, and proper academic and social pursuits, the brain will be wired based on these inputs. If the adolescent brain is engaged primarily in pursuits like watching television or playing computer games or just "hanging out," the brain will be wired up accordingly. One of the dangers of adolescent drug use is that the brain is not only being affected by the activities it is engaged in but also by those that are being missed. Brain plasticity might be viewed as good or bad depending on the influences that are shaping the brain. This ability of the brain to change based on outside influence has sometimes been referred to as a double-edged sword (Healy, 1990; Lerner & Hood, 1986). The wiring will affect the individual for life. A drug such as marijuana may not damage brain cells, but it certainly affects the way neural networks are being formed and structured.

An adolescent using drugs may be missing out on the normal, healthy development of the frontal cortex that is so vital for future success because of its moral, personal responsibility, and executive function components. There is strong evidence that the use of drugs has a direct effect on the way different structures in the brain communicate with each other. This effect is due to the framework of the neural networks that are being structured during the adolescent years. The best drug prevention program in an environment where drugs of abuse are readily available is the strengthening of the frontal function through teaching, coaching, and the presenting of convincing factual information coupled with higher levels of success in the academic, extracurricular, and social arenas.

ADHD

A student with ADHD is at the greatest possible risk for drug abuse (Restak, 2001). ADHD is caused when brain structures responsible for attention operate at less than an optimum level. These structures include the lateral prefrontal cortex and several small structures located deep in the center of the brain. This causes the student with ADHD to experience difficulties with focus, concentration, organization, and managing priorities and time.

Adolescents with ADHD have difficulty focusing on one thing with sufficient concentration to garner the necessary information in an effective way. Because of this situation and the demand that is placed on the adolescent in academic and social settings, chronic frustration can develop into demoralization, loss of confidence, and even clinical depression. Many turn to illegal drugs to relieve the effects of their condition.

The most widely used medications for treating ADHD are Ritalin and Dexedrine. These drugs affect the dopamine system by increasing the availability of dopamine in structures in the brain related to ADHD. In the proper dosages, they bring the functioning of several structures to a level that is typical of a normally functioning brain.

Some studies show that students medicated for their ADHD demonstrate a reduction in risk for the abuse of drugs like alcohol, cocaine, and other stimulants when compared to ADHD students who are not medicated (Restak, 2001). Drugs of abuse also target the dopamine system, but are grossly unregulated and strongly addictive. Many students will finally experience a normalizing of the dopamine system as they mature and will be able to discontinue the use of their medication.

We can conclude that the activities students engage in or do not engage in affect the shaping of their brains. The use of chemicals that change brain functioning also influences the shaping of the brain. These inputs and actions are part of the environment that directs brain plasticity.

ENVIRONMENT

Earlier we considered the work of Dr. Marion Diamond and her team of researchers. They proved that environment could cause changes in the density of brain tissue. Just how powerful is the effect of environment on a brain? Perhaps more than we might think. What about genes? Doesn't our genetic code determine how the brain is shaped and molded? This is certainly true, but environment is now known to have a much larger effect than anybody thought possible.

Genes and Environment

Genes are primarily in charge of constructing the framework of the brain and getting its neural connections established. If we compared brain development to building a house, the genes have the blueprints and take care of the basic construction of things like the foundation, framing, wiring, and plumbing. Genes also produce proteins that act as the workers to carry out the construction. Once the basic construction is complete, environment takes over and does the finishing work. This finishing work has a profound effect on the quality of the finished product.

Environment and IQ

Several research studies demonstrate that environment can affect a change in IQ by 20–25 points (Kotulak, 1996). Researchers doing autopsy studies have shown that the brains of mentally active graduate students could have up to 40 percent more neural connections than the brains of high school dropouts. These astonishing discoveries have underscored the importance of continuing our education throughout life and how much the brain can be shaped by the demands placed upon it by the environment.

The New Brain

The brain of a newborn is estimated to have about 1000 trillion neural connections. By age 10, this number will be reduced to about 500 trillion. This thinning process, as mentioned earlier, is called pruning. Those connections that get stimulated by the environment will get the protection and support they need to stay healthy and useful; those that do not find work will be lost as the brain is shaped and molded by the environment and other biological processes.

This shaping and molding allows a child's brain to adapt to whatever stimulation or lack of stimulation it encounters. It is ready to adapt to its environment and culture. It is as if the brain started as a large block of clay ready to be sculpted; the portions not needed are carved away and other areas are formed and shaped. Environment turns out to be the sculptor. What a marvelous thing this is!

The Child's Brain

The brain exhibits its greatest plasticity from birth to about age 12. During this phase of life, the brain can readily reorganize itself. Between the age of 4 and 12, the brain operates at over a 200 percent energy level compared to a normal adult brain. It is busy setting up and eliminating neural networks. This period is a critical time for learning and a critical time for a child to live in an enriched environment. Although the sculpting continues throughout life, much of the work gets done before adolescence.

Children who have mothers who talk to them frequently demonstrate better language skills. Without exposure to an abundance of words, the networks that are used to construct language may not develop properly, and the child may be robbed of the full capacity to use language (Kotulak, 1996). The brain only sets up networks based on the input it gets through the five senses. Most of this building is done through input received through the three educational channels of sight, sound, and touch.

Children who come from negative environments will frequently have many disadvantages throughout life. Constant stress and anxiety will affect what gets stored in memory and how it is stored. All of this will affect the personality of the child and the cognitive functioning of the brain. If children are subjected to abusive environments, they will build circuits characterized by negative schemata instead of circuits related to positive schemata and optimism.

Enriched Environments

Children who have parents, teachers, and other important individuals who display positive patterns of behavior have the opportunity to wire their own brains in a similar manner. The environment, which includes relationships with people, literally shapes and molds the brain of a child.

A child who comes from an enriched environment has a very significant advantage in life.

An enriched environment should be a place where an adult gives positive feedback and responds to a child's use of symbolic language. Children should be exposed to an abundance of language with a rich variety of vocabulary, and they should be allowed to explore their world. Children should be asked questions and given an opportunity to respond. They should be able to rehearse new skills in a safe and supportive environment where they are comfortable and relatively stress free.

As educators, we pay attention to school environments and classroom climates in a constant effort to keep them positive and supportive. We want students to maintain a resourceful learning state. Resourceful learning states might be described as learning states in which the student feels comfortable and connected with others in positive relationships. In a resourceful learning state, the student is relatively stress free and feels motivated to learn, participate, and cooperate. Fear is minimized or eliminated, and students are confident with the challenge of their learning tasks.

Catalogue of Educational Moves

1. Teach students the material presented in this chapter about the brain and the process of learning. Share what they can understand at their particular grade level. Be bold. Most students can learn the material presented in this chapter before they leave elementary school. You do not have to be a scientist or a science teacher to do this. Students are generally very interested in the brain, and they enjoy discovering how learning takes place. The knowledge will instill a greater interest in learning and will enhance their participation in specific learning strategies and moves. Students should know the "why" behind the learning moves we ask them to use. I have taught this material to elementary, middle school, and high school students. I do this regardless of the other course content I am teaching. I do this because I always teach students how to learn my content. I like to know that my students not only know my content, but also know how to learn.

2. Teach students about the four brainwave states. Let them know the role of delta sleep for supporting learning. Teach them about the theta sleep state and the important functions occurring at this time. Let them know that part of their responsibility as a student is learning to manage their own learning state.

(Continued)

(Continued)

3. Teach students that learning requires work. Teach them what this means from a neuroscience perspective. Teach them that work can be enjoyable.

4. Teach students the neuroscience behind test anxiety. Let them know that you will be sharing strategies to conquer this challenge.

5. Teach students the relationship between picturing and comprehension and the role of habituated behavior. Teach them this: "There is no comprehension without picturing." Share the baby learning language example.

6. Teach students this important concept: "We make meaning by connecting into existing schemata." Define schema and use the navicular paragraph as an example. Help students understand that the more they learn, the more they can learn. Help them understand that, without adequate schemata, learning becomes more challenging. Teach them that all content learned now will be important for future learning as each of their brains attempts to connect to existing schemata to make meaning.

7. Teach students about plasticity and about how the brain changes. Use the story of Leisha and Dr. Marion Diamond. Let them know they are getting denser. Answer questions using your knowledge about neurons and synapses.

8. Teach students the truth about the difference between a high school dropout brain and that of a college student. Teach them about pruning and the concept of "use it or lose it."

9. Teach students the importance of life-long learning.

10. Keep an eye on research findings related to memory.

11. Teach students how their memories are created. Use the picnic example or other examples.

12. Teach students about working memory. Let them see that they must learn to manage working memory in order to learn.

13. Teach students about convergence zones and about the executive control room where thinking occurs.

14. Teach students about the importance of having a rich supply of schemata for higher order thinking to be effective. Use the football example and other examples related to your content.

15. Teach students that they have three educational channels and that almost everything recorded in their brains was received from these three channels.

16. Teach students that content learning is about storing in long-term memory and about recall.

17. Teach students about the memory control center, the hippocampus. Tell them about Henry and explain the difference between declarative and nondeclarative memory. Teach them that the hippocampus is busy during theta sleep and what it is doing. Let them know that they can influence this process to enhance their ability to store memory and to recall information.

18. Teach students about the functions of the emotional control center, the amygdala. Use the snake and dog examples or other examples. Teach them about the high road and the low road, and discuss the amygdala's partnership with the executive control room.

19. Teach students about the bossy nature of the amygdala and how it can commandeer working memory.

20. Teach students about how a phobia is created, and discuss how we can all have some irrational fears based on past experience. Help students understand how these fears might interfere with learning or performance.

21. Teach students that drug abuse is really brain abuse, and explain the effects of illegal drugs on the brain.

22. Teach students about the role of environment in shaping the brain. Help them notice that they can begin to influence their environment by, for example, their use of music and media or their choice of friends, locations, and activities. Help them understand that students are actively involved in shaping their own brains.

LEADERSHIP NOTES

The cognitive connection offers many opportunities for leadership. It is important for stakeholders to know the cognitive foundation of any leadership initiative that is being supported by a school or classroom leader. Individuals gain confidence in their leader when they witness that strong foundational knowledge is guiding that leader's decisions and recommendations.

For the school leader, this foundational knowledge builds confidence with staff, parents, and students. It is a powerful move for a school leader to share up-to-date information from science that has applications in the educational setting. The school leader should be perceived as knowledgeable in this area.

Leadership does not mean forcing strategy on others. This would be a push instead of a pull. Leadership is about getting others motivated and excited about important information that will lead to specific, effective initiatives. Understanding the reasons behind good strategy is a critical move for establishing durable motivation.

RESOURCES

Bear, M. F., Paradiso, M. A., Connors, B. (2005). *Neuroscience: Exploring the brain.* Philadelphia, PA: Lippincott Williams and Wilkins.

Carter, R. (1998). *Mapping the mind.* Los Angles: University of California Press.

Diamond, M., & Hopson, J. (1998). *Magic trees of the mind: How to nurture your child's intelligence, creativity, and healthy emotions from birth through adolescence.* New York: Dutton.

Kotulak, R. (1996). *Inside the brain: Revolutionary discoveries of how the mind works.* Kansas City, MO: Andrews McMeel.

LeDoux, J. (2002). *Synaptic self: How our brains become who we are.* New York: Viking Penguin.

Restack, R. (2001). *The secret life of the brain.* Washington, DC: Joseph Henry Press.

Sousa, D. (2006). *How the brain learns* (3rd ed.). Thousand Oaks, CA: Corwin Press.

Strauch, B. (2003). *The primal teen: What the new discoveries about the teenage brain tell us about our kids.* New York: Doubleday.

Sylwester, R. (2005). *How to explain the brain: An educator's handbook of brain terms and cognitive processes.* Thousand Oaks, CA: Corwin Press.

Wolfe, P. (2001). *Brain matters: Translating research into classroom practice.* Alexandria, VA: Association for Supervision and Curriculum Development (ASCD).

4

The Context Connection

Context for Students

What a pleasure it is to be in a classroom with strong context for students. I have discovered them at all levels of the educational spectrum. I was recently in one at second grade, fifth grade, and one at the high school level where the teacher was teaching advanced placement physics. Just walking into the room gives you a sense of wonder and interest about what goes on.

The teacher exhibits a positive mental attitude and excitement for learning. Students feel safe and supported and have a strong sense of belonging. Respect and rapport between the teacher and the students and also between the students themselves are present and can be observed. Students are engaged, alert, and attentive, and display consistent effort in completing their learning tasks. They believe that what they are learning is important. They can tell you why it is important. The context is down to business, but engaging, comfortable, and motivating.

Our goal is to keep students resourceful and engaged. We want to do what we can to allow them to use their motivation and not have to rely only on self-discipline to accomplish their learning. We want to minimize stress, fear, and anxiety, so we can capture and hold working memory. We want our students participative, interested, and responsible.

CHANGING CONTEXT

Many teacher and leadership moves help orchestrate an empowering context for students. None of them can compare in importance to the positive mental attitude of the teacher, to the excitement an educator feels for learning and for the subject being taught. This enthusiasm is a highly contagious ingredient and is powerful for stimulating interest and motivation in students. It can be spotted immediately when entering the learning environment. This is an educator who loves the art of teaching. This is one who loves working with the rising generation and sees potential in every student. This is an educator who feels passion about teaching and learning and understands well the importance of the profession.

Most educators get excited about trying new things or making improvements that will increase effectiveness. I have often thought that one sign of a great teacher is staying teachable. It is when this growth stops that our battery begins to run down and we lose our love of the profession. You are involved in this investigation and search, and just that act alone is an important step in the process and will enhance your resourcefulness. In order for our students to remain resourceful, we must be resourceful.

We can think of context as the setting we orchestrate for our students. As we have already discovered, it is important for students to feel comfortable in the learning environment, but context can also have a direct role in educating the student.

We learned from the chapter on the brain that a student who is consistently subjected to a positive environment develops a more positive, optimistic outlook on life. Consequently, in the context of the classroom, many important characteristics of human behavior are modeled and developed. In the context of the classroom, healthy thinking patterns about the student's own potential can develop and students come to understand the importance of effort and good strategy.

Imagine a large, sturdy ceramic bowl full of fruit. If we let the fruit be the actual content we teach, then we might think of the bowl as the context. If it is a math class, then the fruit would be the actual math content, and the bowl would be the environment, the relationship with the teacher, the expectation for on-task behavior, student responsibility for learning, the expectation for quality, the focus on consistent effort, specific learning strategies, the way students treat each other, the excitement for learning, the motivation of the students, each student's sense of safety, the way students support each other— in other words, the context within which we teach the content.

Shifting Beliefs

Student may bring some beliefs with them that challenge the empowering context we are orchestrating. Perhaps you want to create a context for learning in which students are comfortable and willing to take risks. You want them to be free to try things without worrying about making a mistake. But you may have some students who have a strong belief that runs contrary to your intended context. The belief may sound something like this: "Mistakes are a sign of weakness." I believe we have all worked with students who hold this belief. If we are consistent with our context, we may begin to change this belief or upgrade the thinking of the student to a more positive context.

We want to shift this belief or context to "Mistakes help students learn." Let students know that your classroom is a "learning" place, not a "knowing" place. Students are not expected to know everything. If they did, they would not need to be in school. You may want to post the saying "Mistakes help students learn" in your classroom. A poster stating "This is a LEARNING place" might also be useful if you teach students its connection with the freedom to make mistakes. In addition to this, you would have to consistently acknowledge students for taking risks whether they make a mistake or not. It should be about acknowledging their effort. Most of all, we must be consistent and tenacious with our context.

If you are working with younger students, you might have students practice making mistakes in the classroom, so they can be acknowledged for their effort. Ask the class a question and have them think of an incorrect answer. Call on various students and have them give their answers. Have the class give each student applause or some other kind of acknowledgement for the incorrect answer and say, "Thank you for playing; that is an excellent incorrect answer." Repeat this with several other students, and then remind them that mistakes help students learn and ask them what kind of a place this is. They respond with "This is a LEARNING place." Help them understand that mistakes frequently guide us to the answer or outcome we are seeking. Let them know that even though we are all expected to do our best, making mistakes is sometimes part of the learning process. You can then maintain this attitude with your students on a consistent basis, constantly reinforcing the context—"Mistakes help students learn."

We may have students who hold other beliefs that conflict with the context we are attempting to orchestrate. Once we identify what these are, we can begin to plan a strategy for strengthening our context. For example, if we have a number of students who feel that the particular content being taught holds no value, we should immediately work to change this context. If a student believes it is the teacher's job to teach and does not recognize it is the student's responsibility to learn, we will want to make moves to change this limiting belief.

We will now begin exploring teacher and leadership moves that help orchestrate an empowering context for students. The importance of context for students cannot be overstated. It can make the difference between success and failure.

This Is Important

The "this is important" move is a communication move, and it lets the students know that what they are learning is important and valuable. The educator can send this message in many ways to students. Telling them how the content will be valuable to them or what they will gain by knowing the information, skill, or process is very helpful for students and can have a significant affect on their learning (Saphier & Gower, 1997). This is sometimes referred to as the "What's in it for me?" move. We can also ask the students why they think a subject is important. Once we have their response, we can add to it if we choose. When students know this information, they become more interested in learning the content. Clearly, teachers who show excitement for their content can make a significant difference to student engagement. The teacher who is excited about his or her content constantly sends the message about its importance to students in direct as well as subtle ways.

When the "this is important" move becomes an area of focus, a teacher will find many ways to communicate it. It can be communicated in the way a teacher grades papers and in how that educator holds students accountable for their learning. It can be communicated in the way a teacher consistently checks for understanding and pays attention to areas that may be weak. It may be communicated in the attitude of the teacher that the possibility of not learning the content would constitute a crisis. It can be communicated in the way a teacher sticks with a student who has answered a question incorrectly in a discussion. The teacher can choose to guide the student to the correct understanding. The other students observe and get the message that this is important and everyone must know it.

One reason we want this message to come across to our students with such clarity is that the brain will be making decisions about what to keep and what to discard during theta brainwave sleep. We do not want our content in the category of the phone number remembered just long enough for us to dial and then forgotten. We want our content encoded into long-term memory. This process begins with a strong message to the brain that "this is important."

We could have our students talk to their brain. It might go something like this:

> "Please pause. Please have a quick conversation with your brain. Please let your brain know that what we just learned is important. Tell it to store this in long-term memory. Have it store the following items." (Here we can do a short recap of the most important items.) "Please thank your brain and tell it to go back to work." (With younger students, I will have them kiss their brain by kissing their hand and touching their hand to their head.) You can also use this as an enrollment move by having them pause and have a conversation with their brain before you deliver some important content.

Reteaching content when students did not learn it the first time sends a powerful message to students. If we assess students and discover that most of them did poorly but we just give them a grade and continue with the curriculum, students get the message that the content was not important. If this happens too frequently, their thinking can form into an attitude about the content taught in school, and, eventually, apathy about learning may result.

Focus on Effort

Let's consider the following question: How satisfied would you be if all you got from your students was 100 percent effort?

There is something powerful about setting a context around a focus on effort. We can let our students know that this is what they do for a living. They give effort. The teacher takes that effort and directs it to maximize their learning. This is the job of the professional educator. The job of the student is to consistently give strong effort.

One important aspect of focusing on effort is the fact that effort is a choice. Students can choose to give effort, or they can choose not to give effort. They can choose to give moderate effort, or they can choose to give strong effort. Effort is always a choice. High performance may not be a choice for a student at a particular time, but effort is a choice.

Effort creates ability. This is because of the plasticity of the human brain. When we give consistent effort, things change. Neural networks are expanded and modified. It is helpful for students to understand this concept. They can relate examples in their own lives when they demonstrated that effort creates ability, for example, when they learned to ride a bike, to play a sport, to divide fractions, or to drive a car.

Opening Traditions

It is helpful to acknowledge effort on a consistent basis and also to recommend strong effort to our students. We might also include this idea in our opening traditions. An opening tradition is a ritual a teacher sets up to get a class started, and this ritual can be a strategy to help students get focused and to set a positive context. One effective strategy is to include opening questions as part of the opening tradition. The teacher asks questions, and the students respond in unison.

Teacher: Why are you here?

Students: To learn.

Teacher: What works?

Students: Effort.

Teacher: What will you give?

Students: 100 percent.

You might consider repeating each question twice or even three times. You can include other things in the ritual like a table clap or a clapping rhythm before and after the questions. A table clap involves the students hitting their desks or tables with their hands and then clapping their hands together in some established pattern, such as table-clap-table-clap-table-clap-clap. (The word "table" in this example means that students slap their desks or tables.) The table clap moves very quickly. I have used it successfully with students at all grade levels, including high school and college. You might also consider having the students return the question to the teacher.

Clapping pattern

Teacher: Why are you here?

Students: To learn. Why are you here?

Teacher: To teach. What works?

Students: Effort. What works?

Teacher: Effort. What will you give?

Students: 100 percent. What will you give?

Teacher: 100 percent.

Clapping pattern

Opening traditions should be designed to fit the particular situation and students. The purpose is to get things started quickly and to set a positive context. If you decide to use an opening dialogue similar to the one above, you will find it helpful to put the questions and responses on a chart and point to each question as you go through the tradition. The questions in the preceding dialogue are designed to create a focus on effort.

Special opening statements by the teacher can also be part of an opening tradition. For example, a teacher might begin with this speech:

Please adjust your physiology. Let's think about how we will show up today. We are all capable of giving 100 percent effort. It is a choice. I want to take this opportunity to encourage you to give strong effort. I am going to give 100 percent and hope you will choose to do the same. Our success in life will be affected by our ability to choose to give strong effort. Let's all choose to give strong effort. Let's begin.

Opening traditions can save time and are effective for setting positive context for learning. They can also help establish that the student has an important responsibility for making sure that learning is occurring.

Inclusive Language

The use of inclusive language creates a more empowering context for students. To accomplish this, we use words that include us in the same group with our students. Inclusive language tends to put everyone on the same team. For example, instead of saying, "I want you to open your books to page 43," we would say, "Let's open our books to page 43." Instead of saying, "I will explain this to you," we would say, "Let's explore this together," or "Let's put our heads together and figure this out." Instead of saying, "I am giving you six problems for homework," we would say, "We have six homefun problems for tonight." The use of this kind of inclusive language helps send the message that we are all on the same team.

It requires practice to get this move well established. Begin by adjusting your thinking, so you actually consider your students and yourself as being all on the same team. Start noticing your noninclusive language and replace it. At first, you may have to catch yourself, pause, and rephrase what you are saying. Once you get through this stage, inclusion becomes a natural way of communicating with your students, and you will discover it is well worth the effort.

Establishing inclusion diminishes the feelings of cultural or other forms of isolation that can deteriorate motivation to learn. It also fosters an environment that encourages students to be their authentic selves, and, consequently, to take the risks necessary for personal development and academic learning (Ginsberg & Wlodkowski, 2000). The following strategy is effective in creating an atmosphere of inclusion and safety.

Home Court Advantage

When a sports team plays on its own home court in its own hometown, the team actually has a statistical advantage. This advantage has become known as the "home court advantage." We can also have a home court advantage in our classroom. The phrase "home court advantage" is very effective with students. We can use it to help define the context we are creating in the learning environment.

To establish the concept of a home court advantage with our students, we can begin by explaining what it is in relation to a sports team. We can then ask students why they think it is true that a team has a statistical advantage when its members play on their home court. Work to help students discover that, when players are familiar with their home location, they feel more relaxed and safe. They feel a greater sense of belonging. They also may enjoy the benefits of greater support from their fans.

The Three Ingredients

In order to get a home court advantage in a classroom, we need the same ingredients. First, we need a team. In other words, students need to feel that they belong. A sense of belonging is one of the necessary ingredients for a home court advantage. We also would need to feel safe and supported. These are the other two essential ingredients for a classroom home court advantage.

Inform students that you would like to work together with them to establish a home court advantage and that it includes the three ingredients of safety, support, and belonging. Take them to the entryway of the classroom and inform them that it is not a doorway. It is called a threshold. Inform them that when they enter through this threshold things change. Whatever goes on outside goes on out there, but, when they enter here, something happens. It is called a home court advantage, and everybody gets it.

Discuss each of the three ingredients of a home court advantage. Ask them what safety looks like in the classroom. What do students do who feel unsafe? What do students do who feel safe? What do we have to do to make sure everyone feels safe in here when each person walks through the threshold?

Discuss support and ask similar questions. What does support look like in a classroom. Where does it come from? How do you know if you have it? What would non-support look like? How would you know if you are supporting others? Be sure they clearly see that support comes from the teacher and from students. Ask them where the teacher will get support. How will students give support to the teacher?

Discuss belonging. What does belonging look like? How do you know if you belong? What can you do to let others know they belong? Emphasize that, on a team, all players must do their part. Ask them what would happen if one member of the team did not do her or his part. Discuss what would happen in here if even one student does not do her or his part.

Ask students if they would rather be in a room with a home court advantage or in one where it is missing. Ask them which room would be better for learning, and ask them why. Reference what we learned about the brain if you have shared this information. Tell them you hope to establish a strong home court advantage in your classroom, or, depending on their age, have them decide they want a home court advantage. Let them know that establishing a home court advantage is everyone's business: "We can make it happen if we want to, and we will all work together to make sure we get it and keep it."

It is helpful to set your doorway or threshold apart in some manner. Placing a mat students must walk over in order to enter is effective. You might decorate the doorway to help remind students.

The HCA Iconic

You can make an iconic poster to represent the home court advantage (HCA) concept and post it at the entrance of your classroom. An iconic poster is a poster with a symbol on it that represents a concept. The symbol would be similar to an icon you might find on a computer. Imagine an equilateral triangle with a circle drawn inside and touching all three sides of the triangle. This graphic could represent the concept of a home court advantage. The triangle represents the three ingredients of safety, support, and belonging, and the circle represents the concept that everyone is included. You could put the letters HCA inside the circle to represent the words "home court advantage."

Figure 4.1   A Home Court Advantage (HCA) Icon

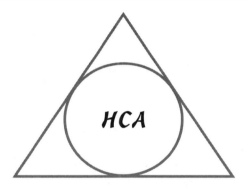

Have a committee of students make a large poster or banner with the words "Home Court Advantage," and post this up front in the classroom. Have a large icon posted in the classroom. On this one, write the three words—"safety, support, belonging"—on the icon by writing one word along each of three sides of the triangle. With younger students, you may want them to have this icon taped to their desks as a constant reminder.

Continue to discuss the concept of home court advantage as you process events that occur in the classroom. Be sure to acknowledge safety, support, and belonging when you see them. Have students report in to assess how strong the home court advantage is. If it is not strong, investigate with students what can be done to strengthen it and to make sure that every member of the class feels it.

The concept of a home court advantage is powerful because it acts as a cognitive anchor. An anchor is something that is attached to something else and holds that thing in place. This particular cognitive anchor provides students something to focus on that feels real to them. It defines what we are attempting to accomplish and allows us to connect important

Figure 4.2   Another Home Court Advantage (HCA) Icon

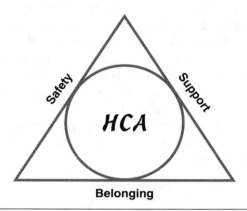

schemata to that definition. It is also powerful because it is easily understood.

The concept of home court advantage is effective for elementary, middle school, and high school students. Of course, it must be presented differently at different grade levels. This adaptability will be true for many of the moves described in this book. Please be cautious about discounting suggestions because you think they might not be relevant for your level of student. If you are an elementary teacher and notice that I am giving a high school example, do not assume that the strategy exemplified is only a high school move. Consider the move carefully before you draw this conclusion. If you are a high school teacher and I include an example that involves younger students, do not assume that the move is not effective at your grade level. We all must adapt these teacher moves to fit our particular situation.

Establishing a home court advantage requires leadership. It requires modeling, motivation, and, of course, using the concept as an initiative for the classroom or school organization. It is also a very powerful ingredient for establishing a system for durable motivation.

ESTABLISHING RAPPORT

Rapport is an important consideration when setting context for students. We all recognize the advantages of having rapport with our students, and many effective teacher moves lead to stronger rapport with students. Some of them are part of the personality of the teacher. An example of this is the use of humor. Some educators are gifted with an ability to use effective humor in the classroom while others have to be more deliberate about how to accomplish this. In either case, humor is an effective tool for building rapport.

Valuing Relationships

One of the most effective steps we can take to develop rapport is to value students in an equal value relationship. This is not the most common relationship between an educator and a student, but it is certainly the most powerful. The most common relationship might be described as a "big me–little you" relationship. This relationship communicates the teacher's importance. "I am more important than you." "What I think is more important than what you think." "What I feel is more important than what you feel." This relationship does not build rapport; in fact, it damages rapport. These relationships exist in the adult communication arena as well as in the classroom arena.

Big Me–Big You

An equal value relationship might be described as a "big me–big you" relationship. I value you, and you value me; our value is equal. And we have an equal value or a win-win relationship. What you think is just as important as what I think. What you feel is just as important as what I feel. This relationship is characterized by attentive listening and respect. A student can feel it immediately. The relationship communicates, "You are important and so am I." Some older students can sit in a classroom for three minutes and determine if the relationship is equal value or if it is a "big me–little you" situation, and their conclusion will impact their achievement.

We want to foster big me–big you relationships throughout the entire organization. We should work to establish them with students, teachers, administrators, and parents. They should be evident when an administrator is talking to a staff member, when a teacher talks to a colleague, when a teacher speaks with a student or parent, and when a student communicates with another student. This initiative should ideally be part of the culture of the school because it creates a climate of mutual support and respect and a sense of safety and belonging. These effects are important for establishing durable motivation in the organization. Also, the "big me–big you" relationship promotes a climate that allows the amygdala to stay calm, so students can maximize their capacity for encoding memory.

Many things can deter the development of an equal value relationship. Such factors as popularity, age, economic status, education, religion, racial discrimination, and authority are examples. The equal value concept might sound something like this: "I don't care how much education you have, or how much authority, or how popular you are, or what your economic status is, or how good you are at soccer, or how smart you are, or what label you wear on your tennis shoes. We have equal value. I value you, and you value me."

Equal Value and Authority

Is it possible to have an equal value relationship and still hold authority properly in the classroom? Yes, and every educator should strive for this dynamic. Maintaining authority within an equal value relationship requires keeping rules and consequences external to the teacher. The idea here is that the rules and consequences operate independently, and the teacher's role is to automatically operate the system. Clarity is essential. Students must be absolutely clear about rules and consequences and know they will automatically operate based on the student's choices.

Another essential ingredient is consistency. A teacher does not have the luxury of applying a consequence to one student and not to another. Everybody is watching. When any inconsistency occurs, the teacher has internalized the discipline system, meaning that the decisions come from inside the teacher rather than from the rules. Now, students may think that decisions depend on whom the teacher likes or on the teacher's mood. This perception by students breaks down the opportunity for equal value relationships and damages rapport. Consistency does not mean that you have to follow the letter of the law. Perhaps a school has a strict policy about being to class on time, but the teacher likes to give one warning. Consistency means that every student gets one warning.

What if a student has just been through the dean of students and is referred to the principal for discipline. Can that principal maintain an equal value relationship? The principal holds the ultimate authority in the school, and the student has broken a very serious rule. Let's slip into a principal's office and listen to a conversation with a student who is in serious trouble:

Jeff, I see you chose to have an illegal substance at school. We have very strict rules about that, as you know. When you pick up one end of a stick you also pick up the other, and now you are going to have to face the consequences for the choice you made. I am disappointed you made this choice, Jeff, and I hope we will still have an opportunity to work together so you can be successful here.

The choice you made has an automatic ten-day suspension attached to it. During the 10-day period, a meeting will be held with the area administrator to decide if you should be recommended for expulsion from the school district. If you are expelled, you will be out of school for one full year.

You must decide if you want to try to stay in our school, Jeff. If you do, I will help you through this process and support you in coming up with a plan for your success. I hope this is the decision you make, but it is your choice to decide if you want to try. We will all be very interested in hearing what you are committed to doing, and I believe it will have an important impact on the outcome.

There is something else you need to know. When a student has an illegal substance at school, I am required to contact the police. I called the sheriff, and he will be here shortly. You can talk to him by yourself, or, if you want me present, I will be there with you. It is possible that he will arrest you. We also must contact your parents, so let's talk about how best to get that accomplished.

This principal is holding and using authority properly and also valuing Jeff at the same time. Notice that the discipline is external to the principal. This leader is not saying, "I am going to suspend you for 10 days." Instead, Jeff hears what the principal must do as a consequence of Jeff's actions and will do depending upon Jeff's choices. Jeff hears that the consequences are a result of Jeff's own choices. It is this automatic system that allows the principal to maintain rapport with the students. The principal is not communicating anger, just disappointment. We have to separate the behavior from the person to accomplish this. It is not Jeff we don't like; it is his bad choice. We value Jeff and hope he will learn to make better choices in the future. Even though Jeff is going to suffer some severe penalties, we can still maintain a big me–big you relationship. These same principles must also operate in the classroom for rapport to flourish and for motivation to be sustainable.

Rapport–Building Moves

Another move that helps to build rapport is attentive, active listening. When we really listen to a student, we send the strong message, "I value you." Giving sincere apologies to students or asking students for advice are powerful rapport-building moves. When something is not working in the classroom, asking advice from the entire class can get some very positive results. It might sound something like this:

Please pause. This is not working the way I had hoped. Something has gone wrong, but I do not know what it is. When I planned this, I thought it would work smoothly, but I may have made a mistake. I am a bit confused. I need some advice. Please help me understand what we need to do differently.

Sharing things about ourselves is another strong rapport-building move. Remembering is also a good move. Remembering might sound like this: "Hey Tamara, did your dad get back from his trip yet?" It may have been a week ago that Tamara mentioned this trip, and the comment you just made says, "You are important." The skill we examined called "inclusive language" is also helpful for building rapport with students. Any time we can bridge to their world, we are making moves that help build rapport. This bridging includes talking about topics that are interesting to them and that are a part of their world, including movies, music, and events.

Strong rapport with students allows us to build a strong context for teaching our content. Some students are affected more than others. Some students might operate from an attitude that sounds like this: "Just tell me what you want me to do, and I will do it." These students may not be nearly as affected by context and rapport as others. However, many of our students are significantly affected by context, and a positive context, including a high level of rapport, can have a dramatic effect on their effort and focus.

ENVIRONMENT

The physical environment of a classroom can have an important impact on setting context (Jensen, 2000). Our classroom or school sends a message. What message does your classroom or school send to students? Let's examine some of the variables we can control related to environment.

Music

Music can be used for setting context and for orchestrating the actions that occur in the classroom. The use of music when students enter the room is very effective. You can also select a particular song as part of your opening tradition. This is a good way to get students started and focused. You would use the same song for several weeks to establish a tradition using the music. You might have music playing before class and then switch to this song to indicate you are ready to start. You can attach other traditions to this opening music if you choose, like a special clap at the end to indicate that class is now beginning. You would then launch into any other opening traditions you have set up.

Managing Mood

Music is an effective tool for managing mood, energy, and attention. With some students, you may want to bring energy down, and soothing music might get just the effect you want. In other cases, you might want to increase energy and would select upbeat music to move students in that direction.

Managing Focus

Music is also helpful to support students in their efforts to maintain focus. This music should have no lyrics. It should not even be instrumental music that your students know the words to, or it may result in distraction instead of focus. Music with words can distract because, when students are reading or focusing on a language task, they are engaging the left hemisphere of the brain, and this hemisphere also follows the lyrics in music. Consequently, when students listen to music that has words, they will be following or inserting the lyrics in the music and may not be able to focus on their work.

One type of music that has been used extensively for focus is music composed during the Baroque period. This period was from about 1600–1750. You might recognize many of these composers, including Handel, Corelli, or Vivaldi. Bach was one of the last of the Baroque composers, and he certainly is one of the most famous. Baroque music is different from other types of music. It is sometimes called mathematical music because it was composed according to formulas that had been handed down through music guilds for several hundred years. It will frequently have more than one musical theme running at the same time, the frequency ranges are different, and much of it is composed at about 60–70 beats per minute, which is the heart's rate at rest.

Just picking up a CD of Baroque music and using it for focus in the classroom will probably not work because you might have an energetic and fast section (a presto or allegro movement) right next to a slower and calmer section (an andante or largo movement). The music has to be arranged to allow you to play slower movements that promote focus without distraction. You can do this if you have a CD burner. Another option is to buy engineered music for the classroom. You will find it at a music store under titles such as "Music for the Classroom" or "Music for Learning" or "Music for Studying" and similar titles. There are also some contemporary composers that are now producing music for the classroom.

If you are using music for focus in the classroom, volume is an important consideration. The music should be barely audible. Once students become familiar with the use of music, they will request it. The focus music helps students deal with distraction and moves them more toward an alpha brainwave state.

Attention Deficit

What if you have a student in your classroom who has attention deficit disorder (ADD)? This student may come to you and inform you that the music makes concentration impossible. Actually, music is a helpful tool for an ADD student, but anything novel or new in the environment will be a distraction for a period of time. A student with an attention deficit will need time to acclimate to the stimulus. You must get through this period, which may take about a week. After that, any students with ADD will have a valuable asset to help them focus.

Transitions

Music can be used effectively for transitions as well. This transition music can be used for clean up at the end of the day or for changing activities during the day. Use the same piece of music each time to create an anchor. The music just comes on in the environment, and the students know what to do. You can use anchored music to let students know that they need to get their vocabulary notebooks and form into their groups. No instructions—just music that is anchored to the particular action. You can also give students a one-song break. It is fine to use music with lyrics and to turn the volume up for musical breaks as well as for transitions or "come-in" songs. One very nice thing about a one-song break is that it has a clear beginning and a clear ending.

Classroom Projects

Music that is more upbeat would be played while students are working on a project in a classroom, and there is activity. It may be better, however, to use classical or other instrumental music instead of music with lyrics depending on the degree of concentration required.

Students' Music

A student may come up to you and say, "Hey, I've got music." Some students will request that their music be played in the classroom, and playing student music can be a positive, rapport-building move. But you might want to observe the following two rules:

- No music with negative themes or bad words is ever played in the classroom.
- Before music is used in the classroom, the teacher must listen to it. If the teacher cannot understand the lyrics, they must be written out, or the teacher must be supplied with the printed lyrics if they came with the CD.

Music is powerful for helping students stay resourceful. It is also powerful for supporting the teacher in staying resourceful. Put on music before school in your classroom, music that gets you energized and ready to teach. The use of music in the classroom is fun and effective, and teachers should carefully consider its use at all grade levels.

Props

Props include objects placed in the classroom to create a special effect. I recently saw an elementary classroom with an antique bathtub sitting in one corner full of pillows. Small self-contained water fountains also create a pleasant atmosphere and are especially effective for students who can benefit from something with a calming effect. Other props might include interesting objects, pottery, artwork, and furniture. They are used to create an interesting and unique environment.

Peripherals

Peripherals include posters and other items attached to the walls and bulletin boards in a classroom or school. One type of poster is an affirmation poster. These can be purchased or made in the classroom. For example, you might have a poster that says "What Works?" or "I Can Do This" or "Learning is Fun."

The use of curricular iconic posters is a move you might consider. These posters have a large icon that represents specific content from your curriculum. Students or teachers can design them and then attach meaning to them. We were considering one earlier to express the home court advantage idea. They can be made to represent important pieces of your content that you want to reinforce. Regular content posters are also useful. These posters are used in instruction and then displayed in the room. Setting aside an area in the room to display student work is also a good idea and sends the positive message "You are important" to students. It can also be used to create a greater focus on quality.

Lighting

Most of us teach under fluorescent lighting. Educational studies involving lighting have shown that fluorescent lighting is the least desirable lighting for students because it cycles just barely above the conscious level. Some students are sensitive to this cycling and will experience fatigue. The best lighting would be indirect, full-spectrum lighting, perhaps mixed with some natural light coming from windows if possible. Of course, sometimes what we want is not what we get. There are some effective moves we can make, however.

Lamps that can be purchased at garage sales or discount stores can be used in a classroom to change the entire feel of the room. About three or four lamps can have a significant impact on classroom context. Depending on the size of the room, you may even be able to operate for short periods with only your incandescent lamps. Mixing fluorescent lighting with incandescent lamps creates better light for learning. The use of lamps creates a more relaxed and pleasant work environment.

How about a blue light special? The students come into the classroom and immediately notice that all the lamps have blue lights. You can anchor this unusual lighting to special events that occur in the classroom.

You could shed some light on an important idea. Perhaps a student asks a question and you say, "Let me shed some light on that." You then hand a powerful flashlight to one of your students and have the student keep it focused on what you are showing at your white board. This spotlight will change focus and pull all attention to the instruction.

Plants

The use of plants in the environment will have a calming effect on many students. Their use can help overcome the institutional look of many school classrooms, creating a more pleasant workspace. The effect of a plant in creating a positive environment can be enhanced when the plant is near a table lamp.

Classroom Maps

Classroom maps are diagrams of various arrangements of classroom furniture. The concept behind this move is flexibility. Students are trained to change the room to different configurations in a matter of seconds. This change can be anchored to a particular piece of music. Let's consider a classroom where the student desks do not have a chair attached, which is a favorable situation because it allows for much more flexibility.

This classroom could have several different classroom maps. Perhaps one could be desks in straight rows. Suppose the teacher wanted students in this configuration, but wanted something different for the next activity. Music comes on, and the students are informed which map should be followed. They would have between 60–90 seconds to change the room. Let's say they are told to change to classroom map B, so the desks are all pushed to the side, and the students bring their chairs to the front and form them around the teacher in a theatre style arrangement. Another possibility would be to have desks arranged in groups or perhaps to have no furniture at all with students seated on the floor.

Our classroom environments should be clean and organized. They should be full, but orderly. Color should be used for accent and for visual stimulation. For general themes in the classroom, pastels and softer colors should be used including blues, greens, or pinks. Bright colors like reds and oranges should be used more sparingly for accent or impact.

Room temperature is also an important consideration. We should do everything we can to keep the temperature of the room comfortable. You might consider aromas as well. Think about what a pleasant sensation you get when you walk into a room that has a pleasant aroma. Aroma can be very effective for strengthening context, and many educators make this move to create a more pleasant environment.

Catalogue of Educational Moves

1. Continue to work on staying resourceful and consistently display a positive mental attitude in the classroom. No context move is more important.

2. Be a discriminating shopper, and select moves that will work for you, but be bold. Begin with the implementation of one or two moves as soon as possible.

3. Make the "This Is Important" theme prevalent in the context of your classroom. Consistently let students know how they will benefit from learning the content. Demonstrate this theme in the way you grade papers and handle student responses. Let students feel your excitement for your content, and hold them accountable for learning.

4. Have students talk to their brain to let it know what is important. Use this opportunity to recap your content. Have them kiss their brain.

5. Use reteaching when students fail to master content to help them get mastery and to demonstrate the importance of learning the content.

6. Create a "Focus on Effort" initiative in your classroom. Teach students that effort is a choice and that giving effort is what they do for a living.

7. Teach students that effort creates ability and relate this to brain plasticity.

8. Consistently acknowledge strong effort in your classroom.

9. Use effective opening traditions. Include opening questions to set the context. Use table claps or other forms of physical action. Use standard opening comments.

10. Use inclusive language to create a more friendly and engaging context for learning.

11. Teach students that your classroom is a LEARNING place and that "Mistakes help students learn."

12. Consistently acknowledge students for taking educational risks.

13. Establish a home court advantage in your classroom. Reinforce safety, support, and belonging.

14. Create a "threshold" that one crosses to get into your classroom.

15. Use humor to build rapport.

16. Maintain equal value relationships with students. Teach students about equal value relationships, and encourage this kind of relationship between students.

(Continued)

(Continued)

17. Model attentive listening in the classroom.

18. Externalize discipline to maintain equal value relationships.

19. Maintain clarity and consistency to foster equal value relationships.

20. Separate behavior from the student to maintain equal value relationships.

21. Give sincere apologies to students when needed.

22. Ask students for advice.

23. Share yourself to strengthen rapport.

24. Use "remembering" to strengthen rapport.

25. Bridge to the interests of students to strengthen rapport.

26. Use music to manage student and teacher states.

27. Use anchored music as part of opening and closing traditions.

28. Use music to support student focus.

29. Use anchored music for transitions.

30. Use music for one-song classroom breaks.

31. Use peripherals and props (including affirmation posters, iconic posters, instructional posters, and student work) to help create context.

32. Use lamps in your classroom to create a comfortable context.

33. Have a blue light special.

34. Shed light on instruction using a large flashlight.

35. Use classroom maps for instructional flexibility.

36. Maintain a clean and well-organized environment.

37. Use color in your classroom environment for visual stimulation and impact.

38. Maintain a comfortable temperature in your classroom.

39. Use aromas to create a pleasant classroom context.

LEADERSHIP NOTES

The home court advantage can be a powerful initiative and can set an effective context for an entire school. Everyone can get involved including the parent community. It can become a focus for newsletters and special assemblies for students. The concept of the equal value relationship can be easily tied in with the same theme. The "Focus on Effort" concept can be used as a schoolwide initiative as well, one that supports motivation because of its relationship with self-efficacy. Effort is something that is within the power of the student to choose.

A strong educational leader must maintain equal value relationships. The classroom leader maintains equal value relationships with students, and a school leader must maintain equal value relationships with staff. These big me–big you relationships are important because the big me–little you relationship destroys teamwork, sets up barriers between people, and frequently creates school politics. A school leader should also model equal value relationships with students and parents. A school leader is there to serve staff, students, and parents.

The physical environment of the entire school can become a leadership initiative. We should work to maintain an environment that is pleasing and stimulating, and one that students, parents, and staff view with pride. Have an environmental committee and involve the parents. If the parent organization has any interior designers, get them involved. Have the parent organization divide the school up into sections and assign them to smaller committees or groups of families. Maintain careful control of the entire project, and use parent coordinators for quality control. Have the parent organization raise money to make the school an exceptional environment for learning. Be bold and be creative.

Many of the moves suggested in this chapter make work more enjoyable, and we discovered earlier that our enjoyment of work has a direct effect on motivation. It might be helpful to review the moves listed in this chapter and notice how many of them relate to direction, self-efficacy, support, or value. Also, notice those moves that are effective for capturing and holding working memory or for creating a climate in which stress and anxiety are reduced.

RESOURCES

Noddings, N. (2005). *The challenge to care in schools: An alternative approach to education* (2nd ed.). New York: Teachers College Press.
Seligman, M. (1995). *The optimistic child.* Boston: Houghton Mifflin.

5

The Character Connection

The process of building a strong character connection for students begins with setting in place effective cognitive anchors that can be used to define and strengthen specific character themes. A cognitive anchor is an overarching principle around which we can develop the schema that supports students in building strong character. The anchors discussed in this chapter are "the line," "the gold coin of respect," and the "four gems of excellence": the gems of integrity, ownership, positive mental attitude, and perseverance.

Anchors should be clear and precise enough for students to picture their own positive behavior and strong character. Once the anchor is in place in the student's thinking, we continue to reinforce it with ongoing curriculum to develop and strengthen the anchor. Stated another way, we help students establish a positive neural network and then assist them in building that network over time until it becomes powerful in guiding choices and actions.

This chapter reads differently from the chapters you have already explored because of the special nature of our topics. You will discover several stories that teachers can use to introduce and reinforce the principles. They are included as resources to be used with students. These stories and examples are only to get you off to a strong start. You will want to continue to collect examples and stories that reinforce these concepts and to tap into those already in your repertoire. We will also listen in on some actual dialogs with students to assist our understanding of how we might better establish these anchors.

As you explore this material, consider how you might use it with your own students. Perhaps you will modify specific stories or examples to fit your particular situation. You might be reminded of your own experiences or of a different story, one you know that would be effective in establishing or reinforcing the anchors.

THE LINE

Let's begin by learning about "the line." This concept sets up a powerful framework for students. When introducing it to students, you might draw their attention to a poster with a solid, bold line drawn on it. Tell them that what they are seeing may look like a line, but that it is not *a* line. It is *the* line. Let them know that each of us can choose to live our life above the line, or we can choose to live below the line. Each of us must choose every day where we will live.

This concept creates an immediate and strong anchor for students. They can easily picture a line, and students of all ages can begin to define what kind of behavior is below the line and what kind of behavior is above the line. When introducing the line, allow students to share their understanding of above and below-the-line behavior. It is also helpful to put them into groups and have them make their own posters with a bold line drawn through the center and above and below the line behaviors stated or illustrated in their proper locations in relation to the line.

This anchor has been tested with students of all ages, from elementary school children to adults, with excellent results. The anchor is powerful because it is clear and easy to understand. Students will normally have a desire to live their lives above the line. Once established, "the line" concept can be used in the dialogue of the student and the teacher or administrator. We might ask, "Is that action above the line or below the line?" "Were you speaking above the line or below the line?" "Is that kind of thinking above or below the line?" We can use it in discussions that focus on personal actions, school situations, or local and world current events. These discussions are designed to strengthen the anchor.

For students who have been taught the "law of source and resource," this concept can be used to define the line. If what we are saying, thinking, or doing is building the source, then we are above the line. If we are diminishing the source, we are below the line. For example, if we tell the truth, we are above the line. This behavior builds the source because it builds our reputation with others and ourselves. If we are telling a lie, we diminish the source. Even if we get away with lying, the act diminishes our reputation with ourselves.

Once we have the concept of the line well established, we can begin to establish additional cognitive anchors that define above-the-line thinking and behavior. There are many possibilities for principles that could be the foundation of a character program in a classroom and school community. I have selected the five that I feel are the most powerful and most essential: respect, integrity, ownership, positive mental attitude, and perseverance. These principles describe thinking and behavior that build the source, and they set the stage for building strong character in students.

When introducing the "gold coin of respect" or the four "gems of excellence" to students, we want to begin by setting a powerful context that creates a feeling of value and importance about the principles. Giving a brief history of success principles is helpful in creating this strong context.

SUCCESS PRINCIPLES

The idea of isolating the characteristics of successful people has been an area of focus for a long time in America. Perhaps it all got started with Andrew Carnegie, who believed he had in his possession a formula for success. Andrew Carnegie was known as "The Steel King" in America and was considered very successful. He donated millions of dollars to support the arts and education. (It might be helpful to have a group of students study and report on his life as well as on the lives of the other successful individuals mentioned in the paragraphs that follow.)

Andrew Carnegie believed that, if you studied the lives of successful people, you would find common characteristics that made them successful. He believed that any individuals who put these characteristics to work in their own lives would be uncommonly successful as well. He wanted to test his theory and interested a man by the name of Napoleon Hill in conducting a research project. Andrew Carnegie asked Mr. Hill to interview and research the lives of the five hundred most successful people in America to discover what traits they had in common that had contributed to their success.

Napoleon Hill agreed to do this project, but it took him twenty years. By the time he was finished, Andrew Carnegie had passed away. Some of the individuals on Hill's research list you may recognize: Henry Ford, William Wrigley, Jr., George Eastman, Charles Schwab, Theodore Roosevelt, Wilbur Wright, King Gillette, Thomas Edison, F. W. Woolworth, Clarence Darrow, Woodrow Wilson, and Alexander Graham Bell.

When Napoleon Hill finished this project, he published a massive volume of his research findings. It has been out of print for many years, but his conclusions stirred up great interest in the topic of success. Many researchers have continued the search and much has been written to identify the traits necessary for success and strong character.

The five principles presented here come from this tradition of isolating character traits that lead to success. The idea of studying successful people to discover what they have in common is a powerful one and a concept that students can grasp. Use this idea to create interest in the principles and to emphasize their importance. Let's begin with the most essential principle: respect.

THE GOLD COIN OF RESPECT

Respect is a critical theme for the classroom and for the entire educational community, so it should be the primary foundational principle for character education. This principle should be defined as respect for people, property, and self. Respect is the master principle that grounds the other character building principles.

Imagine a gold coin. There is something engraved on both sides. On one side is engraved the words people, property, and self. When you turn the coin over, you find the words life, liberty, and pursuit of happiness. This is the "gold coin of respect."

Figure 5.1   The Gold Coin of Respect

Credit: Anadine Burrell, 2006.

Without respect as a grounding principle, other principles in our character program may float and create confusion for students. If you are teaching in a private religious school, you could ground the success principles in the laws of God. But this cannot be done in a public school. To understand why respect is the grounding principle of character development, consider the event that has come to be known as 9/11, the act of terrorism that caused the two World Trade Towers to collapse in New York City.

Were the terrorists in alignment with the principle of integrity? We can define integrity as aligning your actions with what you believe to be right. Yes, they were in alignment with integrity. Was it an act of courage? Many would argue that it takes a lot of courage to die for what you believe in. Were they in alignment with the principle of ownership? In other words, did they take responsibility for their actions? Yes. Were they in alignment with the principle of commitment? I think we can agree that they were committed. Were they loyal to their cause and the members of their group? Yes.

These are important principles and could be included in a character program, but there must be a foundational principle to tie these principles to for the program to be well grounded. Respect is the most powerful grounding principle. The terrorists were in violation of this basic principle. They did not have respect for people, property, and self. They did not have respect for life, liberty, and the pursuit of happiness. We are never above the line when we are out of alignment with the gold coin of respect. Even if we demonstrate other important principles, we cannot violate this grounding principle and be justified. Students must never lose this coin.

It is powerful to give each student a plastic gold coin with these words on it when this important principle is taught. Tell them to keep the coins safe and to always live by this principle. The definition of respect as described here must be firmly planted in their thinking, so it can serve as a grounding principle of success for their lifetime.

Clarity

Students must have a clear definition of respect. This definition should be reviewed and reinforced on a regular basis. Here is one definition that works well: to show respect means to show consideration, honor, and esteem for people, property, and self. If you have established the anchor of "the line," it is valuable to have students brainstorm what respect and disrespect look like and to work in teams to create a "line chart" showing their descriptions above and below the line. When discussing respect for people, it is also helpful to include the broad concept of respect that includes respect for life, liberty, and the pursuit of happiness.

Respect for Self

Helping students understand what is meant by respect for self may require some brainstorming and discussion. Help them bring their own meaning to the concept. This investigation may uncover concepts related to believing in ourselves, positive self-coaching, honesty, maintaining good health, the use of drugs, doing our best, looking our best, or maximizing our potential. Establishing awareness of self put-downs is helpful too, and may be necessary for particular students.

Quality work is a sign of respect. It demonstrates respect for self and for the teacher. It builds the source and is above the line. Poor quality work is a sign of disrespect. It shows disrespect for self and toward the teacher.

It does not show consideration, honor, and esteem for self. It diminishes the source and is below the line. Students should show respect for their talent and ability by always doing their best and producing work that is commensurate with their ability. The teacher should view quality work as a sign of respect and train students in this thinking and constantly acknowledge that doing one's best is a sign of respect. Educating students to respect themselves by producing their best work can be a powerful act of leadership and can set in place an important foundation stone for durable motivation.

We want students to live above the line and to build a positive reputation with themselves. Any behavior they engage in that diminishes their reputation with themselves is considered disrespect for self. Students who consistently demonstrate self-respect are more positive and excited about who they are and tend to have higher levels of self-efficacy. We have already noticed the relationship between self-efficacy and motivation.

Human Dignity

Respect for other people includes the concept of human dignity. The following story can be used with students to demonstrate and reinforce this concept.

A very elderly woman slowly stepped off a bus in Denver, Colorado, and walked up to a gentleman waiting at the bus stop. She looked up at him and asked, "When does bus 17 come?"

The gentleman looked down at the aged, kind face and said in a polite but concerned tone, "Ma'am, you just got off bus 17."

The old woman then explained what had just happened on the bus. A boy about 15 years old had gotten on the bus. He was crippled and walked with the kind of crutches that attach to the wrist. He had been shopping and was hanging on to a shopping bag in one of his hands.

The boy had difficulty getting on the bus. The other passengers were impatient. The old woman watched as he struggled to position himself for the bus to move. The bus was packed with people. She was amazed that nobody offered to give him a place to sit. He attempted to hang on to the overhead bar, but this was difficult because his crutches would swing, and he was having difficulty managing his package in that position. The old woman watched as embarrassment swept over this teenage boy. Still no one offered him a place to sit.

When the bus got to its next stop, the old woman slowly got off the bus.

The old woman looked up at the stranger standing at the bus stop and said, "I knew that young man would be so embarrassed if an old woman like me got up and offered him a place to sit. So I just pretended it was my time to get off the bus. I was wondering when bus 17 comes by again."

The old woman believed in something called human dignity. Because of her belief, she showed respect toward the boy and toward herself. She honored her belief. She showed consideration, honor, and esteem toward the boy. When we are in alignment with the gold coin of respect, we are above the line and building the source.

Who got the reward in this situation? Both the boy and the old woman were rewarded. It was a win-win situation. The boy got a place to sit and perhaps some relief from his embarrassment, and the old woman got the good feeling and the strength that comes from living in alignment with what she believes is right. Her actions and behavior lined up with her beliefs and values. This alignment is called integrity, and it is an important part of self-respect.

GEMS OF EXCELLENCE

Once the gold coin of respect is well established, we can add other principles that guide students in living above the line. We will now begin our exploration of the four "gems of excellence." To add importance to them, we want to be sure to set the proper context once again. One way to do this is to use a powerful story. I created the "Gems Story" for this purpose and have used it successfully with hundreds of groups of students from elementary school to college. Following the story are notes with additional suggestions on how to use the story.

The Gems Story

The sun was high, and the sun was hot. The traveler had been traveling all day. He was seeking treasure. Obtaining the map had required much sacrifice, and now, after years of effort, he would find success. At first, everything had been new, and he loved the adventure of walking a trail upon which he had never before set his foot. Each rock, each flower, each new smell held an excitement for him. His walk was marked by frequent stops to examine the world of the ancient forest through which he passed.

But the excitement of the morning fled, and the wonder of this strange world gave way to his concern for reaching his destination. An uncomfortable feeling had begun to whisper a warning in his mind. At first, he had been able to send it away, but now it refused to leave. "Something isn't right," it whispered.

Perhaps he was on the wrong trail! The thought burst upon him without warning and caused his breath to catch. It started his mind racing back again over his morning travels. He knew about the fork in the trail. Had he missed it? Had he been so

---

(Continued)

(Continued)

intrigued with the magic of this ancient forest that his eyes had failed to show him the correct path?

He continued to travel and fell deep into his own thoughts. He had to be on the right trail, but why had he not met another traveler? He was so focused on his thoughts that he was only slightly aware of the forest and the sides of the trail.

Something caught his attention from the corner of his vision. He hesitated and turned to look. When he did, he was so astonished he backed up in surprise. There, along the trail's edge, leaning against a small tree, was an old, old man. His body was limp. His head was down. White silvery hair dangled down around his face. He gave no sign of life. "Perhaps he is asleep," thought the traveler.

The traveler walked toward the old man and stopped right in front of him. He blurted out "Excuse me, are you all right? Are you okay?" The old man did not move.

The traveler got down on one knee and reached out ever so gently and touched the old man on the shoulder saying again, "Are you okay? Are you all right?" The old man failed to respond.

The traveler stood up and continued to stare at the old man wondering what he should do. Then the old man began to move. His head slowly came up, and he fixed his eyes on the traveler. He stared deep into the traveler without expression. His eyes did not move.

The traveler, shocked by the old man's face, moved a step backwards and blurted out, "I was just wondering if you were all right. I have been traveling all day, and I haven't seen anyone, and then I saw you, and I was surprised to see you here, and I was just checking to see if you were all right."

The old man did not move. He said nothing, but continued to stare. The traveler stated in a nervous voice, "Well, I didn't mean to wake you up, I just was wondering if you were okay, and I guess you are, and I must keep traveling." He didn't know what else to say and wanted to find comfort away from the staring eyes. He looked at the old man for a few more seconds and then began to turn away.

As the traveler began to take his first step, the old man began to speak. The traveler froze. The old man creaked out ever so slowly in an old ancient voice, "When you get to the river, gather up what is there before you cross." The traveler once again engaged the old man's stare. The old man repeated his stern message, "When you get to the river, gather up what is there before you cross." As soon as the words escaped his lips the second time, his head fell to its original position, and his body went limp.

The traveler stood and watched. The old man did not move. Anxious to get away, the traveler turned and quickly continued his journey. He began to consider what the old man had said. "When you get to the river, gather up what is there before you cross."

"I think the old man has been in the sun too long. Maybe he's crazy! I'll bet there isn't even a river." But the traveler was wrong.

As he cleared the crest of a long steep hill, he stopped and gazed at the river winding its way through the bottomland before him. He was hot and tired. The sight of the river gave him new energy. He hurried his pace and sometimes broke into a run in his eagerness to reach the water. When he finally had gone the distance, he rushed into the water with a splash and began to cross. Oh, it felt so good! With his hands and arms, he scooped deep into the river and threw water into the air laughing as it rushed back to soak his head and shoulders. By the time he reached the middle of the stream, the water was about waste deep. It felt so good.

It was then that the words of the old man came back to him. He stopped. "When you come to the river, gather up what is there before you cross." The traveler turned, his eyes sweeping the shore. "There is nothing there," he said right out loud. He turned to continue his journey, but the words of the old man came back to him again. "There is nothing there," he said in a loud, aggravated voice. But as he did, he turned and walked back to the shore. "The old man is crazy," he said as he began to look around.

There was only what you would expect to find along a riverbank. There were stones, pebbles, twigs, sticks, and clumps of grass. There was a large bush very near where he had crossed, and the traveler walked around it carefully searching for something hidden. He said again, "There is nothing here." He began to look at the stones along the shore. "I suppose the only thing here that you could gather are these stones, but why would you want to?"

Certainly, the old man seemed to know something. Perhaps the old man had traveled this path and knew what was ahead. Perhaps the old man knew about the treasure! Nothing along the riverbank looked worthy of gathering. He studied the bank again. He bent down, scooped up a small handful of stones, and crammed them into his pocket. As he did, he shook his head as if he couldn't believe he had been so silly. "Now who is crazy?" he asked the water.

He crossed the river and continued his journey. As he did, he quickened his pace because he was losing his light. He checked his map again. Before long nightfall would be upon him.

He felt a concern that gained momentum until it consumed his attention. Where was the fork in the road? He had to find it to be sure of his destination. What should he do? He stopped, searching for a decision. His mind whispered a warning. It was too risky to continue. Night was already settling upon the land, and the trail was beginning to hide itself. He would have to spend the night on the trail and start out again with the morning sun. "I should not sleep right on the trail," he thought. "There could be another traveler in the night. Wild beasts might use the trail."

He found a place he felt was safe at some distance from the trail and prepared a quick meal from the provisions he had with him. Weary from the day's long journey, he soon fell fast asleep. He slept very soundly until about midnight. He was awakened by something, but he did not know by what.

(Continued)

(Continued)

He stood and looked about. He could not believe what he saw. There was a huge, bright moon, and it was casting a silvery sheen over all the land. It was a beautiful and strange sight. Then he realized what had awakened him. He had rolled over onto his side and was sleeping on the stones in his pocket. Suddenly he felt the pain of it. He reached into his pocket to throw the stones away.

As he brought out the stones, the moonlight caught them. His eyes became wide as he fixed his gaze on them. He stared at the stones in his hand and did not move. "This is impossible!" he finally exclaimed right out loud. "This can't be true." He held the stones up higher in the moonlight. With mounting excitement, he reached into his pocket and brought out the remainder of the stones. His astonishment at what he saw caused him to talk right out loud again, "This can't be true, it just can't happen."

The stones had turned into precious gems—diamonds, emeralds, rubies, and sapphires. The traveler held each stone up to the moonlight again and again. He then cried out to the moonlight and the silent forest, "Oh! I wish I had gathered up more stones before I crossed the river!"

The possibility of sleep had fled. The traveler knew he had found his treasure. He knew his treasure could have been greater if he had gathered more abundantly, but this did not lessen his excitement for what he had gained. As the night wore on, he began to settle into his thoughts. He realized that the stones had not looked like treasure when he first gathered them. He could have passed by them and never known what a difference they might make in his life. He traveled over the course of his life and wondered if there had been other missed opportunities to gather gems. He wondered if he had ever had gems in his hands and let them go.

Using the Gems Story

Telling the story using your own words may create the greatest impact with your students. Create an outline of what you will include, and rehearse it a few times. Using movement helps. For example, getting down on one knee to touch the old man is effective. Digging into the water and throwing it into the air or getting down on your knees and gathering stones add power to the story. When I come to the part of the story where the traveler pulls stones out of his pocket, I pull gems out of my pocket. I use glass globs, which can be purchased at a hobby store and at stores that carry supplies for making stained glass. I buy them by the pound or sack, and I mix many colors of glass together. I let the students know that there are four important gems that we will be gathering. You can do this as an ending to the story. Here is a sample script for ending the story.

We are each a traveler much like the traveler who crossed the river. You are gathering. I am gathering. Perhaps some of the things we gather will just look like stones at first. Some of the things you gather are more important than others. In the days ahead, we are going to gather four gems of the greatest importance. These gems are precious. You are preparing to cross the river. You will finish school here and cross the river into a new step in your life. I hope you are wise enough to take these gems with you.

Each time I introduce one of these gems I am going to give you an opportunity to gather a gem like the ones I have in my hand. Each time you select a gem, you will pick one of a different color from the ones you have already gathered. You will gather four gems in all. I already have my four gems. (Show them your gems.) I also have my gold coin of respect. These physical gems will become an anchor for another kind of gem called the gem of excellence. Each time you see or touch your physical gem, it will remind you of the gem of excellence. Be careful. One or two may look like an ordinary stone to you at first. But if you put it to work in your life, I can tell you that it will turn into a precious gem. You will know you have found treasure. You may carry it with you when you cross back over the river.

You do not have to gather these gems. This is a personal thing. Nobody can make you do it. But let me be honest with you. If you do not gather them now, the day may come when you will look back and say, "Oh! I wish I had gathered more stones before I crossed the river." Perhaps it will be because you are looking at others who did gather and have a higher quality of life. Perhaps you will see then that you could have been more successful if you had gathered them when you had the chance.

If you choose to gather them, then they will belong to you. Nobody can take them from you. You are free to put them to work in your life. Let's take an opportunity to gather our first gem should you make that choice.

If you use the "Gems Story" in this way, I recommend that you give students their first gem on that same day. You can introduce any one of the four gems. Once you have introduced the gem, give them one of the glass gems to keep as an anchor. They can carry it with them or place it in a location where they will see it on a regular basis to remind them of the principle. Once they have their first gem, you can decide when you will introduce another. Perhaps you would do one a day for three days or maybe one a week for the next three weeks. The students will be anticipating the gathering of the other gems. Each time you gather a gem, work with students to define it and to give this definition concrete meaning that relates to your shared experiences. Let's turn now to the process of gathering each of these gems.

The Gem of Integrity

Integrity means that our actions and behavior line up with our beliefs and values. Integrity can be viewed as part of self-respect. In fact, it is one of the highest expressions of self-respect because our beliefs and values are such an important part of who we are. When our actions and our beliefs are in alignment, we build a positive reputation with ourselves and get a good feeling about who we are. When we do not live in alignment with what we believe to be right, we do not feel self-respect. Living in alignment with integrity often requires commitment and courage. This is especially true when peer pressure is pushing in a different direction. Because this concept is so important and so powerful, I recommend you present it as a separate gem even though it can be considered a component of self-respect.

The most effective way I have seen for teaching this concept to students is the way we do it in our Quantum Learning Network programs.

Have students put up one hand, palm facing them with the fingers spread apart. Model this. Have them take the index finger of their other hand and trace the letter "B" on the palm of the hand that is out in front of them. Have them trace over it a couple times. Teach them that this "B" stands for "Beliefs and Values." Ask them what it stands for and have them repeat it back a couple times.

Have them drop that hand, and have them put the other hand in front of them with the palm facing them and fingers spread apart. Model this again. Have them take the index finger of their other hand and trace a large "A" on the palm of this hand. Have them trace over it a couple times. Teach them that this stands for "Actions and Behavior." Ask them what it stands for and have them repeat it back a couple times.

Next, have them put both hands in front of them with the palms out and the fingers spread apart. Have them rehearse with you what each hand stands for a couple times. Have them bring their hands together with the palms touching and the fingers perfectly lined up with each other. Teach them that this is integrity. Integrity means that our actions and behavior line up with our beliefs and values. Integrity is when what we do is in alignment with what we know to be right.

This method of teaching integrity creates a strong anchor for students. It is simple and powerful. It should be reinforced frequently. It can be used with students of all ages. If you use the story about the lady on the bus, you can help students see that her actions were in alignment with her beliefs and values. By demonstrating respect, she was also demonstrating integrity. You will also spot a theme of integrity in many of the stories and examples used to demonstrate the other three gems. Be sure to help students see this connection to reinforce the integrity gem.

The Gem of Ownership

The principle of ownership sounds like this: "I am responsible for me, no more excuses." To a cognitive psychologist, this statement means the student has an internal locus of control. Students with an internal locus of control recognize that they make personal choices and are responsible for the choices they make. Students with an external locus of control feel that control of their lives is outside themselves. They do not understand that they make choices and are responsible for what they choose. Things that go wrong are not their fault. It is not their fault that they were late to class or came in without their homework finished. It is not their fault that they were unkind to another student.

Choice Talk

An effective move for helping students take ownership is choice talk. Let's see how this works. Consider the following dialogue.

"Why did you choose to hit Jimmy?"

"I didn't choose to hit Jimmy, he hit me first!"

Do you hear anything amiss in this response? Let's try another one.

"Why did you choose to be late?"

"I didn't choose to be late, I accidentally overslept."

In these dialogues, both students demonstrate an external locus of control that denies the students' ability to choose. The students are telling us that they are not in control. I once responded to a student's comment about being late with the following dialogue.

"I will give you a $100 bill if you can be on time for the next three days."

"Are you serious? You are going to pay me to be on time?"

"That's right, I will pay you $100 if you are on time for the next three days. Do you think you will be on time?"

"Well, of course I will be on time if you really pay me $100."

"I am just kidding, I cannot actually pay you $100 to be on time. I just wanted you to notice that you can choose to be on time if it is important to you."

Helping students learn that they make choices in everything they do is the pathway to the principle of ownership and to an internal locus of control. We can begin to use the words *choice* and *choose* with our students on a consistent basis as a training tool to help them learn about ownership. Introducing and reinforcing the idea that we each have the power to choose is a powerful teacher move for building strong character in students.

First, we must teach students the principle of ownership. Once they have a basic understanding, we consistently use the words choose and choice when communicating with them. To demonstrate this to my students, I will sometimes ask a student to volunteer to argue with me. Let's step into this situation in a high school English classroom and eavesdrop on the conversation. Dillon has volunteered to argue with me.

"Dillon, let's pretend you were assigned a short essay yesterday that is due today. I notice you did not do your essay and am going to ask you why. Please do not take any responsibility for the fact that the essay is not done. Just come up with whatever you can to avoid taking ownership." Let's begin.

Dillon, why did you choose not to do your essay?

"It wasn't my fault. I had to go to soccer practice, and it got out really late and I didn't have time to do the essay."

"So you chose to go to soccer and that's the reason you chose not to do your essay."

"I didn't choose to go to soccer, I have to go. If I did not go, I would get kicked off the team."

"So it is because you were worried that you might get kicked off the team that you chose to go to your soccer practice, and this is the reason you chose not to write your essay."

"Well, I had to go to soccer practice."

"What did you do when you got home?"

"Well, I had to eat dinner and then my mom said I had to clean up my room and bring all my laundry downstairs."

"So you chose to clean up your room and bring your laundry downstairs, and that is the reason you chose not to write your essay."

"I didn't choose to clean up my room, my mom told me I had to."

"So you chose to obey your mom and that is the reason you chose not to do your essay."

"If I didn't obey my mom, she would ground me."

"So, because you were afraid your mom would ground you, you chose to obey your mom and not do your essay."

"Well it would not be worth getting grounded over."

"What did you do after you cleaned up your room?"

"It was really late, and I went to bed."

"So, you chose to go to bed and that is the reason you chose not to write your essay."

The purpose of this move is to help students understand that they make choices. Not doing the essay may have been a good choice under certain circumstances. It is not so much about good and bad choices as it is about helping students understand they are choosing. What if Dillon just comes back with the response "I forgot." Many students think that forgetting is not a choice and is outside their control. It is important that we clarify this issue and never let them use forgetting as an excuse for nonperformance. Even though the response "I forgot" has the word "I" in it, it demonstrates an external locus of control. Students believe that forgetting is something outside their control and may use it as an excuse. Our response might sound something like the following.

"Dillon, why did you choose not to do your essay?"

"I forgot?"

"What things did you do to remember?"

"What?"

"What are the things you actually did to remember?"

"Nothing, I guess."

"Choosing to do nothing is not good enough when it comes to remembering. By choosing to do nothing to remember, you chose to forget to do your essay. What things can you choose to do in the future that will help you remember?"

It is true that many things are out of our control. But our goal here is to help students begin to take ownership for the choices they do make. In the elementary school, students may have less control over some of their choices. However, we should start very early assisting students to develop an internal locus of control. Suppose you ask an elementary student named Julie why she chose to be late.

"Good morning, Julie. How are you today?"

"I'm late."

"I see you are late. Why did you choose to be late?"

"I didn't choose to be late. It wasn't my fault. My mom dropped me off at school late as usual. I was ready on time."

"What kinds of things are you doing to help your mom get you to school on time?"

"I keep telling her we are going to be late."

"Is that working?"

"No."

"What other things can you do that might help solve this problem?"

It may be that there is nothing Julie can do to get her mom to drop her at school on time, but we want Julie to take as much ownership as she can. Her mother may be rehearsing her in the art of excuses. It is also possible that Julie can change the situation with her mom, once her mom sees how important being on time is to her daughter and that Julie is being proactive about solving the problem. It is never the intention to frustrate students by asking them to take ownership for something that is beyond their control. Sometimes, we have to acknowledge that circumstances are out of our control. This is also an important lesson related to ownership.

Reason or Excuse

It may be helpful to create a distinction between a reason and an excuse and to declare that excuses are illegal in the classroom. In order for educators to know the difference between a reason and excuse, they must listen for the location of the locus of control. An excuse has an external locus of control, and a reason has an internal locus of control.

If we are getting an excuse from a student, we can say, "Please pause." With some students, we may want to suggest that they remove the whine from their voices. Have a student begin again with the words, "The reason I chose. . . . " These four words work like magic, transforming an excuse into a reason. Younger students may need coaching.

Acknowledging Positive Choices

We have been focusing on situations in which students may not want to take ownership. It is also important to consistently use choice talk in acknowledging good choices. Here are some examples:

"Phil, I see you chose to put some extra quality into your essay. Great choice. Thank you."

"Sara, I noticed that you chose to help Kim with the directions. Thank you."

"Ben, I see you chose to line up your data so it is easier to read. Good choice."

If we help a student move the locus of control from the outside to the inside, we have accomplished an important educational victory. We have built the source and great benefits, or resources, will result for the student. Students with an internal locus of control can set goals and learn to be responsible. They can begin to feel that they are in charge of their lives, and this can result in higher levels of motivation and energy. Having an internal locus of control can support them in making good choices and becoming proactive in making changes that result in greater effectiveness and higher performance.

The Gem of Positive Mental Attitude

Staying positive is something that can be learned. We should do everything we can to help students stay optimistic and maintain a positive view of their future. Such a view can have a powerful effect on their performance at school (Levine, 2002). Perhaps nothing will affect the success and quality of life more than this gem of positive mental attitude. It should be considered a precondition to academic success (Ginsberg & Wlodkowski, 2000). I learned this lesson well in working with students who had sustained head injuries. Those who could maintain a positive mental attitude demonstrated quicker and more complete recoveries compared to those who could not align themselves with this important gem.

One of our goals at Colorado NeuroLearning Center was to strengthen three critical paradigms that support a positive mental attitude. A paradigm is the model of thinking through which students view the world, themselves, and their situation. Strengthening these three paradigms is an effective strategy for upgrading attitude and strengthening durable motivation. In concert with this approach, we add training in positive self-coaching. This strategy will result in remarkable results with students.

The three paradigms we will work to shift and upgrade are the potential paradigm, the failure paradigm, and the problems paradigm. We will consider each of these paradigms and discover stories and examples that have proven effective with students. Following this, we will explore the subject of positive self-coaching for students and present a sample script helpful for getting started.

Potential Paradigm

A student's concept of his or her own potential is closely associated with self-efficacy. We want to strengthen and upgrade this paradigm, so the student understands the incredible extent of her or his own potential.

We want the thinking of students to encompass the idea that they have unending potential.

The following sequence of stories and examples is powerful in shifting and upgrading this paradigm. Be aware, however, that this sequence does not have to be presented all at the same time. In fact, there is too much material here for that approach in most cases. I have used this sequence with students in the elementary, middle, high school, and college arenas. I then continue to reinforce it with other examples and stories. You could use part of the sequence or the whole thing. Also, use your own examples and stories, and allow students to share examples and stories of their own that strengthen and shift this paradigm.

The Potential Questions

Let me ask you a few questions. Just answer right out loud with a yes or a no. Can you wind surf? Okay, I heard lots of no's and I think I may have heard a few yes's. Let's try a new question. Can you keyboard on a computer at 80 words a minute? *(Response.)* Can you speak three languages fluently? *(Response.)* Can you build an engine from the ground up? *(Response.)*

The correct answer to each of these questions is yes when we are talking about potential. What I mean is "Could you do it if you choose to do it?" The answer is yes.

Do you have the potential to do it? Yes! I am going to ask each of these questions again and give you an opportunity to answer correctly with a "Yes!" Please answer boldly. Ready, here we go.

Can you wind surf? *(Response.)* Please give your answer a little louder. Can you wind surf? *(Response.)* That is much better. Can you keyboard on a computer at 80 words per minute? *(Response.)* Good! Now you might be thinking, "I'm no good at keyboarding." That's okay. We are not talking about that. But do you have the potential? Do you have the potential? *(Response.)*

Can you speak three languages fluently? *(Response.)* You might say, "I would never choose to do that!" That's okay. But could you do it if you chose to do it? Yes. You might say, "In my lifetime the most important thing I am going to accomplish is to speak three languages fluently." What if you went after this as if your life depended on it? What if your life did depend on it? Would you do it? Can you speak three languages fluently? *(Response.)* A little louder please. *(Response.)* Can you build an engine from the ground up? *(Response.)*

How many questions are there that you would honestly have to answer yes to? *(Take some responses.)* There is no end to the questions because your potential is unlimited. There is no end to the things you can choose to do. If you started right now and decided you were going to develop all of your potential, you would never be able to stop. You cannot develop all of your potential in a lifetime. It cannot be done. You have so much potential that you must pick and choose. Your job is to continually improve using your unlimited supply of potential. Your job is to stay green and growing.

Roger Bannister

How many of you have ever heard of a man by the name of Roger Bannister. Roger Bannister was the first man in the world to run a four-minute mile. Nobody thought it was possible. Roger was a medical student, and he got the idea in his head that he could run a mile in four minutes. He was training for the Olympics and really believed it was possible.

He was sitting at lunch one day with some other students and made the comment that he thought he could run a four-minute mile. One of the other students looked at him and said it was impossible. Roger said he thought it was possible and that he could do it. Another student said, "No, Roger, you cannot run a mile that fast. If you even come close, your heart will burst and you'll be dead."

Roger Bannister did not believe it. Instead, he continued his training. He got up in the morning and ran. He ran at night. He ran in the heat and in the rain. And then the day came. While the world watched, Roger Bannister ran a four-minute mile. It was unbelievable. But something even more interesting happened after that.

As far as we know, nobody on the face of this earth had ever run a four-minute mile before Roger Bannister did. But then, in the months that followed Roger Bannister's record breaking run, sixteen other runners also ran a four-minute mile. How can this be?

Take an opportunity for students to explain what happened and how this was possible.

Training Elephants

How do you train a bull elephant? A bull elephant can weigh thousands of pounds. How do you get him to do what you want him to do? What if you want him to stay, but he decides to leave? What are you going to do? Do you jump in front of him and throw up your fists to scare him? I don't think so.

You need to train him to stay when he is little. When he is just a baby elephant, you take a chain and wrap it around his leg and padlock it on. *(Use motions to show this.)* Then you take the other end and put it through an iron ring that is imbedded in a piece of concrete and you padlock it.

The baby elephant will not understand at first. He will attempt to leave, but his leg won't come with him. After a while, he will really put some effort into it, but his leg still will not come with him. Then he will get angry. He will tug and pull. He will scream and try again and again. And then, finally, he will quit. You take off the padlock and remove the chain from his leg.

(Continued)

(Continued)

Now all you need to tie up the elephant is a piece of clothesline attached to a stake about 15–20 inches long. The elephant won't go anywhere; he's tied up. *(It is very effective to have a stake with a piece of rope attached to use as a prop.)*

Now he is a full-grown male elephant in a circus and weighs thousands of pounds. He is just standing around minding his own business when a little girl comes along with a bag of popcorn. She is running to catch up with her mother when she trips and falls. Popcorn from her bag falls out on the ground. She looks at the popcorn on the ground and begins to scoop it back into her bag just as her mother turns around. Her mother yells, "No, no, that's dirty!" She rushes back and grabs the bag and dumps considerably more of the popcorn on the ground. The little girl and her mother continue on, leaving the popcorn on the ground.

The elephant just watches the whole thing. He loves popcorn. He can smell it. It is not far away, and he decides to have some. But he can't quite reach it. He will stretch out as far as he can, but the popcorn is just out of reach. He can't get it. He's tied up. *(Show your prop.)* That piece of clothesline is tied around his leg, and it is attached to a wooden stake that has been pounded into the ground. He will never be able to get any popcorn because he is tied up. He is what? *(Response.)*

Question! Watch out! This may be a trick question. CAN the elephant get the popcorn? *(Response—Yes.)* I have another question. Watch out! WILL the elephant get the popcorn? *(Response–No.)* He will not because he believes he cannot. Let me say that again. He will not because he believes he cannot. I will say it to you, and then you say it back. He will not because he believes he cannot. *(Response.)* He is tied up.

What about you? Are you ever tied up? What beliefs do you have that hold you back from your potential? Are you green and growing or are you ripe and rotting? To stay green and growing, we must always be working to develop our potential. It is a lifelong endeavor.

Perhaps one of the most compelling stories for helping students strengthen their paradigm regarding their potential is the classic story of Annie Sullivan and Helen Keller. This story can have a powerful impact. Do not tell students whom the story is about until you introduce Helen in the story.

Annie and Helen

Annie's life is one of the best examples of what is possible for each of us. She was born in Ireland where she lived in abject poverty with her family. Her father was an alcoholic and did not provide for the family. Her mom did everything she could for the family's five children. Annie's mom wanted to go to America, and, one day, she finally got her opportunity, and the family sailed for the Promised Land.

The mom felt things would be better once they got to America. They arrived in Boston and immediately both parents looked for work. The father was not responsible and, before long, they were in worse shape than before. The mom lost three of her children in the first two years to diseases related to poverty.

That left Annie and Jimmy, who were both in bad shape. Jimmy had a hip disease and had to use a crutch to walk. He was in pain much of the time. And Annie had suffered from trachoma, which left her legally blind. She could only see shadows. Annie did everything she could to help her mother and took care of her little brother, Jimmy.

During the third year of the family's stay in America, the mom got sick and died. That left Annie and Jimmy in the hands of their father. But the father did not take care of them. The State of Massachusetts found out about the two children and, hoping that someone would adopt them, took them away from the father and put them in the custody of the state. But nobody wanted them. Annie was legally blind, and Jimmy was sick and had a hip disease. So the state officials did a horrible thing: they put the two children in a place called Tewksbury, a place for people who had nothing or who were insane and sick. It was no place for two children.

Fortunately, Annie made friends with an old woman who was there. Annie took care of Jimmy and tried to keep him alive. She was able to do it for one year, and then Jimmy died leaving Annie by herself at Tewksbury. The old woman told Annie to get out of Tewksbury somehow, but Annie had nowhere to go. She had no idea what had happened to her father.

During that next year, Tewksbury became a political issue in Boston. Some people said something had to be done; that it was a disgrace to the State of Massachusetts. Others said that the people who lived there deserved what they got and that the state could not afford to spend money on these people. The State of Massachusetts decided it would investigate Tewksbury, and sent a delegation of four representatives to check it out.

Annie discovered that they were there and, although she could only barely see shadows, with the help of her friend she located the delegation. She went up to them and literally begged them to get her out of Tewksbury. She told them she was smart and would go to school. She said she would work hard doing anything if they would get her out. One of the women in the delegation spoke to Annie and said she would check into it. The delegation then went about its business.

Several weeks later, that same woman showed up at Tewksbury and said she was looking for the girl named Annie. Annie was brought to the woman who informed her that the state had decided to sponsor Annie to get an education at the Perkins Institute for the Blind and Deaf. Annie could not believe her ears. The woman told her to get her things. Annie did not own anything of value, but needed to say goodbye to her friend.

(Continued)

(Continued)

When she told the old woman, they both celebrated the moment. Tears of joy came to the old woman's eyes. Annie gave the old woman a hug and then turned to leave. But, she did not get far. The old woman reached out for her and pulled her back, saying in a stern voice, "Annie, make me a promise. Promise me that when you leave this place, you will never say the word Tewksbury again. Never let anyone ever know you were here. Promise me, Annie."

"I promise," Annie replied. She hugged the old woman and turned to leave again.

Annie was so excited that she was going to attend a school. She had never been in a school. She was totally unprepared for what was going to happen. Annie did not know her letters and numbers. She was street wise, but did not have even the basics for school. The other students made fun of her and thought she was stupid. The ridicule became intense.

Annie had to make a decision. She had the opportunity to feel sorry for herself, but that was not the choice she made. She decided to win. She decided she would continue to improve herself. She stayed up late to study secretly, although it was against the rules of the school. She did not need any light because she was blind and could study with her fingers. She got up early, worked hard in school, and studied after hours night after night. She was a fighter, and the other students learned to leave her alone. She got the nickname of "Miss Spitfire."

A couple of her teachers did not like her because she seemed to get into trouble. One day in her English class, her teacher asked her in front of the class, "Annie, when does your brain ever wake up?" Annie stood on her feet to reply. She was required to do so. She said with a defiant tone, "My brain wakes up the minute I walk out of your classroom!" The teacher was furious and tried to get her expelled. But Annie stayed at the Perkins Institute and graduated the valedictorian of her class.

Because she was the valedictorian, she was required to give a graduation speech. About 1,800 people attended, including the governor and other dignitaries and many people who had donated money to the Perkins Institute. The graduation was a big deal.

Annie gave an excellent speech with confidence and determination. There was a thunderous applause. Annie stated in her speech, " We can build for ourselves true and noble characters, and because we can, we must." Listen to that statement again. "We can build for ourselves true and noble characters, and because we can, we must."

There was a doctor in the audience who came up to congratulate Annie on her speech and also to ask her about her blindness. She told him about the trachoma. He said that he would like to examine her eyes in his office, so the following week she went for an appointment. She was informed about a new surgery that might be effective in her case. The doctor felt Annie was a good candidate and would get some if not most of her eyesight back after the surgery.

A few weeks later, Annie had the surgery, and, when they removed the bandages, she had regained most of her eyesight. With glasses, she was able to see well enough to learn to read with her eyes.

She began looking for a job after graduation. One of the teachers who had become Annie's close friend agreed to loan her summer cottage to Annie until Annie found employment. Annie lived there and wrote letters and learned to read with her eyes.

Meanwhile, in the state of Alabama, a father was pacing back and forth outside his little girl's bedroom door. She had taken sick during the night with a high fever. Her temperature was so high that she had begun screaming out and hallucinating, so the doctor was sent for immediately. He was in the room with the mom and the little girl. When the doctor came out, the father looked directly into his eyes to see what was written there. The doctor said that the little girl might not make it through the night. He said he suspected scarlet fever.

The little girl fell into a very deep sleep, and the father stayed by her bed all night long, listening to her breathe. Sometime during the night, he fell asleep with his head on her bed. When the little girl woke up in the morning, all signs of the fever were gone. She was hungry and wanted something to eat. The mom and dad could not believe this good fortune. They felt they had witnessed a miracle. But they didn't know.

A few days later, they discovered that their little girl was not able to hear. And, within a week, they discovered their child was also losing her eyesight. Within a couple weeks, the little girl was totally blind and deaf. What's her name? *(Response.)* That's right, Helen Keller.

The mom and dad didn't know what to do. They took Helen to doctor after doctor trying to get help, but nobody could help the little girl. The parents were told to put her in an institution where she would be fed and kept clean, but the mother would not hear of it. "I will not put my little girl in an institution like an animal," she yelled at one doctor. "My little girl is trapped in there. There has to be a way to reach her." Helen's parents decided to raise her at home.

As Helen got older, she became almost impossible to manage. She would have severe temper tantrums if she did not get what she wanted. One day her father came home and said, "If we don't do something with Helen, we are going to be living in a pile of sticks. She will destroy everything." They decided to look for a doctor who would help. But it was the same. One doctor told Helen's father that you could teach a horse to fly before you could teach Helen anything.

There was one doctor who was helpful, however. He said there was nothing he could do, but he recommended that they travel to visit with a man by the name of Dr. Alexander Graham Bell. So Helen's parents took her to see Dr. Bell. You know his name because he invented the telephone, but Dr. Bell also worked with people who were deaf. He met Helen and was impressed with her. He said, "I think you are right. There is a bright little girl trapped in there. I don't think I can help you, but I might know someone who can. He is a friend of mine and is the director of the Perkins Institute in Boston. I would like you to contact him."

(Continued)

(Continued)

Helen's parents contacted the director of the Perkins Institute and the director told them about a girl named Annie who had just graduated and was the valedictorian of her class. He said she was living in a summer cottage that belonged to one of his teachers. He said that if there was anyone who could help Helen, Annie could. He talked to Annie and she accepted the challenge. When she got off the train in Alabama, there stood three people to greet her: a dad, a mom, and their girl named Helen.

Helen Keller was tough. She was really tough. But Annie was tougher. Annie went to work with Helen and would not give up until she had a measure of success. But success required months of failure. Helen would throw things, bite, and have long and wild temper tantrums. She was dangerous, but Annie would not be defeated. Then the day of the breakthrough came. Annie taught Helen one word. The word was "water." From that moment on, the whole world opened up to Helen Keller, and learning that word provided the foundation for a relationship of respect and friendship with Annie that lasted a lifetime.

Helen Keller never saw Annie Sullivan. She never heard her speak. But Helen went on to accomplish some amazing things. With the help of Dr. Bell, Helen and Annie worked out a system of communication. Annie communicated by making symbols in the palm of Helen's hand. Helen graduated from Radcliff College with honors. Annie sat beside her and communicated what the teacher was teaching. Helen then would use a typewriter to communicate her knowledge of the subject.

Helen Keller learned to read in five languages. She wrote eleven books. One is called *The Story of My Life,* and it is in almost every library in America. Helen learned how to talk. This was a difficult process. She placed one hand on Annie's throat and with the other hand placed two fingers on her lips with her thumb under Annie's jaw. She would then imitate the movement of the jaw and lips and the vibrations in the throat. Helen Keller gave lectures all over the world and raised millions of dollars to help those who were less fortunate. Helen Keller died in 1968 at the age of 87.

I believe that Helen Keller and Annie Sullivan were great ones. When I think about what they were able to accomplish, it makes me stop and wonder. If Helen Keller, blind and deaf, could accomplish all that, what could I do with the talents and abilities I have? What could you do with your potential? Their story provides strong evidence that we can all accomplish more than we ever dreamed possible.

Who can stop you? You can. We need to get excited about who we are and what we can do. Don't wish you were him or her. You are never going to be him or her. You are going to be you every day while you walk on the face of this earth. You have what it takes. Get excited about your own talents and abilities and be the best you can be.

SOURCES: Keller, H. (2002). *The story of my life* (100th anniversary ed.). New York: Penguin Group; Hickok, L. (1961). *The touch of magic: The story of Helen Keller's great teacher, Anne Sullivan Macy.* New York: Dodd–Mead.

When you use a story to teach an important concept, it is a good idea to allow students to share their reactions. I usually follow a story with a short discussion and capitalize on opportunities to reinforce the main concepts of the story. In the sequence already described and in any discussions that follow from it, we want to keep strengthening the potential paradigm. We should ask students what we can learn from the story and help them develop their ideas. Our goal is to help students make a connection between the characters in the story and themselves. One way we can help students accomplish this transition is to connect elements of the story to events or situations in their own lives. For example, we might have them share situations where they were unwilling to try something because they thought they could not do it, or experiences when they felt the excitement of accomplishment after sustained effort. Let's now turn our attention to another important paradigm.

Failure Paradigm

A student's view of failure is an important factor for developing a positive mental attitude. A fear of failure can kill motivation because of its relationship to self-efficacy. It destroys hope. We can teach students that *failure is for feedback and learning.* I teach students that a failure is something that you try that does not turn out the way you want. Failure is frequently necessary for learning to occur. I like to teach the following saying:

It's okay to try, and fail,

And try, and fail again.

But it not okay to try, and fail,

And fail to try again.

I usually require my students to memorize this saying and be able to say it faster than I can. They get very fast, and we would sometimes race. One of my students cross-stitched this entire saying, had it framed, and gave it to me as a gift. I have it hanging on my wall at home.

It is helpful to collect stories that demonstrate how individuals have had to take a positive view of failure in order to succeed. There are many of these stories available. The story of Thomas Edison is probably one of the most common and still one of the most effective.

Thomas Edison

Thomas Edison was one of the greatest failures who ever lived. When he was attempting to invent the light bulb, he knew exactly what he wanted to do. Other scientists believed it was an absolute waste of time, but Edison ignored their position

---

(Continued)

(Continued)

and set up the first experiment. He believed that, if he could take two metal rods and connect them with a fine substance (a filament), he could run electricity up one side, across the filament, and down the other side. He believed the filament would try to burn up, but he would not let it burn because he would remove all the oxygen from the container. It could not burn without oxygen. He just had to find the right substance for the filament.

Edison set the whole thing up and ran the electricity through the filament. But his experiment did not work. So, he tried it again. But that did not work. He documented the two attempts and then tried it again. But it did not work. He wrote down what he did and tried it again, but it did not work again. So he tried it again. But it didn't work. So he tried it again. But it didn't work. He repeated this process more than nine hundred times, and he wrote every one of them down! None of them worked.

Thomas Edison was well known in his own day. Another scientist made a comment about Mr. Edison in a scientific journal. I would like to quote it for you: "Mr. Edison is a fool."

A young reporter wanting to do an article on Thomas Edison got permission to interview the inventor. The first question he asked is interesting, as was Mr. Edison's response.

The reporter asked, "Mr. Edison, why do you persist in this foolishness with electric light when you have already failed more than nine hundred times? Why don't you spend your time doing something more valuable than that?

I think the question made Mr. Edison angry. He looked at the reporter and gave the following response, "Young man, you do not know how the world works. I have not failed at all. As a matter of fact, I have *successfully* identified over nine hundred substances that don't work! Therefore, I'm nine hundred substances closer to the one that does work."

I don't know how Thomas Edison got his hands on this great concept. Maybe he learned it from his parents or perhaps from a teacher. But he had it and put it to work in his life, and that made all the difference.

SOURCE: Adapted from Josephson, M. (1992). *Edison: A biography*. Indianapolis, IN: Wiley. Used with permission.

When you share this story with students, it is important to give them the definition of failure. As stated above, a failure is something you try that does not turn out the way you want it to. That's it. It is not some horrible thing. It is just something you try that doesn't turn out the way you want it to. It could be a math problem, a spelling word, or making a new friend. Failure is for feedback and for learning.

Two Exceptions. There are two exceptions to the statement "Failure is for feedback and learning." I usually like to be right up front with my students regarding the exceptions. I know sooner or later I will get a question about these exceptions. Below is a sample of how I might present these exceptions to students.

There are two exceptions. How many? *(Response.)* Exception number 1: If you try something, and it does not turn out the way you want it to, and it kills you, then this is not for feedback! Let me say that again. If you try something, and it does not turn out the way you want it to, and it kills you, then this is not for feedback. This is exception number 1.

Please stand. Please put your hands out in front of you with palms out. *(Demonstrate.)* Now flip your hands around. *(Demonstrate flipping your hands around so the palms are facing you.)* I am now going to turn this definition around and say it in a different way. Here we go. If you try something, and it does not turn out the way you want it to, and it does *not* kill you, then this is for feedback. Let me say that again. Ready? Flip your hands around again. If you try something, and it does not turn out the way you want it to, and it does *not* kill you, then this is for feedback. In other words, if you try a math problem and fail to get it correct and your vital signs are still stable, then this is for feedback and learning. Thank you, and please be seated.

How many exceptions are there? *(Response.)* How many do you have? *(Response.)* How many are left? *(Response.)* When you are ready, say "ready." *(Response.)* Here is exception number 2. If you try something, and it does not turn out the way you want it to, and you keep doing the same thing over and over that you already know does not work, then you have gone beyond the concept that failure is for feedback and learning. Would you agree with this? *(Response.)* Let me say that one more time in a slightly different way. If you try something, and it does not turn out the way you want it to, and you keep doing the same thing over and over that you already know doesn't work, you are ripe and rotting instead of green and growing.

Thomas Edison said, "You show me a thoroughly successful person, and I will show you a failure."

We might say today, "You show me a thoroughly successful person, and I will show you someone willing to fail."

Henry Ford said, "Failure is only the opportunity to begin again, more intelligently."

Perhaps the following information regarding Abraham Lincoln would be helpful in relation to the two quotations above:

Abraham Lincoln was born into poverty and was faced with defeat throughout his life. He lost eight elections, twice failed in business, but he never gave up.

1831–Failed in business

1832–Defeated for the Illinois legislature

1833–Second failure in business

1838–Defeated for Speaker of the Illinois General Assembly

1843–Defeated for Congress

1848–Defeated for Congress

1855–Defeated for Senate

1856–Defeated for vice president

1858–Defeated for Senate

1860–Elected president of the United States

Problems Paradigm

Strengthening this paradigm is a powerful move for upgrading attitude. Teach students that problems are challenges and opportunities to grow, and a normal part of life. I usually get a little dramatic with this. I stand in front of them and pretend I am doing curls with a weight. I ask them to guess what I am doing. A student will usually say immediately that I am lifting weights.

What if you walk up to someone that you see doing this and ask, "What are you doing?" The person turns to you and says excitedly, "Oh, I am building up my muscles." You stare back and say with surprise, "But you don't have any weights!" The person turns to you and exclaims, "Yea, I know. Weights are heavy!"

I ask my students if this makes any sense to them. I explain that, in order to build up muscles, you must have resistance. Without resistance, you cannot get stronger. The weights provide the resistance. I ask them, "What are the weights that build strong character?" I lead them to understand that problems are the weights. You might then introduce them to the following quotation by Jacob Braude:

> Life is a grindstone. Whether it grinds you down or polishes you up depends on what you are made of.

Discuss with your students what Braude means. Teach them that life polishes you up when you look at problems in the correct way. We must learn to see problems as challenges. Many people think problems are bad when, actually, problems are an important part of life. I tell my students that, if they do not have any problems, they might want to go get some. Without problems, you cannot grow and get stronger. Problems are the weights that build character. Problems are challenges and for growing.

The Butterfly Analogy. The following story is a good way to help students begin to capture the vision of this new way of thinking.

Nikka was a little girl who just loved the forest. Everything was a wonder to her. She would go into the forest often to explore. The forest held no fear for her. One day, on a journey near the old pond, she discovered something. She did not know what it was, but sensed it was important. She scooped it up, cradled it in her hands, and began to head for the village in search of Buracca.

Buracca was an old man who was quite patient and friendly with the children. Nikka believed he knew everything about the forest. When he spotted Nikka coming toward him, he smiled. She was one of his favorites.

"Buracca, Buracca, look what I found," she excitedly called out, holding her treasure in front of her. "Look at this, Buracca."

"Oh," replied Buracca. "That is an important find."

"What is it?" inquired Nikka.

"That is called a chrysalis."

"What does it do?" Nikka asked.

"Well," explained Buracca, "It has a butterfly inside. When the butterfly is ready, it will come out of the chrysalis.

"Oh," exclaimed Nikka with renewed excitement. "Can I keep it?"

"I don't think that would be a good idea," replied Buracca. "You should put the chrysalis back in the forest. You can check on it to see how it is doing."

"Oh no, Buracca, I want to keep it and watch the butterfly come out. I won't hurt it."

"Well, if you do that you must make a promise."

"I will promise," Nikka replied before Buracca could finish.

"You must promise you will not help the butterfly when it is trying to get out of the chrysalis. It must be allowed to get out of the chrysalis on its own."

"I promise, Buracca," Nikka replied as she turned in the direction of her home.

Nikka prepared a special place for the chrysalis in her room and checked it frequently to see if anything had changed. But nothing changed. It seemed to her that it was taking the butterfly forever to come out of the chrysalis. Then she noticed that a crack had formed in the chrysalis. She was so excited. She could not wait to see the butterfly. By the next day, she could see the butterfly moving inside the chrysalis and trying to get out. She watched in anticipation, but the butterfly could not get out. She almost reached down to help it, but then Nikka remembered her promise to Buracca.

The next day she watched the process intently, growing more impatient for the butterfly to break free. The crack was larger. She could see the butterfly struggle, and then it would rest. Then it would struggle again. She grew more impatient and said out loud, "It can't get out." Without even thinking, Nikka reached down and pulled the chrysalis apart and the butterfly fell out.

She watched as the butterfly began to unfold its wings. She witnessed the color of the wings for the first time and was fascinated. The butterfly would vibrate its wings, and then it would rest. Then it would vibrate again, and then rest. It kept repeating the process. Each time the butterfly stopped vibrating its wings, it would rest a little longer. Then the butterfly quit moving.

(Continued)

(Continued)

> Nikka picked up the butterfly and the chrysalis and headed out in search of Buracca. When she found Buracca, she held up the dead butterfly and the chrysalis. She said, "Look what happened."
>
> Buracca looked at the butterfly and then at Nikka. Still looking at Nikka he said, "You did not keep your promise."
>
> Nikka looked at Buracca and then looked down and said nothing.
>
> Buracca explained, "It is important to let the butterfly struggle to get out of the chrysalis. By doing this, the butterfly has an opportunity to build up its own strength. When it has enough strength to get out of the chrysalis, it also is strong enough to survive in the world. The butterfly must be given an opportunity to build its strength by overcoming the problem of getting out of the chrysalis."

After telling the story, I have my students break into groups and discuss how this story is like life. I ask them to find analogies. Once they have had some time to do this, I bring them back and discuss their findings. Young students might immediately suggest that you should keep your promises. Guide students to see that the butterfly had to struggle in order to get free of the chrysalis. If the butterfly just quits, it will not be prepared for life. Make sure they notice that the butterfly had to struggle in order to be successful. Help them to use this story to strengthen their problems paradigm.

If you are using this story with a group of teachers or parents, there are several other analogies that can be discovered. For example, somebody will probably mention that sometimes a parent or teacher should not jump in too quickly to give help, but should let the student or child struggle for a reasonable time. They must understand that problems are the weights that build character. Parents and teachers sometimes feel that confusion and frustration are signs that they have not done their job. We should view these conditions as a natural part of the learning process (Stigler & Hiebert, 1999).

Sarah's Story. The story of Sarah Kellett is powerful for helping students understand the concept that problems can be viewed as challenges. This story demonstrates the power of a positive mental attitude. It can be read or told to students.

> When Sarah was still in grade school, she was already dreaming about becoming a professional athlete. When she was in sixth grade, she actually wrote down her goal and put herself on a training program. She pursued swimming, running, and cycling. She trained in one of these every afternoon, weather permitting.

One day, she was riding her bicycle on her route and stopped at a stoplight to wait for a green light. She was on her bicycle and had one foot on the curb as she waited for the light to change. An automobile going 30–40 miles per hour over the speed limit swerved out of control and went right over the top of Sarah.

Three different doctors struggled to save her life. After hours of surgery, it was necessary to remove one of Sarah's legs. It was obviously not possible to prepare Sarah for this because she was still in a coma. Sarah was a long time in recovery and went through months of painful physical therapy.

One of the physical therapists said it was part of her job to cheer Sarah up, but it was impossible to cheer Sarah up. The physical therapist explained that people would go into Sarah's room to cheer her up, but, instead, Sarah would cheer them up. You could not cheer Sarah up because she was already too cheerful.

Once Sarah was fully recovered, she stayed with her goal to become an athlete. She decided to take up a new sport—skiing. Sarah skied on the United States Olympic handicap ski team and won both gold and silver medals. Later, Sarah decided to become a physical therapist. A new job took her to Washington State where she decided to take up a new sport called mountain climbing.

Sarah picked out a mountain and climbed all the way to the top. You and I might look at that mountain and say, "Sarah, that is not a mountain. That's a hill." But it was a mountain to Sarah, and she climbed all the way up and came all the way down.

Sarah then picked out a taller mountain. We would still say, "Sarah, that is not a mountain. That's a hill." But it was a mountain to Sarah, and she climbed all the way up and then came all the way down.

Sarah finally began climbing mountains we call fourteeners in the West. These mountains are higher than 14,000 feet above sea level. Some of these peaks are very difficult to climb. Sarah started going on climbs with professional climbers who sponsored climbs in the mountains where she lived. She designed special equipment to assist her with her handicap. Sarah had a dream, and she was preparing to reach it. For several years, she didn't let anyone know what she wanted to do.

Sarah had decided to climb to the top of Mt. McKinley. This was her dream. Mt. McKinley is located in Alaska, and it is the tallest mountain on the North American continent. It has the greatest vertical rise of any mountain in the world. Its summit is over 20,000 feet above sea level and is extremely difficult to reach partially because of the adverse weather conditions that prevail on Mt. McKinley starting at about 10,000 feet.

Sarah had shared her dream with several professional climbers who had become her friends. After three years of waiting and preparation, Sarah got her chance. She got a call from a climber who was doing an equipment test and promotional climb, and he invited Sarah to join the team. He had climbed with Sarah on several occasions, and was impressed with her determination and positive mental attitude. He had already checked with the other members of the climbing team, and they were all

(Continued)

(Continued)

excited to have Sarah along. Asking Sarah to join the climbing team was an important decision because, on a climb like this, you literally put your life in the hands of the other members of the team.

The team was flown to the base of Mt. McKinley. At the base camp, they distributed the equipment. Some members offered to carry additional weight to lighten the load for Sarah, but Sarah would not hear of it. She said she would not climb that way. So Sarah got her fair share for a total weight of 85 pounds. The team planned to reach the summit in about 20 days if everything went well.

On day 12, a severe storm blew in on Mt. McKinley. Temperatures dropped to minus 50 degrees Fahrenheit and visibility was zero. Sarah dug in under the snow. The storm lasted for three days. When it was over, Sarah climbed out of her hole bringing with her a positive mental attitude. Team members had to decide if they would continue the assent or head back to base camp. They decided to continue.

They had good climbing until they came to the wall—a huge wall of rock. If you could see the climb from a distance, you would see five tiny specks on a massive wall of rock. This would be Sarah and the other four climbers. Sarah said the problem with the wall was the wind, which was blowing straight up the mountain with gusts sometimes estimated at 80–100 miles per hour.

At one point, Sarah was blown completely off the mountain and to the top of her rope. Contemplate this picture. Sarah was tied in and was blown straight up the mountain and was suspended in midair at the top of her rope. She hung up there long enough to realize that when the wind broke she would fall. She would not fall to where she was, but would fall all the way to the other end of her rope.

When the wind broke, Sarah came crashing down. Fortunately, she was able to get her pack between herself and the cliff when she crashed into it. The other climbers saw her fall, but could not see her at the other end of her rope. They yelled down at her, "Sarah, are you all right?" There was no answer. They called to her again and again as they made preparations to rescue her.

Finally, Sarah was able to get her breath back. She called up to the members of her team to let them know she was all right. She yelled up, "I'm all right. Just having a little challenge with traction!"

In the three days that followed, Sarah climbed to the top of Mt. McKinley. And then she climbed all the way down.

Sarah Kellett later made a comment to a newspaper reporter worth remembering. She said, "We all face great possibilities brilliantly disguised as impossible situations."

Sarah had an unusual way of looking at the world. She saw problems differently than the way most people do. She believed problems are challenges. When she lost her leg, she did not see a problem. She saw a challenge. When she climbed her first mountain, she did not see a problem. She saw a challenge. When the storm blew in on Mt. McKinley, she did not see a problem. She did not say, "I will probably freeze to death. We will never make it to the top. This isn't fair. I should have known we would have bad luck." No, she did not say these things. She did not see a problem. She saw a challenge, and she stayed focused on the rewards of success.

This is a choice every person must make in life. You can see life as a series of problems or as a series of challenges and possibilities. This choice will make a significant difference in the quality of your life and will be a major factor determining what you accomplish. It will have a profound affect on your motivation. Choose to see problems as challenges and opportunities for growth. It may determine whether you are green and growing or ripe and rotting.

Get excited about what you can do and who you are. Your potential for good and for accomplishment cannot even be measured. Both are unlimited. Like everyone else, you face great possibilities brilliantly disguised as impossible situations. Problems are challenges and opportunities for growing.

SOURCE: Adapted from Haily, P. (1987, July-August). Sarah's incredible climb. *Youth, 87*, 11–12.

Positive Self-Coaching for Students

We have explored the three paradigms used to strengthen the attitudes of our students. Let's now turn our attention to positive self-coaching. In Chapter 2, we examined this strategy of positive self-coaching as a tool that teachers can use to help sustain a positive mental attitude. It is also a powerful tool for helping students build character and stay focused on the rewards of success. I use it with individual students, but I have also had entire classrooms using the same script. A script can also be individualized to focus on a particular challenge or goal important to a student.

Following is a script that includes some positive self-coaching I have used with students. It is only a sample. I have sometimes used this entire script or just portions of it. I have, in some situations, made tapes of it that a student listens to on a regular basis. It is also effective to have them read the script on a regular basis. You can read it to them on a daily basis and then have them read it at home once a day on their own. This works if you have a group on the same script.

Another effective approach is to take statements from the script for use in an opening tradition. You and your students could read the statement or paragraph together. You can then change the statement or paragraph every few weeks. When you have finished presenting the whole script in this way, you can cycle back to the original statement or paragraph again to reinforce it. Using the script as an opening tradition in this way can work as an effective step in supporting a positive mental attitude and for upgrading motivation. When motivation is upgraded as a result of a changed paradigm in a student, it is more sustainable.

If you are going to have students use a self-coaching script, you will have to sell the idea. I tell my students that it is a technique used by high performance human beings. All Olympic athletes are required to learn how to coach themselves properly. I let them know that this is a tool I personally use. I let them know that using it is voluntary and that it is normally only used by adults, not kids.

They do not have to use it if they don't want to. But, if they want to learn how to use this powerful strategy, I will teach them how. I ask how many are interested. I tell the ones that are interested that they must not waste my time. I will help them, but it requires a commitment on their part. They must use it two times a day for thirty days. They must make this commitment or they are not in. After the thirty days, they can decide if they want to continue. After thirty days, they may want to customize their script.

Here is the sample script.

Great Day

Today is a great day. I feel great. I am full of life, energy, and enthusiasm. I can choose to have a great day, and I choose to have a great day today.

Self-Esteem

I am positive, confident, and in control. I like who I am. I like how I think, and I like my style. I would rather be me than anyone else in the world.

   I am smart. My mind is quick and alert. My mind makes things work right for me.

   I have many wonderful talents and abilities. I have unlimited potential and am always improving. I like who I am. I am a very special person living at a very special time.

Positive Attitude

I have a positive mental attitude. I see problems as challenges and opportunities to grow. I see the good in others, and I am excited about life. I am happy on the inside, and I am happy on the outside. I am persistent; I just do not give up easily. I stay focused on the rewards of success.

School

I am a good student. Being a good student is no problem for me. I stay organized, and I do my work on time and in the right way. I am alert and active in class. I like to participate. I enjoy answering questions and taking part in discussions. My teachers see me as an interested, hardworking, positive student. I take pride in what I do, and I like to do my best.

Treating Others

I am a great friend. I make people feel good about themselves. People like to hear what I have to say and to know what I think. I can always see the good in others, and I treat people with value. People are important to me, and it shows.

Good Decisions

I make good choices. I do things that make me feel good about myself. I know right from wrong, and I choose the right. I have plenty of courage, and standing by what I believe is no problem for me. I have integrity. I am a winner, and I prove it every day.

The Gem of Perseverance

Perseverance is also an important concept, whether it is perseverance in learning new skills or content or perseverance in reaching a worthy goal that will improve the quality of your life. Point out the role of perseverance in the Roger Bannister and Helen Keller stories if you used these with your students. Let students give their own description of what perseverance is and have them give examples of it from their own experience or from what they have observed in others.

Share a story of perseverance from your own life or a story about someone who accomplished something through perseverance.

Although you may have to invest some effort in learning stories and examples, once you have memorized them, they become a permanent and valuable part of your repertoire. They can be used over and over again. I have used them to strengthen the paradigms of thousands of students. For me, taking time to add stories and strategies to my inventory has been well worth the investment a hundred times over. Putting power behind stories and examples can leave a lasting impression with students. I have discovered this when I run into them 20 years later, and they still remember these examples and talk about their impact.

Stories can teach us important lessons about perseverance. You would need a *definite purpose* and a *strong desire* to achieve success. Without a definite, well-defined purpose, you are not able to persevere. You need *faith* that, if you keep doing the right thing in the right way, you will win. You need to take *consistent action* toward your goal. You have to be *resilient* against opposition and discouragement. An *alliance* with one or more persons who can offer you support, perspective, and encouragement is very helpful and in some cases might be critical to ensure your success. Let's look at the elements of this perseverance formula:

1. *Purpose:* A definite, well-defined purpose

2. *Desire:* A strong desire for success

3. *Faith:* Faith you will succeed by doing the right thing in the right way

4. *Action:* Consistent action supported by clear purpose

5. *Resiliency:* Resiliency against opposition and discouragement

6. *Alliance:* An alliance for support, perspective, and encouragement

Learning the six ingredients of this perseverance formula is very helpful and will support you in staying in alignment with the important gem of perseverance.

The six ingredients in this perseverance formula could become an important focus in the classroom for a period of time as you reinforce this gem. If you have introduced the "home court advantage" to your students, you might want to establish a connection between the home court advantage and the ingredient of alliance. One of the necessary ingredients of a home court advantage is support. Creating an alliance as part of staying in alignment with the gem of perseverance is easier when a home court advantage exists in the classroom.

Another concept that is helpful in reinforcing the gem of perseverance is systems thinking. If your students are old enough to understand it, I highly recommend teaching this approach. Use the bicycle example given in Chapter 2. Help students understand that perseverance is about getting personal victories and that they will need to have personal victories to win the race of life.

Recap

This completes our investigation of the four gems of excellence and the gold coin of respect. The gems we studied included

- The Gem of Integrity
- The Gem of Ownership
- The Gem of Positive Mental Attitude
- The Gem of Perseverance

There are many other important principles that could be included as part of a character program. We do want to be careful not to include so many principles that the focus of our program becomes too broad to create the impact we are seeking. In their excellent book, *Built to Last,*

James Collins and Jerry Porras point out that most very successful companies have between three and six core principles (Collins & Porras, 1994). Having too many might weaken the focus and impact. Many schools have adopted character principles as a foundation for an entire school. If this is the case in your school, use the examples given here to reinforce your school's program and continue to look for additional examples.

Eight Keys of Excellence

As part of our character building in the Quantum Learning Network (QLN) SuperCamp programs, we teach students the "Eight Keys of Excellence" (DePorter, Reardon, & Singer-Nourie, 1999). This is a powerful combination of success principles originally assembled by Bobbi DePorter and includes

- Integrity
- Failure Leads to Success
- Speak With Good Purpose
- This Is It
- Commitment
- Ownership
- Flexibility
- Balance

These keys are self-explanatory except for the key, "This Is It." This key means that you live in the present moment and live each moment fully. A student may walk into a math class and think, "This is not it." The concept of the "This Is It" key is that we can make whatever we are doing "It."

If your school has not adopted a formal character program with well-defined principles, then, by all means, create your own or adopt one. Select the principles you feel are most useful for building character in your particular students. Be sure your program is anchored with the principle of respect as described in this chapter. Make your program a regular and vibrant part of your school and classroom culture.

Catalogue of Educational Moves

1. Introduce the cognitive anchor of "the line" to students.

2. Have students work in small groups to create a "line poster" showing examples of above and below the line behavior.

3. Reinforce the line concept when discussing current world, local, and school events.

(Continued)

(Continued)

4. Use the law of source and resource to define the line with students who are old enough to understand the law.

5. Set a strong context for introducing the four gems of excellence.

6. Use the story of Andrew Carnegie to set context for teaching the gold coin of respect and the gems of excellence. Place emphasis on the concept of studying successful people to identify traits that contribute to success. Discuss with students why isolating these traits might be useful.

7. Teach students about the gold coin of respect. Give them a plastic gold coin if this is possible in your school. Have them work in groups to discuss what respect means. Teach and reinforce a clear definition of respect that includes respect for people, property, and self, and also includes respect for life, liberty, and the pursuit of happiness.

8. Expand students' understanding of the concept of respect for self. Teach them about the relationship between respect and quality. Guide students to understand that quality work is a sign of respect for self and respect for the teacher. Help them understand that poor quality is disrespect, diminishes the source, and is below the line.

9. Guide students to understand that respect for people includes the principle of human dignity. Use the "bus story" to help students understand this important concept. Discuss the story to help students see that both the boy and the elderly woman got a reward.

10. Have students work in groups to develop a "line chart" for respect. Encourage them to include the three aspects of respect: people, property, and self.

11. Guide students to understand that anything that diminishes their reputation with themselves is a sign of disrespect toward self.

12. Introduce the concept of the gems of excellence. Use the "Gems Story" to set a powerful context for teaching the four gems of excellence. Use glass globs as gems, and inform students that they will be receiving these gems each time you introduce a gem of excellence. Explain the concept of using a physical object as an anchor for a concept.

13. Teach students that their beliefs and values are an important part of who they are. When their actions and behavior are in alignment with their beliefs and values, it is a sign of self-respect. Teach them that self-respect often requires courage.

14. Teach students about the gem of integrity using the alignment of hands strategy.

15. Reinforce the gem of integrity concept often. Direct student attention to this principle as you teach them the other gems of excellence. Reveal it when discussing news and current events or events in the lives of your students.

16. Introduce the gem of ownership. Use your own examples and stories to help students understand this important gem.

17. Introduce "choice talk" to students. Help them understand their power to choose. Use the concept of internal locus of control with students who are old enough to understand.

18. Use "demonstration arguing" to help students understand the concept of ownership.

19. Use choice talk consistently with students to help them learn to take ownership.

20. Teach students that forgetting is a choice and should never be used as an excuse for nonperformance. Teach them that, when forgetting occurs, they should examine what they chose to do to remember. Help them understand that choosing to do nothing may not result in remembering.

21. Teach students the difference between a reason and an excuse.

22. Consistently use choice talk to reinforce the good choices students make.

23. Teach the gem of positive mental attitude. Teach students that being positive is something that can be learned.

24. Help students develop and maintain a positive mental attitude by strengthening and expanding their potential paradigm.

25. Use the yes-no question sequence to expand your students' view of their potential.

26. Use the Roger Bannister story to reinforce students' views of their own potential.

27. Use the "Training Elephants" story to help strengthen students' potential paradigm. Have students find connections between this example and the Roger Bannister story.

28. Use the Annie and Helen story to strengthen your students' concept about what is possible for them and to strengthen their potential paradigm.

29. Help students develop and maintain a positive mental attitude by strengthening their failure paradigm.

(Continued)

(Continued)

30. Teach students, "A failure is something that you try that does not turn out the way you want."

31. Teach students that failure is for feedback and learning.

32. Have students memorize this saying: "Its okay to try, and fail, and try, and fail again. But it's not okay to try, and fail, and fail to try again."

33. Collect and share stories of individuals who overcame failure in order to succeed and improve the quality of their lives.

34. Use the story of Thomas Edison to strengthen your students' paradigm about failure.

35. Teach students the two exceptions regarding "failure is for feedback and learning."

36. Help students understand how a proper attitude about failure is related to the gem of positive mental attitude.

37. Display the quotation by Henry Ford—"Failure is only the opportunity to begin again, more intelligently."

38. Share the information about Abraham Lincoln to strengthen students' paradigm regarding failure.

39. Help students develop and maintain a positive mental attitude by strengthening and expanding their problems paradigm.

40. Teach students that problems are challenges and opportunities to grow, that they are a normal part of life.

41. Use the weights example to teach students that problems are the weights that build strong character. Use the quotation by Jacob Braude and discuss its meaning with students. Reinforce the idea that problems are challenges and opportunities to grow.

42. Share the "Butterfly Analogy." Debrief to create the analogy. Help students understand that struggling to solve problems and to learn new things is a natural and important part of life.

43. Share the Sarah Kellett story to help students understand the powerful paradigm of seeing problems as challenges.

44. Encourage students to see life as a series of challenges and opportunities.

45. Display the quotation by Sarah Kellett—"We all face great possibilities brilliantly disguised as impossible situations."

46. Help students develop and maintain a positive mental attitude using positive self-coaching as a training tool.

47. Introduce students to the gem of perseverance.

48. Remind students that they are either green and growing or ripe and rotting.

49. Teach students that there is little you can accomplish by doing nothing.

50. Use stories to teach the gem of perseverance.

51. Use an inspiring story to strengthen your students' concept of perseverance.

52. Teach students the perseverance formula, and discuss each aspect of the formula with them. Make this a focus for a period of time to help build strong schemata connected to perseverance.

53. Explain the relationship between the perseverance formula's concept of alliance and the "home court advantage."

54. Teach students the importance of staying focused on the rewards of success instead of on the penalties of failure.

55. Relate the principle of perseverance to systems thinking and to achieving personal victories if you have shared the systems thinking model with your students.

LEADERSHIP NOTES

Orchestrating a strong program for character development is an essential part of strong leadership in the educational arena. This is true in the classroom and at the school level. The principal should be proactive in developing and maintaining the program. Administrators, all support personnel, students, teachers, and parents should embrace the specific initiatives that are part of the program. The program should be simple and straightforward. The parent organization should be instrumental in helping to promote the program.

The cognitive anchors introduced in this chapter are excellent for schoolwide initiatives. They can be introduced in individual classrooms or at schoolwide assemblies. They can be included as newsletter topics and reinforced at staff and community meetings. They can be promoted in the environment of the school using posters and banners. Constant recognition of students who embrace these principles can help reinforce their adoption by other students, and visits to classrooms by administration to reinforce the importance of these initiatives can be powerful as well.

Emphasizing the uniqueness of the school because students live by these critical success principles is also helpful.

Leadership can be detected when these initiatives are coupled with modeling and motivation. The character connection should involve all stakeholders in the educational community including administration, staff, students, parents, and, in some cases, local business leaders.

6

The Classroom Connection

The classroom connection begins with a focus on the elements of effective teaching that are essential for maintaining resourceful learning states and are directly related to durable motivation. We begin by examining the "connected quartet" and then turn our attention to ALERT, a tool designed to help students take responsibility for managing their own learning states. Following this, we focus on the management of learning states and build an extensive catalog of effective teacher moves. We end our exploration by learning a powerful new strategy for expository reading called PAGES. Many of the suggestions in this chapter are powerful leadership initiatives. We examine this issue in the leadership notes at the end of the chapter.

THE CONNECTED QUARTET

The "connected quartet" is a model that includes four essential elements for establishing durable motivation and making certain that learning has been encoded in long-term memory. These four elements are described by four short words: engage, chunk, diversify, and reinforce. Their importance cannot be overstated. They should be woven together and connected throughout a lesson. They are important building blocks for masterful teaching.

Engage

We must capture and hold the attention of our students if we are going to educate them. Stated another way, we must capture working memory and hold it long enough to facilitate the encoding of long-term memory. Masterful teachers will always be thinking about this important step as they plan how they will present new material to students.

The purpose of the engage step is to capture student attention and connect with previous experience or schema. This step stimulates student interest in the content and prepares the brain to learn. Although engagement is a beginning step in instruction, it should be viewed not only as an initial step but also as one that continues throughout a lesson or unit.

Know the Why

There are many different ways engagement can be accomplished. Guiding students to understand the "why" behind what they are learning is important and should be considered an ongoing move to help students maintain their focus and motivation.

Teacher Enthusiasm

A teacher's level of enthusiasm is a powerful tool for motivating students and capturing their attention. It is communicated through the verbal and nonverbal expression of the teacher. As well, the energy level displayed by a teacher has a significant effect on students and on their ability to focus their working memory on the subject.

Lesson Example

A lesson on calculating slope might start with a sequence of engaging questions and discussion. Let's step into a classroom to see how this might work. The teacher begins with some questions: "Has anybody in here ever been on a steep hill?"*(Responses.)* "How did you actually know you were on a steep hill?" *(Responses.)* "Has anybody in here ever ridden on something going down a steep hill?"

The teacher notices at this point that the students are becoming engaged. The questions have created interest, and students are relating their own experiences. Students who are not responding are also connecting into actual experience. The teacher may now begin directing the questioning toward the desired outcome. For example, she might ask, "How can we know whether one hill is steeper than another?" She might then direct them to the idea that we can measure the steepness and then compare the results.

"How do you measure the steepness of something?" She will try to elicit the concept of slope. If the students do not go there, the teacher can tell them about slope and have students show respect by standing up or by using some other tradition to create emphasis on the importance of the idea. She can then teach that slope equals rise over run by having students make motions with their hands and arms. For rise, students would make a vertical motion with one arm and hand, and, for run, students would make a horizontal motion with their other arm and hand.

Actual Experience

Another approach to engaging student interest before teaching the concept of slope might be to give the students an actual experience that they can relate to this idea. For example, the teacher might have a student crouch on a portable table with the table legs folded up. The student's shoes would have been removed, and his or her hands and feet would touch the table. Other students could then lift one end of the table and continue lifting until the student began to slide. Then, the rise over run could be measured, and another student could take a turn on the table. Students could compare results. Students are quickly engaged by this activity. Of course, we always have to consider safety and what a particular group can handle. Perhaps demonstrating the calculation of slope by sliding objects down an adjustable incline plane would work well to engage students.

Keep Engagement Active

As the teacher continues to teach this lesson, she selects some slope problems that the students can relate to, and, when the opportunity presents itself, she asks students if they have ever experienced a similar problem or been in a similar situation. She keeps the engagement step active and continues to connect to her students' actual experiences whenever possible. She keeps her own energy and excitement level high enough to stimulate energy and motivation in her students.

Teaching the Mundane

What if you are teaching something particularly mundane? We should still look for ways to engage our students through questioning, an activity, a demonstration, or a prop, and by connecting to their experience. I watched a teacher doing a grammar lesson recently. He had already taught his students to identify nouns and verbs in context, and he was now ready to teach them to recognize prepositions and prepositional phrases in context.

He began the lesson by setting a large box front and center in his classroom. Just the use of a prop like this is frequently enough to engage the interest of the students and motivate them to attend. He got into the box and asked the students where he was. A student raised her hand and declared that he was "in the box." The teacher excitedly jumped out of the box, went to the white board and wrote the words "in the box." He told his students to write this phrase down in color. Next, he asked his students to tell about some things that they can get in. This further engaged the students by connecting the preposition "in" to their own experience.

He repeated this process by lying on the floor and putting the box on top of himself. His students came up with the phrase "under the box." He wrote this phrase on the white board and had his students change color and write it on their own sheets. His students then shared with the class things they can get under. He repeated this process several times and captured a number of phrases.

The students next worked on a paragraph together that had the exact same phrases hidden in the context. He then challenged his students to work on their own looking for these phrases in another paragraph, but he informed them that the phrases were better hidden, so the task would probably be challenging for them. The students were learning about prepositional phrases and were very engaged throughout the entire process. This teacher had captured and held their working memories.

Contrast this with the following introduction to a lesson on prepositional phrases. "Today we are going to be learning about prepositional phrases. Please turn your books to page 148." I am not suggesting that we should not use a book, but starting in this way may not engage our students. We should engage them by capturing their interest and connecting into their experience.

Chunk

Chunking means breaking our content into small segments to ensure that the content does not initiate a fear, stress, anxiety or threat response in our students. We keep our content from activating the amygdala, so we can capture and hold working memory. Chunking also functions to help facilitate the encoding of long-term memory by breaking content into segments that can be easily handled when memory is consolidated.

I had a request from one of my teachers when I was a principal of a middle school to come into a particular classroom to observe and make suggestions. The teacher stated that the students were "good kids," but indicated he was having trouble keeping them on task. I told him I would be happy to come in and that we could put our heads together and figure out "what works."

He was a science teacher and liked to do hands-on lessons with his students. The first day I came to observe was on a Monday, and he was introducing a new three-week physical science unit focused on forces and other topics such as buoyancy. He did an excellent job of engaging the students and connecting into their own experience. He had them engaged within a few minutes of starting the lesson. He then handed out some materials for the three-week unit. It was well organized. He handed the students their vocabulary list for the unit. There were 60 words on the list.

I noticed a change in many of the students when they saw the list. They looked at the list, and it seemed endless to some of them. They did not know the words. Many students saw the list as a threat. Their stress and anxiety response kicked in, and their excitement about the unit was diminished.

After the lesson, I had an opportunity to discuss this with the teacher. I complimented him on the many excellent moves that he made in introducing the unit. I then suggested that he consider chunking his vocabulary list, and I explained what I had observed. He indicated that it was a three-week unit, so he could do 20 words per week.

I told him he was on the right track, but that he could chunk the word list down even more. He said he could break it down to four words per day. I told him four words per day would not be threatening for his students, but I also suggested that he could chunk it down even more. For example, he could say to his students excitedly, "We are going to learn two words in six minutes. How many minutes?" (*Response.*) "How many words?" (*Response.*) "Raise your hand if you think you can learn two words in six minutes." (*Response.*) "Please adjust your physiology and tell your brain to capture these two words."

The teacher could also stress the importance of these two words and might even do so in a humorous way:

> These words are important. You are going to need these two words to survive effectively in the world. If you choose not to learn these two words, you will have a serious pothole in your schema. Someday in the future, you will be in a conversation with another educated person such as yourself, and you will stop mid-sentence. You will have to say, "I apologize. I have a major pothole in my schema." Whatever you do, do not let these two words get past you!

The students in this class might not see the entire list of words until the end of the unit, when they are celebrating what they have learned and are being acknowledged for what they have accomplished. They will see the list building as the words are reinforced, but learning the list will feel like an accomplishment instead of a threat.

Diversify

The subject of diversification brings us to the topic of brain dynamics. The study of brain dynamics got started with the research of Dr. Roger Sperry. It is interesting now to look at what happened.

Dr. Sperry was a medical doctor who was doing research on the brain. He was very interested in the corpus callosum, a huge bundle of nerves that crosses over between hemispheres deep in the center of the brain. He wanted to know the function of the corpus callosum, and decided he would cut the corpus callosum on some laboratory animals. He noticed little change in the health or behavior of his animals as a result of this procedure. Dr. Sperry's work was written up in several scientific journals.

A few years later, a situation developed involving a woman who had a tumor deep inside her brain. The tumor was affecting several important structures in her brain, causing severe seizures, and it was spreading across the corpus callosum. Her doctors gave a grim prognosis unless the tumor's growth could be arrested before the tumor spread to her other brain hemisphere.

One of her doctors was familiar with Dr. Sperry's work, and suggested she might contact him. She contacted Dr. Sperry and subsequently requested that a surgery be performed to sever her corpus callosum in an attempt to arrest the spread of her tumor. The surgery was performed, and, as far as we know, she became the world's first split-brained patient.

Right Brain–Left Brain Distinctions

This surgery and the subsequent research conducted by Dr. Sperry (and later by others) initiated all the right brain–left brain distinctions and models (Gazzaniga, Ivry, & Mangun, 2002). We learned for the first time that the two hemispheres in our brains are specialized, and later that each of us has our own balance of preferences for how we use these hemispheres. Dr. Sperry conducted sophisticated experiments, and his discoveries and research earned him a Nobel Prize in science. There are more than a hundred split-brained patients in the world today.

Brain Dynamics

These discoveries stirred up interest in how the brain functions, and further research revealed that we have different categories of brain preferences. These brain preferences are what create brain dynamics. The term "brain dynamics" refers to the balance of the preferences in our own particular brain. One of these dynamics is our preference for the use of our sensory input channels.

Modality. We already learned that we have three sensory educational channels. These include the visual channel, the auditory channel, and the kinesthetic channel. Each of us has our own unique preference for these channels. For example, you may prefer your visual channel and learn best by seeing things. Or perhaps your preference is for listening or for doing. These sensory input channels are called modalities, and your balance of preferences for these channels is called modality balance.

Style. Another important dynamic is style. You have a teaching style, learning style, working style, and thinking style. This dynamic is created by the brain's preferences for processing and storing information. There are four basic styles identified by a number of different educators and researchers. The terms we will use to describe these four style categories include structured, analytical, affective, and original.

Having accurate knowledge of our own individual modality and style balance is a valuable asset to an educator. It allows us to understand and gain insights into our natural tendencies regarding the presentation of content, communication, classroom organization, and expectations for students. An understanding of our modality and style balance gives us important knowledge about how to diversify.

Brain Preferences Survey. Located in the resource section following this chapter ("Teaching Resources for Chapter Six") is an inventory for measuring modality and style balances and our right brain–left brain preferences. It is called the Brain Preferences Survey. This survey, although it takes only about fifteen or twenty minutes to complete, has been shown to be very accurate with thousands of students and educators. Instructions for completing the instrument are included as well as several resources that can help us determine how we might best diversify our style. Make a copy of the inventory, and just follow the directions.

The Brain Preferences Survey is also designed to be used with students from middle school to college and can be powerful in shifting their view of themselves as learners. You are allowed to make as many copies of this survey as you need for your students. It can be used with students in fifth and sixth grades with assistance from the teacher. These students can usually complete the modality portion of the instrument on their own, but, when elementary students are completing the style portion, the teacher may need to read each of the 15 groups of phrases and sentences with their students, discuss these, and answer questions before students make their selections.

The inventory gives students valuable information about how they learn. Once students finish the inventory, they should discuss it and perhaps compare results. It is important for the teacher to have students notice that all the style traits are positive. Help students discover that it takes all styles to make the world work, and tell them that they should be excited about their own style. I tell students that they should not wish they were somebody else because they are not going to be somebody else. They should get excited about who they are and strive to be the best they can be.

Teaching the Power of Diversity. Ask students if they would want all the same modality and style in the members of a group or if it would be better to have a diversity of modality and style. Have them give reasons for their answers. Help them discover that the power of any group is in the differences of the individual members. Of course, it is more challenging to get members with strong differences to work together effectively. The first step is to have them understand these differences and honor them based on knowledge about the power of diversity in a group.

Responsible Use of Data. A student must never be allowed to use data from the inventory as an excuse for nonperformance. For example, a student who scores low in the structured area might say, "Well, the reason I don't bring my stuff to class is that I am not strong in the area of structure. It is just not my style." This must not be permitted. We never talk about style or modality as areas of strength and areas of weakness. We should present the inventory as giving information about areas of strength and areas of challenge, or areas of strength and areas for growth, or areas of strength and areas of opportunity. Remember that the brain is constantly changing through the process of plasticity. Because of this plasticity, it is possible to strengthen our non-dominant style through focused effort and the demands placed on us by the environment. The use of a non-dominant style is called style flexing, and this conscious style flexing is an effective strategy for self-improvement.

Using the Preferences Survey. I have personally used the Brain Preferences Survey with hundreds of students and found it to be effective and valuable. I have had many students say to me, "You mean to tell me there is nothing wrong with me?" I would respond that we all have areas of strength and areas of challenge. They have their own style and their own opportunities for growth and improvement.

I have also used the survey in counseling teenagers and their families. I have all family members who are old enough complete the survey. It has frequently been a source of revelation for both parents and children, giving important insights for solving conflict and accepting differences.

There are many important outcomes that might encourage use of this inventory with students. It gives both the teacher and the students important insights about how they learn, which can help them adapt learning strategies and methods. It also helps them understand that each person in the classroom is a unique individual with special strengths as well as areas of challenge. But, perhaps most important of all, it helps them see the differences in people and the importance and value of diversity. It increases tolerance as they learn that it takes all styles to make the world work. They come to celebrate this diversity as they learn that, in any group, the strength of the group is in the diversity of the individual members. They see the evidence of this strength in diversity based on real data.

I used the survey with an entire school staff when I was serving as a principal, and I witnessed many positive results. The staff exhibited greater tolerance of differences and were better able to work together effectively when armed with this data about themselves and others. Diversity in people came to be regarded as a valuable asset.

The Brain Preferences Survey actually measures three things including, modality balance, style balance, and right and left brain dominance. Following the survey are some very important resources for educators and their students. The instruction page in the resource section explains how these can be used.

VAK Teaching

We have been focusing on the topic of diversity as part of the connected quartet. One important teaching move we should make on a consistent basis is called VAK teaching. VAK teaching means that we consider the visual, auditory, and kinesthetic modalities when planning and delivering lessons. The use of all three channels helps to ensure that we are maximizing the learning for all students and giving them as many tags to memory as possible.

Flexing Style

We should also flex our style to be sure we are meeting the needs of all students. Those of us with a strong preference for a particular style, as indicated on the Brain Preferences Survey, have to exercise the greatest caution. We may have a tendency to operate in our style and forget that we are significantly mismatched in style with a large population of our students. The resources in the resource section titled Student Preferences, Teacher Preferences, Parent Preferences, and Learning Methods Preferences should be helpful for guiding us in the process of diversification.

Reinforce

The final player in the connected quartet is the use of proper and adequate reinforcement. To a neuroscientist or cognitive scientist, the issue of reinforcement might sound something like this: "How many times do we need to fire electricity over a new neural pathway to ensure it gets consolidated as long-term memory."

10–24–7

In the Quantum Learning for Teachers programs, we use the formula 10–24–7 as a protocol for proper reinforcement. The 10 refers to a ten-minute window. This window occurs right after we have introduced new content to our students. It means that, within 10 minutes, we should be firing electricity over the new pathway again to reinforce it. This translates to the concept of continuous review while teaching new material to students. In the 10-24-7 formula, the 24 means that we should review the new material the following day. This is a critical time to reinforce our content because the process of consolidating memory should be underway. The student has entered into sleep states. Following this initial sleep by the student, we should be sure to fire electricity over the new neural pathways to reinforce learning and send an additional message to the brain about the importance of the learning.

The 7 in the 10–24–7 formula indicates a seven-day window following the first day of reinforcement. Only the professional educator will know how to determine the frequency and intensity of reinforcement required during this window. It will depend on the difficulty of the content and the ability of the group to learn the material being presented. With one group, a teacher may elect to reinforce the material two or three times during the seven-day window to ensure that the content is consolidated into memory. With another group, perhaps just one quick review during this window is all that is necessary.

10–48–7

If we are teaching in a block schedule, the formula will have to be modified to 10–48–7 to accommodate the fact that we do not see students every day. A block schedule places an extra burden of responsibility on the educator for reinforcement. It is essential that the material be reviewed and reinforced when the students return to the classroom. It would also be most ideal to assign homefun that is broken into two parts and designed to reinforce what was learned in class. In this ideal situation, the student would do the first part of the homefun on the first night after class and do the second part of the homefun on the second night after class. This would help facilitate the encoding of memory as the student sleeps on both nights before the next class.

Twenty Effective Reinforcement Moves

Below is a list of effective reinforcement moves. It is helpful to have a rich supply of these moves in our repertoire.

- **Teacher Recaps.** Teacher recaps are quick recaps of content. The teacher just briefly recaps what was just taught or taught the day before. The use of a hat called a "recap" is effective. I have two types. One is called a "standing recap." Whenever I put this cap on my head, my students automatically stand up. From there, I might do several of the moves in this list of suggestions. I also have a "sitting recap." Just the use of the "recap" changes state in students.

- **Partner Recaps.** Students quickly recap, with a partner or in a group, what was just taught. This forces them to use their own language centers in their own brains to express the content. Whenever they use their own language centers, they are involved in a different cognitive activity and one that is helpful for encoding memory.

- **Random Recaps.** Random recaps are effective for getting students to attend to content when it is being presented. The teacher draws a name after a short chunk of content and has a student recap for the class what was just taught. The name then goes back into the pool of names, so the same name could be drawn twice. This move requires a safe and supportive classroom climate. The focus of the students will tend to be very intense during a session involving random recaps. You could also have this anchored to a particular anchor cap that you wear. Any time students see you wearing this "random recap," they know what process you are using. It is important to keep the chunks that you ask students to recap small. During random recaps, you might also allow the "phone a friend" move that lets the student doing the recap confer with a friend if help is needed. If a student's name is selected for a recap, that student must give the recap. Saying "I don't know" is an illegal move. It is legal for the teacher to assist the student, however.

- **Summary Reviews.** This is a timed event. Students have a brief amount of time to summarize in a group or with a neighbor what has just been taught.

- **Turn to Your Neighbor.** This is a very quick and usually spontaneous moment when a student turns to his or her neighbor for a response or to repeat something just taught. For example, the teacher might give this direction: Please turn to your neighbor and say, "Gravity is the attraction between two objects." Remember that the purpose here may be to get students to quickly process the information using their own speech centers.

- **See-Say-Do Reviews (SSDRs).** This is a powerful method of review because it involves all three educational channels. These reviews are done by the student and should become a standard study method. The student sees something that has a strong graphic component to it, such as a content diagram, content map, picture, or some other graphic. They *look* at the item (*see* it) and *speak* the concept it represents out loud (*say* it). They do not just think it, but actually say it or whisper it. The sound must come out of their mouths, into the air, around the corner, and into their ears so it can activate the temporal cortex of the brain. They also must perform a *kinesthetic motion* that helps express the concept (*do* it). They can use their own natural signing (larger content motions) or elect to use fine motor actions by pointing with a pen in motions that quickly recreate the original graphic representation of the idea. This strategy should be used extensively at home when they are studying, but it can also be used at school in the classroom.

- **Content Diagrams.** A content diagram is a diagram that is created by the student to represent a concept just learned. For example, perhaps a student is going to make a diagram of the following statement because it is part of some content that must be remembered: "The troposphere is the lowest layer of the atmosphere and the place where the earth's weather occurs." The student would quickly draw a picture of this concept.

This is not about making drawings that are suitable for framing. The student should complete this diagram in about 30 seconds. It is essential that the drawing is done in color, however, and that more than one color is used because using various colors creates contrast and helps stimulate the visual cortex of the brain, which will enhance the encoding of memory. Students may use words in their drawings, and it is often essential that words be included. In the example just given, it is necessary for the student to include the word "troposphere" in the drawing.

The use of content diagrams causes students to use the cognitive process of picturing that is so essential for encoding memory. They enjoy this process and will discover that they are learning and retaining better because of it. When they complete their drawings, the teacher might have them do an SSDR (See-Say-Do Review). If they are collecting a number of drawings in a notebook, they might go through a quick process of doing SSDRs for each of the diagrams. This is a powerful study process when preparing for a test. If they are doing more than one, they will need to say the phrase "Got it" between each review to give a clean ending to the review before they begin reviewing the next diagram.

Content diagrams can be used in the 10-minute window or as a review strategy the next day. A teacher may ask students who are learning math to stop and draw a content diagram of what was just taught. In a social studies class, perhaps a teacher will assign content diagrams as homefun.

• **Homefun.** Homefun is the assignment of schoolwork to be done at home. It has more frequently been referred to as homework. I prefer to use the term "homefun." When I tell students that they have a homefun assignment, they are absolutely required to cheer. If I tell them that they do not have any homefun, they are required to moan. I have done this with students in elementary school, middle school, and high school. I once had a student come up to me at the high school level and say to me, "That thing you do with homefun is really stupid." I replied, "Thank you for sharing. You are correct about it being stupid. That is why I like it so much." This was the end of the conversation.

• **Content Mapping.** Content mapping is a powerful reinforcement tool and should be used frequently. Content maps begin with a main idea in the center and then work out toward more and more detail. Content maps can include lines hooked to lines, lines hooked to boxes, lines hooked to pictures, pictures hooked to pictures, lines hooked to circles, etc. Each box, picture, or line should represent one idea only, although it might be broken into supporting ideas as the map is developed. It is best to use only one or two words to express the idea if possible.

We start with the most important or general ideas in the center and work outward toward the details. Students should be encouraged to use color, draw pictures, use symbols, and be creative. After some practice, students will begin to develop their own personalized style of content mapping. It will become a powerful resource for them. Content maps can be developed in teams, done as homefun, or developed with the teacher when new content is presented. They are a valuable study aid and can be used to define what is important. They are open ended, and ideas can easily be added as new material is introduced. They can include a combination of material taken from assigned reading and content presented in class by the teacher.

- **Circuit Learning.** Circuit learning is a pattern students follow for review. It involves reviewing what they know and then adding a chunk. They then review what they know including the new chunk and then add another chunk. This pattern can also be an instructional model. Suppose a teacher is teaching events in a chronological sequence and wants students to remember the chronology. The teacher would present the first chunk. Next, the teacher would review that chunk with students and add the second chunk. The teacher would then review chunk one and two and add the third chunk and then continue with this pattern through the content. If the teacher has 20 items for students to learn, he or she may group them in fives for learning. In this case, when the teacher has taught chunk 6, the class would review chunk 6 and then add chunk 7, and follow this pattern until chunks 6 through 10 are complete. Then, the learning and review would start with the next group, i.e., chunk 11. Circuit learning is a powerful process for students and ideally will become a regular part of how they study on their own. Whether students are learning the chemistry of the digestive system or math proofs, whether they are doing geography, memorizing sight words, or learning aspects of the democratic process, circuit learning will prove a valuable asset for encoding information into long-term memory.

- **Fast Forward.** A fast forward is similar to a student recap except that the student goes through the recap process as quickly as possible. The fast forward causes students to process the content intensely in order to accelerate the use of their language centers.

- **Gallery Walks.** A gallery walk would be similar to strolling through an art gallery looking at the artwork on display. The classroom becomes a gallery of content graphics. For example, suppose you have been using flip charts to show things related to your content. You could then hang these charts throughout your classroom and do a gallery walk. Students might be placed in trios and then move from chart to chart discussing what the chart represents and what they remember about the concepts involved.

Another effective way to do a gallery walk is to assign students to create charts of specific content in preparation for a gallery walk. Each group of three students is responsible for producing a chart of an important portion of content. You might indicate that these charts should be suitable for framing. On the day of the gallery walk, all the charts are displayed, and students move from chart to chart. Each chart has the names of the students who created it prominently displayed.

Once the gallery walk is completed, the charts become the property of the teacher. They can be used later to reinforce concepts in another review, or they may become teaching aids for future groups of students. I have seen some amazing instructional charts created by students. These become a valuable resource for the teacher.

• **Gallery Scans.** In a gallery scan, the teacher shows several graphics related to previous content in a review format using an overhead, flip chart, or some other electronic media. The students work in teams to remember the content. The teacher can also make review comments. These graphics might include overheads created and saved, pictures that were previously shown and that are anchored to content, or previously used flip charts and posters created by the teacher or students.

• **Content Map Reviews.** In a content map review, students study their previously created content maps, perhaps working in pairs to compare maps and add distinctions. It is a powerful move, and students should be encouraged to review their content maps frequently.

• **Theta Scans.** The use of theta scans is a relatively new technique that helps the brain know what is important for memory encoding. We can let students know the school day is divided into two parts. The first part is when they are physically at school, and the second part is the last five minutes of the day just before they sleep. We can train younger students that the last five minutes of the day belong to the teacher.

We know that the brain is busy consolidating memory during sleep as the hippocampus flashes memory up to the cerebral cortex. The hippocampus must decide what is important enough for long-term memory and what needs to be discarded as irrelevant information. Having a student review content from the school day at the very end of the day may increase the likelihood that the material will be processed into memory.

Perhaps a student comes home from school and gets homefun completed right away, according to the house rule. But later that student uses powerful media like television or watches a DVD or plays a computer game. If the student plays the computer game just before bed, guess what gets processed during theta brainwave sleep. Perhaps you have experienced this effect after watching a powerful movie just before you slept. You may have discovered you were processing the movie while you were sleeping and caught yourself thinking about it during the night.

By doing a theta scan before sleeping, a student comes back to what is important for long-term storage. It could be a list of new sight words or three new theorems in geometry. Perhaps it is some new vocabulary for science or a sequence of events in history. Doing a quick theta scan will give the student an edge by sending a strong message to the brain, "This is important."

The implication here is not that television or other powerful media are bad. These media do have an impact on children's learning and should be taken seriously, but they are neither inherently beneficial nor harmful. The effects of media on learning depend on how the media are used (National Research Council, 2000).

- **Teacher Reteach.** Teacher reteach is a common practice in which the teacher reteaches the content presented previously, but in a different way or format and usually putting emphasis on different modalities or styles.

- **Student Reteach.** A student reteach involves students working in pairs to teach their partners something that they have been learning in class. One effective way to do this is to have the student in the role of the teacher pretend that the student being taught is much younger. This role-play will cause the "student teachers" to attempt to simplify what they are teaching and to create analogy. It encourages them to reteach using methods and words that differ from what the teacher was using.

- **Reflect.** Reflecting is an effective reinforcement tool. It is a quiet process in which the student reflects on what has been learned and perhaps expresses feelings about new insights and different aspects of the content. We have students ponder a question or write in a journal. Perhaps they pause to think before writing a reaction paper about what they have learned.

- **Standing Down Strolls.** This is a quick stroll down memory lane. A standing down stroll begins with all students standing. Students raise their hands, and, when called on by the teacher, each student reviews a small chunk of the content, usually by making one statement. Once a student has given a micro-review, she or he is allowed to sit down. Students are not allowed to repeat what another student has already reviewed. If another student reviews their chunk, they must quickly select another chunk for review. This review is meant to be fast and high energy. The teacher may make quick comments to emphasize certain content during the review, but without breaking the momentum of the review. Each time a student gives a review of a chunk of content, that student receives applause or some other acknowledgement as he or she sits down.

- **Game Reviews.** Having students play a form of Jeopardy or some other competitive game to review content is very effective. Based on the nature of your content, you can design a competition that will work well with your students.

This completes our exploration of the connected quartet. We looked at four important teacher methodologies—engage, chunk, diversify, and reinforce. These elements of the quartet should always be present in our planning and teaching. We will now turn our attention to a powerful strategy designed to assist students in understanding their important responsibility in making sure learning occurs.

ALERT

Students should feel responsible for their learning. Learning is what they do for a living. We want them to see learning as their profession. The teacher is there to help and works in a partnership with the student. This concept of students being responsible for their own learning should be a theme consistently present in the context of the classroom. We can even use the term "professional students" when students are old enough to understand its meaning. We should let them know that we will help them be the best professional students they can be. These attitudes can be fostered at an early age, and can serve the students well throughout their educational careers.

ALERT is an effective tool for creating a focus on the student's responsibility for learning. This is an acronym for a strategy used by students to enhance their attention and ability to learn.

A   Adjust

L   Look and Listen

E   Encourage

R   Reframe

T   Take Ownership

Adjust

The first step is to prepare for learning. Students adjust physiology and attention. They notice their posture and sit up in an attentive manner. To have them activate their ALERT strategies, you might just point to a chart outlining the steps of ALERT. Another way to do this is to remind them of the first step.

Adjust Attention

One method for reminding students to activate their ALERT strategies might sound something like this. "Please be ALERT. Adjust your physiology; sit up straight. Adjust your attention." Adjusting attention means to begin an effort to keep working memory focused on the content or the communication in the classroom. I use the phrase "adjust your physiology" even with very young students by teaching them what it means and having them practice it.

Adjust Physiology

Students that change their posture to one that is more attentive send a powerful message to two brains, their brain and the teacher's brain. The executive control room of the brain is always aware of our position in space. An attentive posture affects the ability of working memory to focus and can change brain chemistry.

The best posture is to sit up and lean slightly toward the teacher. Point out to students that, since they were small children, when they were carefully attending to something, they had a tendency to lean toward it. It is a natural physiological response to attention. Have students practice this move. Have them demonstrate the worst posture for learning, so they can feel the difference it would make in their attention. Tell them that their brain will thank them for supporting it with proper posture for learning.

Elbow Disease

It is helpful to eradicate "elbow disease" from the classroom environment. Tell them that elbow disease is illegal in the classroom because it is very contagious and dangerous to learning. If a student has this disease, before long others will also come down with the symptoms. The disease can be spotted when students place bent elbows on desks and use their hands to support their heads. When one student gets both elbows involved, we have advanced stage elbow disease, and drastic action is needed.

If you spot elbow disease, let the entire class know that there is illegal activity in the room. "We have two cases of elbow disease. We cannot continue due to the threat to other students. Please check your neighbors to see if they are okay."

Students are responsible for their learning, and being responsible for assuming a learning posture is an important first step. The first step of ALERT requires that students adjust two things—their physiology and their attention.

Look and Listen

Learning requires work. Students must begin this work by using their two symbolic language educational channels to receive the proper sensory input. These two channels are the visual and auditory channels. They should stay visually cued to the activity of instruction and take control of their listening. They must activate working memory with the content being taught in order for anything to be encoded into long-term memory. Students start this process with the look and listen step, which requires effort on their part and begins with a reminder that looking and listening is what is expected at the present moment. This is their job and responsibility as a student.

Encourage

Students should encourage themselves to learn. They should think, "I can do this." They should use positive self-coaching. Also, students should share some responsibility to encourage the students around them to attend. I will frequently pause and ask students to check to see how their neighbors are doing with their attention. It might sound something like this: "I know you are trying to learn like a professional student. Thank you. Please check your neighbors and see how they are doing." Another important action in the encourage step is for the students to encourage their teacher. This is done with the nod.

The Nod

The nod is an essential part of the ALERT process. The nod is a small nod up and down with the head. We are all familiar with this nod. It is usually done when an important point has been made. It is powerful and sends an important message to two brains, the student's brain and the teacher's brain. This nod should be a requirement in the classroom. It is used to support the teacher and other students in discussions, answering questions, and presentations. If I am not receiving this nod from my students, I let them know I am noticing a famine of nods. I tell them that a deficiency of nods cannot be tolerated and that I would expect some action from them immediately. I ask them to please be ALERT. The room will change instantaneously once they are trained in the process.

The nod has a powerful effect on the teacher and is a valuable source of encouragement. It can affect the quality of instruction and the energy and excitement of the teacher. It can also affect where the teacher directs his or her instruction. We once tested this with student teachers. We trained all students in the ALERT process and then had five students on one side of the classroom use it. We discovered that the student teacher began to teach to that side of the room with greater frequency. Then, without the knowledge of the student teacher, we switched sides of the room with a signal the students knew. We now had five students on the opposite side of the room using ALERT, and the original students quit their use of ALERT. The student teacher began to teach to this new side of the room with greater frequency. Both the students and the teacher learned the power of this important move.

Pretend to Learn

I sometimes tell my students that the very minimum requirement in my classroom is that they at least pretend to be learning. They can pretend to be learning by sitting up and leaning in just a little. They must look and listen and give me a nod when I make an important point. This is the very minimum they must do. (Pretending to learn is very difficult without actually learning.)

Reframe

The art of reframing is the art of picturing. There is no comprehension without picturing, so students must picture the content and concepts being taught. Picturing is a separate cognitive activity required for learning.

When students are picturing, they are reframing the content in their own words and connecting it to their own schemata. When picturing is not working, they are raising their hands and asking questions. Any time students raise their hands to ask questions because they are confused about the content, we may be sure that they were engaging in the process of picturing and connecting to existing schemata and that this process broke down somewhere. We can thank them for being ALERT.

Reframing Moves

Many teacher moves are helpful for supporting students with the reframing process. We can have them turn to a neighbor and explain a small chunk of the content. It might sound like this: "Please check with your neighbors to see if they understand the difference between those two terms. If not, help them out." We might use sentence completions to check their understanding and involve them in picturing. It might sound like this: "The force moving away from the center is ___." They then would supply the answer in unison.

We might do a "pause and picture" move. This means that we pause and have them get a picture and then see if they have any questions. We could ask a student volunteer to reframe for the entire class, using her or his own words, what we had just taught. We might have students write something down. The second a student is involved in writing something down or in using the speech centers of the brain to process ideas, that individual is using an important cognitive process and must rely on picturing an existing schema. We might have students draw a quick diagram. This will help them encode the information into memory. Reframing requires work. In many ways, it is the work required for memory storage.

Using Analogy

The use of analogy is especially powerful in helping students learn to picture. When we use analogy, we take something in our students' common knowledge and use it to explain something more complex. This is like using the idea of speedboats and docking stations to explain synaptic chemistry or talking about construction workers to describe the action of proteins. The effective use of analogy is part of the art of excellent teaching. We should employ this powerful strategy as often as possible to facilitate picturing and to enhance understanding.

It is helpful for students to create their own analogies to explain what they are learning. This can be done in small groups and will often result in the creation of analogies you might never have discovered. Once students complete the creation of an analogy, their learning will be solid because of the intense picturing required. You might ask them to come up with a way to explain what they just learned to someone much younger than they are. This task will usually involve them in the process of creating analogy.

Take Ownership

Ownership in the ALERT process means that the student takes ownership to make sure learning occurs. If the process of reframing is not working, students take ownership and raise their hands to ask questions. You can then thank them for taking ownership and being ALERT.

If students are assigned homefun to reinforce what was learned in class, they take ownership for making sure it gets done. They bring their completed homefun assignment to class the next day, so their learning can be confirmed or expanded. They don't just complete their homefun assignment for credit; they actually check themselves to be sure they understand and that learning is taking place. This is ownership. It comes from the concept that students are responsible for their learning. The teacher is there to help and assist with the process.

Quality is also an important consideration and is part of ownership. There should be an expectation in the context of the classroom that students will produce quality work. The teacher should constantly define what is meant by "quality work." Poor quality work is a sign of disrespect. It demonstrates disrespect toward the student and toward the teacher. This should be made clear to students and reinforced regularly.

ALERT is a powerful teacher move and can be introduced at the elementary level. It is very effective with middle school and high school students, and helps students maintain a more resourceful state for learning, which is another important step for durable motivation. Teach your students to be ALERT. Once they are trained and this tool has been reinforced, it will be a valuable asset for you in maintaining resourceful learning states.

STATE MANAGEMENT

The term "state management" refers specifically to the management of our students' learning states. The word state refers to the physical, cognitive, and emotional state of our students. The objective of state management is to consistently move students to resourceful learning states. An ideal resourceful learning state might be described as one in which students are attending, motivated, and engaged in their learning. A classroom teacher uses effective state management moves to orchestrate resourceful learning states.

State Changes

One immediate concern in state management is holding student focus and attention. We have all noticed that attention falls away over time, and sometimes over a very short period of time with some students. To counter this problem, a teacher can use state changes to support student attention. When we change state, the student will refocus attention. The teacher always monitors student states and initiates moves to continually keep them resourceful.

An example of a state change might be, "Please turn to your neighbors and check their understanding of the formula." A simple callback can be a state change. A callback might sound like, "It is called the amygdala. What's it called?" We can have students stand to show respect for very important ideas in our content. This is a state change and sends a message to the brain that "this is important." We might have them stand and do a motion related to the content. We could tell them that we are going to stretch their thinking and have them stand up and stretch and then sit down.

Upon learning the four steps in a process, we could have them stand and give four people a high four. We could say the words, "Be ALERT." We could compliment them on their effort and have them give themselves finger snaps, a round of applause, or another form of acknowledgement. We could say, "If you've got it say 'I Got It.'" We could say the words, "Please let me see your nod." We could say the words, "Why are you here?" and receive their habituated response. We could say "What works?" or "What will you give?"

Sixty Effective State Management Moves

The constant managing of student state plays an important role in maintaining proper context for learning and is a powerful classroom management tool. It also has a direct effect on student motivation and on the success of the brain in encoding long-term memory.

Below is a list of effective moves for helping orchestrate resourceful student states. The idea is for each of us to build a rich repertoire of effective moves that change student learning states. The list is somewhat comprehensive and includes more than 60 valuable moves. It is not my purpose to overwhelm my readers with possibilities, but I do wish to provide a resource that can be used for several years. Effective state management is essential to accomplishing durable motivation and encoding memory, and state management is improved one move at a time. It is also true that the best way to gain a deeper understanding of state management is to examine the moves associated with it.

I invite you to read carefully through the moves and identify the ones that would be most valuable in your repertoire. Once you have accomplished this step, pick a couple moves from your list for implementation. After these are well established, identify a couple of new ones for implementation, and so on.

If our students are trained in ALERT, they are working to maintain their own resourceful state while the teacher is consistently influencing them with effective state management. This is an ideal partnership for learning.

- **VAK Teaching.** VAK teaching is an important teacher move that involves teaching in a format that allows students to use all three of their educational channels when learning new content. This is a diversification move. The three educational channels include the visual, auditory, and kinesthetic channels. The teacher keeps these three channels in mind when planning instruction and reinforcement.

- **Pause and Look.** This move helps students with attention. It functions as a pattern interruption that tends to capture attention. The teacher pauses and looks at students without saying anything. Students check to see what happened. The teacher may follow this with a comment such as, "Thank you for your attention. This is important. Do not let it slip past your brain." The teacher then continues with instruction if satisfied that attention is at a level necessary for encoding memory.

- **Name Dropping.** Name dropping is an effective attention move. The teacher just drops the names of students right into the instruction. I might sound like this: "The use of the first term, Julie, is what guides our thinking to the proper subject." Julie's name was dropped into the instruction without warning and without any apparent reason. It will tend to change Julie's state and possibly the state of those around her. It is possible that the teacher had a very good reason for selecting Julie's name. The teacher continues to drop names occasionally into the instruction. For this move to be effective, it should not be overused.

- **Touch.** Touch is a strategy to help students maintain a resourceful learning state. This strategy works especially well with students who are struggling with focus and attention. The teacher simply touches the student on the shoulder or arm during instruction. This touch is usually used as a signal to work harder to maintain a learning state, and the teacher can set this up as a signal with students in advance. In this case, we would explain to students the importance of maintaining a proper learning state and attention. We would let them know that this is their responsibility but that we will do everything we can to support them. Tell them that touching them is one way you can remind them and help them to stay resourceful. In some situations and cultures, however, this move may not be appropriate because teachers are not allowed to touch students or it violates cultural traditions between certain groups of people.

- **Proximity.** Moving close to a student or group of students during instruction will tend to shift their state. This is done to help students maintain attention and focus.

- **Future Pacing.** Future pacing gives students a preview of coming attractions. The teacher drops hints and gives little previews about what is coming up in the curriculum. These are positive and motivating commercials that create anticipation or suspense for students. This anticipation helps to motivate them when the time arrives to learn the content. Future pacing can occur anywhere in the presentation of content. Perhaps the teacher is explaining something and gives a preview of something new to be presented the following day related to what the students are learning at the present moment. A teacher may elect to do some future pacing at the end of a class to create interest in the topic for tomorrow. When done effectively, future pacing is upbeat, motivating, and designed to capture the interest of the students.

- **Unison.** Unison means that students say important portions of the curriculum together as a group. The teacher will frequently make the statement first and then have students say it together as a class with the teacher also participating. The purpose of this move is to reinforce learning by having students process using their speech centers. It is also a technique that is effective to put emphasis on important ideas that need to be encoded into long-term memory. It also functions well to induce a quick state change.

- **Callbacks.** Callbacks involve having students repeat back to the teacher a word or short phrase. For example, a teacher may say, "These systems working together are called an ecosystem. They are called a what?" The students would then answer back with the word "ecosystem." This changes the learning state, puts emphasis on the term, and allows students to process the word in their own language centers. Callbacks can be used frequently and help students hold working memory on the content.

- **Incomplete Sentences.** This teacher move helps keep students involved in the content by having them complete sentences left open by the teacher. This is similar to the callback. It might sound something like, "These systems working together are called _____." The teacher pauses and waits for students to finish the statement. Incomplete sentences can be used frequently to encourage a state change and to reinforce learning. Many of these moves can be used together. For example, following the use of an incomplete sentence, the teacher might have students write the word in color, take 45 seconds to decorate it, and share their work with a neighbor.

- **Random Response.** This is a powerful move to focus the attention of students. The teacher establishes a random method of selecting names of students for giving responses, such as drawing their names from a container. The teacher asks questions during instruction and draws names out of the container to decide who will have an opportunity to answer the question. When a name is selected, the student answers the question if this is possible. The teacher can assist if necessary. The response "I don't know" is illegal. If a student does not know the answer to the question, she or he may respond with "I need time to think" or "I need to check my notes" or "I would like to phone a friend." This activity should be kept upbeat and positive. The questions should tend to review and reinforce things the students know. The "random response" is similar to the "random recap" move described previously as a reinforcement strategy.

• **Shifting Instructional Position.** Shifting instructional position means that the teacher moves around while presenting content to students. The purpose of this move is to help students maintain a resourceful state. Change tends to help focus working memory, and students will be better able to attend effectively if a teacher changes position.

• **Eye Contact.** Maintaining eye contact with students is helpful for maintaining attention. Using this strategy effectively may require some practice because it is easy to center our teaching on students who are better at attending. This can happen without any intention on the part of the teacher. We need to diversify our eye contact in the classroom to include all students. We sometimes may have to remind all students to establish eye contact. This can be accomplished by using various phrases: "Please pause. Please gaze into my eyes." Or "Open your eyes to really see." Or, simply, "Let me see your eyes."

• **Voice Variety.** Changing vocal inflection, intensity, or volume is an effective practice for helping students maintain attention. It is better to error on the side of exaggeration when it comes to vocal variety. The practice of speaking in different voices, perhaps imitating different characters, is also a powerful move and may involve speaking with an accent or switching to a different dialect. The use of props like a puppet or an object that has been characterized is effective too.

• **Silence.** The effective use of silence can be powerful for holding student attention and for managing their learning states. Silence speaks. Use silence just before making a major point in a presentation. Use it to bring variety into your presentation.

• **Gesture.** We should all learn to use effective gestures as we present content to students. Once again, it is helpful to error on the side of exaggeration. The use of gesture helps to hold the attention of students. Freezing gestures with silence is effective.

• **Challenges.** Giving students challenges affects the motivation system in their brains. A challenge is a goal that individuals or whole groups strive to accomplish. The teacher acts as a coach giving direction and encouragement in order to challenge students and motivate them to greater performance and more focused participation.

• **Time Targets.** Time targets are challenges with time as the focus of the challenge. "Let's see how many we can accomplish in six minutes." "You will have exactly 4 minutes and 38 seconds to complete the three items listed on this overhead." Time targets are powerful for changing state and for creating greater focus and attention in students. The purpose is to motivate, not create stress, so the teacher must be effective in setting targets that are within reach of students.

- **Props.** The use of props during instruction is a powerful way to help students focus their attention, especially if the prop used is something not normally seen in the classroom. Novelty tends to focus attention. Props can also be an effective way to connect content to real-world schema.

- **Acknowledgments.** Acknowledgments are effective for motivating students to greater performance. Acknowledgments can come directly from the teacher or from the entire student group. The practice of establishing acknowledgements as a group response is very effective and is useful for managing learning states. Below are some suggested moves we might use for acknowledging student effort and accomplishment.

Applause

Students look at the person receiving the acknowledgement and applaud. This move is also effective as an acknowledgement for the entire group. "Well done. Please give yourself a hand."

Round of Applause

This is an applause that plays on the common phrase "round of applause" and is applause done while moving the hands and arms in a circular motion. It can be used to acknowledge an entire group or an individual.

Finger Snaps

All people in the class snap their fingers on both hands continuously to acknowledge an individual or the entire group.

Microwaves

Students wave at the person receiving the acknowledgement using only their index finger.

Sitting Ovation

Students hold their hands over their heads forming a large "O" and make the sound "ohhh." Of course, everyone looks at the person receiving the acknowledgement.

Power Woosh

Students look at the person receiving the acknowledgement, clap three times, and extend their arms in the direction of the person while making a "whoosh" sound.

Public Posters

These are posters giving acknowledgements to individuals, small groups, or large groups.

Private Notes

These are teacher notes giving acknowledgement to individuals or small groups. This is a very powerful acknowledgement.

Classroom Conspiracies

A classroom conspiracy is a secret plan by a small group or entire classroom to do something nice for a member of the class. The plans must be kept secret. Students enjoy receiving and being involved in classroom conspiracies.

High Fives

High fives, high tens, high sevens, etc., are a great way to change learning state and can be used as an effective acknowledgement for an entire classroom or as a quick celebration of learning. If your students just solved four math problems, you might have them give four people a high four as a celebration.

Pat Yourself on the Back

Students reach around and pat themselves on the back.

Teacher Acknowledgements

These are acknowledgements given by the teacher to individuals or entire groups.

Creative Acknowledgements

Students can design their own acknowledgements. I recently visited a second grade classroom where they had invented 15 different acknowledgements that the whole group could use to acknowledge individuals. Students were sometimes allowed to pick the acknowledgement they would receive.

- **Encouragement.** Giving students regular encouragement is helpful. Keep students focused on the rewards of success instead of the penalties of failure. Keep a strong focus on effort. Remind students that effort is a choice. Notice their effort and acknowledge it.

- **Teacher Enthusiasm.** There is perhaps no individual factor that influences the resourceful states and durable motivation of students more than the ingredient of teacher enthusiasm. It is so significant in the classroom that it becomes a professional responsibility.

- **Humor.** Humor is a powerful tool for managing learning state and capturing and holding working memory. Humor also has the added benefit of building rapport with students because the students and the teacher laugh together.

- **Sound Effects.** Sound effects work well for capturing attention and for changing state.

- **Music.** Music is a powerful tool for managing learning states. The moves related to music are described in detail in Chapter 4.

- **Dramatizing.** Drama is a powerful tool for capturing and holding working memory, and it can be used in many different applications in the classroom. Students can create skits to review content, or teachers can use drama by assuming different characters to teach content.

One powerful application is mixing drama with vocabulary. Students can act out vocabulary words showing the meaning of the word and giving hints about what the word is by using "sounds like" words. We call these "mystery words" in the Quantum Learning Network programs. For example, students could do a skit showing the meaning of "disperse" by spreading things throughout the room from a purse. A student could continually say, "Wow, we have a lot of stuff to spread out in "dis purse." Using a purse in the skit, and frequently using the phrase "dis purse" and phrases like "spreading things out" or "sending items in different directions" would show the meaning and also give a clue about word's identity.

The students should show and tell the meaning. If "tangible" were the vocabulary word, the skit could center on a "tan gerbil" with a focus on touching it to show the definition. Students would push the phrase "tan gerbil" and also the definition by saying how they love to touch it or by using such phrases as, "Oh, it is so touchable." The skit must do two things. It must incorporate a "sounds like" word and also emphasize the definition.

After students do the skit, the teacher would teach the word and have the students write it with the definition. They could then be given an opportunity to write a couple of sentences using the word in context. The next step might be to have them turn to a neighbor and share their sentences for reinforcement and clarity.

Mystery words can be assigned in advance to small groups of students who then have a day or two to prepare a skit. The skit should not last more than two minutes. A teacher may elect to do one or two a day or to do four or five on a regular day each week.

- **Frequent State Changes.** The frequency of state changes is an important consideration. Only the professional educator knows how to manage this frequency for the optimum effect. Doing state changes too often will interfere with the flow of instruction, and doing them too infrequently will allow the working memory of students to wander. The proper balance is contingent on many factors including time of day, ability of the group to attend, student interest level in the material, and enthusiasm of the teacher. Getting the proper balance is very helpful for maintaining attention and focus.

- **Storytelling.** Storytelling is a powerful tool for holding attention and is effective for all types of learners (National Storytelling Association, 1994). Professional educators should continuously strive to improve their storytelling skills.

- **This Is Important.** This move lets students know that what they are doing is important. The teacher strives to communicate the importance of specific content and of learning in many ways and with high frequency. Telling students why what they are learning and doing is important will result in better attention and participation. This is the "What's in it for me?" move (DePorter, Reardon, & Singer-Nourie, 1999; Jones, 2003).

- **Big Picture.** Giving students the big picture of a unit of study or even of a daily lesson is helpful because knowing the big picture allows them to feel grounded as they are learning and allows their brains to better organize the schema as it is learned. The big picture can be viewed as a list, a content diagram, or some other graphic organizer. It is helpful to come back to the big picture during instruction to reground students in the proper organization of the content. It is also a form of future pacing, allowing the students to know what is coming.

- **Enrolling Questions.** Enrolling questions are questions asked of students related to content that tend to tap into their curiosity and interest.

- **Enrolling Statements.** Enrolling statements are statements made by the teacher related to the content that tend to enroll students by tapping into their curiosity and interest.

- **Connecting to Experience.** This is an important move for motivating students to learn. The teacher continuously connects content being learned into schema or experiences to which the students can relate.

- **Color.** Using color is a valuable move for encoding memory and also helps to enroll and motivate students. Students should learn to work in color frequently and always have colored felt-tipped markers with them. The visual cortex of the brain is stimulated by color and is especially sensitive to color diversity and contrast. For this reason, students should use at least two colors when using this strategy.

- **Spotlighting.** Suppose a student asks a question and the teacher says, "Let me shed some light on that." The teacher then hands a large flashlight to a student and has him or her shine the light on the explanation being given at the white board. Where do you suppose all the attention of the students will be? This is called spotlighting.

- **Drum Rolls.** Drum rolls are done as a tradition that is anchored to some move the teacher makes on a regular basis. For example, every time the teacher pulls down an overhead projector screen or flips over a sheet on a flip chart pad, the students automatically do a drum roll. They do this by "drum rolling" on a table or on their legs while seated. The purpose is to change state and to focus working memory.

- **Natural Signing.** Research studies have shown that normal hearing students can benefit by learning American Sign Language (Daniels, 2001; Dennis & Azpiri, 2005). What an advantage this would be if it were taught to all students when they first started school. Knowing sign language would allow students to use their kinesthetic modality to reinforce their learning throughout their educational career. Although teaching American Sign Language may be impractical as a strategy for changing learning state, teachers can use "natural signing" to enable students to learn through motion. The term natural signing refers to the use of motions that are connected to the content or express the content. Students have enough natural gestures in their body to express almost every concept we can teach them. Help students learn to talk with their hands by using their own personal signing. Use signing with the whole group. Use a motion to express something in the content and have them imitate it back. The use of natural signing helps to manage student state and reinforces memory.

- **Graphic Organizers.** A graphic organizer is a tool used to organize content in such a way that the learner can get a picture of its organization. It can be done by content mapping the curriculum or by using some other device. Sticky notes attached to a white board can be effective. Formal outlines can function as graphic organizers. Physical objects such as cans or small boxes are effective in some cases.

Graphic organizers are effective for showing students the big picture. A teacher can get quite creative with graphic organizers. For example, in one classroom, a teacher had six inflated balloons taped to the wall in a circular configuration. Each balloon had one of the six main concepts related to the unit written on it. As students completed learning each new concept in this mini-unit, the teacher popped the balloon related to that concept, doing so with plenty of fanfare and celebration. The students immediately drew the balloon, wrote the concept they had learned in the center, and then discussed it with their neighbors to make sure their neighbors understood it and would "never-never-ever" forget.

- **Timed Instruction.** Timed instruction involves letting students know how long a particular chunk will last. It might sound something like this: "We will now explore this concept for 7 minutes 15 seconds. Please prepare yourself. You will want to give this your full attention." The teacher then sets a timer and begins the instruction.

Timed instruction has a very positive effect on students because it lets them know that there is a beginning and a reasonable end to instruction. It sends a strong message that they must give strong effort, holding their attention on the topic. Timed instruction lets them know that the chunk for instruction is reasonable. It functions like a goal or target. The teacher must never extend beyond the timer. The instruction should be followed by something that changes state. Perhaps students will create a content map, create diagrams of what was taught, or work with other students to prepare something or expand the topic.

- **Checking Questions.** This is a technique Madeline Hunter refers to as "dip sticking." It means that the teacher asks frequent questions to check students' level of understanding. Students come to know the process and contribute valuable information about their level of understanding on a particular topic. It might begin like this: "I would like to check your understanding. Please help me with the following checking questions." The teacher then asks a question, and the students respond. Next, the teacher surveys the group to see how individual students feel about their understanding and asks, "What questions do you have about this topic?" If answers to student questions are brief and their questions of a minor nature, they can be answered, and then the teacher can move to another checking question. In some cases, the teacher may decide to do some additional instruction or reinforcement on the topic at a later time. Students learn to examine their own learning.

- **Choice Talk.** Choice talk was covered in Chapter 5, but it is listed here as an important state management tool. It functions as a reminder that the student is always making choices and can take ownership of effort and level of attention. "Almost every student in this room has chosen to give full attention to this discussion. Thank you. You have made an excellent choice. Those who are not fully attentive are invited to make that choice at this time. This has been a public service announcement."

- **Clap It Shut.** This move is an ending tradition that occurs after a chunk of instruction. Students hold one hand out in front of them in a cupping position with palms up. Using the other hand, they pretend they are putting each of the concepts away by putting them into the hand held out in front of them. The teacher does this with the students saying the item to them and having the students say the item as they pretend they are placing it in their hands. For example, the teacher might say, "Let's put our three new vocabulary words away. Please stand up." (*Students are standing with their hand held out as modeled by the teacher.*) "The first word is "deficit." It is the amount an expected sum of money falls short. It is called a deficit. Please put this word away." The students say the word in unison and pretend to put it in their hands. The teacher and students then move to the next word. Once all three have been put away, the students, as a group, clap the words they have learned shut by moving their free hands in a large arch and clapping them together with their hands holding the concepts. The students can then be seated, or they can move directly into their next learning task. "Clapping it shut" creates a clean ending to a segment of instruction and also functions as an excellent learning state change.

- **Celebrations.** Celebrations are moments in the classroom when the teacher and the students pause and notice and celebrate their learning and accomplishments. A celebration might begin with the following comment from the teacher. "Please pause. Please notice how well everyone is working in this classroom. The scores from yesterday's quiz were excellent. You are all doing a great job. Please take a moment to give everyone at your table a high five." If a bigger celebration is called for, the teacher might give the students a "one-song break" to celebrate their accomplishments. We want the celebration to occur inside the students. We want them to get the good feeling associated with accomplishment. The teacher orchestrates these internal celebrations, and they should occur frequently in the classroom.

- **Talk to Your Brain.** Have your students talk to their brains. Pause just before you make an important point in your instruction and have them tell their brains, "This is important."

- **Talk to Your Neighbor's Brain.** Have students talk to their neighbor's brain to remind it to be resourceful or to attend with full power for the next 67 seconds.

- **Partner Shares.** Partner shares are opportunities for students to spend several minutes with a partner to discuss an aspect of the curriculum or to get another person's opinion on a particular topic.

- **Student Movement.** Balancing body movement with focus and attention is an important teacher skill related to learning state management. We should watch the attention of students carefully and use student movement to help them manage their learning states. Using movement can mean something as simple as having them stand up and reach for higher ground or doing a movement that causes them to cross the midline. The midline refers to a plane that runs through the center of the body dividing it into a right and left side. The left hemisphere of the brain controls the right side of the body, and the right hemisphere of the brain controls the left side of the body. When we do a movement that moves an arm or a leg to the other side of our body across the midline, it helps to energize both sides of the brain. (LeDoux, 2002; Wolfe, 2001).

- **Shifting Student Location.** Having students move to new locations during instruction can work as an effective state change strategy. It might sound something like this: "Please stand. Please look at your chair and say, 'Thank you for supporting me.' When I say 'new perspective,' find a new place to sit in a new neighborhood. Be seated in your neighborhood and immediately begin starring at me. New perspective."

- **Elbow Disease.** Declare elbow disease illegal in your classroom. Elbow disease, whose symptom is heads resting on hands supported by elbows propped on desks, is contagious. Let students know it is dangerous and can quickly spread throughout the room. Elbow disease sends messages of inattention in many directions: to the students' brains, to their neighbors' brains, and to the teacher's brain.

- **Echo Claps.** The use of echo claps is a handy teacher move for bringing the attention of the group back to the front of the room. The teacher claps a pattern, and the students echo back the pattern. Once students are trained, the teacher can begin echo clapping with only a few students toward the front of the classroom, and then, by the time the teacher claps a second pattern, the entire room will be attentive and will join the clapping. You can clap several patterns.

- **Instant Replay.** In this move, the teacher repeats back exactly what she or he just said using the same words and expression. It might sound like this: "Wow. That was important. Let me do an instant replay. Please push the pause button. Now push the instant replay button." *(Students pretend to be pushing a button in the air.)* The teacher then does the instant replay and might elect for students to do the same replay with a partner.

- **Adjust Physiology.** The words "adjust your physiology" mean to shift your position to one that is more attentive. Once the room becomes anchored to the phrase, you will see the entire room change when the phrase is used.

- **Nods.** Remind students to give nods. Let them know when there is a famine of nods.

- **Reframing.** Remind students to reframe content using their own thinking. This will involve pausing and saying to students, "Please reframe."

- **Thinking Aloud.** Thinking aloud is an effective strategy for capturing attention. The teacher talks as if he or she were alone and thinking right out loud. It might sound something like this: "Wow, this is going to be really important for my students. I wonder how I can convince them this homefun assignment is critical for tomorrow's lesson on fractions. Let me try to convince them." Or perhaps it would sound like this: "This is really risky. If one of my students does not understand this point, she or he might get lost on our field trip. I'd better make a really big deal out of this." The teacher, once finished thinking aloud, communicates directly with students.

- **Early Finisher Routines.** Early finisher routines are important for good classroom management. When students are working individually on a learning task, they will usually not finish at the same time, so it is helpful for the teacher to establish what students who finish early will be doing once they do finish. Having a task to engage their focus can help keep them from engaging in their own sometimes less desirable activity. An early finisher routine should include tasks that students enjoy doing or that will easily keep them occupied for a few minutes. It is also effective to give them a choice of two or three early finisher routines, perhaps including silent reading as an option.

- **Classroom Maps.** Have students switch to the classroom map that is best suited to the learning task. Aligning the proper classroom map with an activity can make a significant difference in student focus and classroom management. Classroom maps were discussed in Chapter 4.

- **Tiebacks.** Use tiebacks to continue to help students connect to existing schemata and to motivate. There are four important tiebacks to keep in mind.

Payoff Tiebacks

This is the "What is in it for me?" tieback. Frequently remind students about the payoffs of their learning. Create clarity about how their learning will be valuable for them now and in the future. Remind them about the importance of building schemata now to allow for future learning.

Objective Tiebacks

These tiebacks connect students to the objective of the lesson. The teacher makes the objective of a lesson or the objectives of a unit of study clear and frequently references these objectives to demonstrate the progression of instruction. This helps students hold the big picture and gives them a feeling of accomplishment.

Prior Learning Tiebacks

Keep connecting into the students' prior learning by using prior learning tiebacks.

Student Setting Tiebacks

Frequently connect the content being taught with the students' world. Seek and use examples from the students' own world to teach and to reinforce learning.

- **Signal Phrases.** Signal phrases are useful devices, especially when giving directions. A signal phrase might sound like this: "When I say go" or "When I say 'proofs,' get into your groups and do the following . . ." The signal phrase lets students know when the action begins. This allows them to hear the directions in their entirety before they move or begin the action. It allows the teacher to make sure the directions are understood by asking checking questions or just asking students what questions they have. This is a very effective classroom management technique.

- **Mnemonics.** Mnemonics can be very useful for helping students learn in certain situations. They also affect motivation because of the success that most students have with these learning devices. Mnemonics can include acronyms (ALERT), acrostic sentences (Every good boy does fine), rhyme and rhythm, or song mnemonics. A narrative chain is a powerful mnemonic and has many applications in the classroom. Students can create a narrative chain by creating a story out of the content being learned. For example, if they were learning countries in the Middle East, they might make up a story something like this: "I had lunch in a restaurant and ordered a large bowl of *turkey* soup. I tasted it, and *oh man* it was good. But right after my first taste, *I ran* out of there because *a rock* came through the window. I jumped to the side and tripped on an *afghan* belonging to a lady seated right next to the door and . . ."

• **Reinforcement moves.** The moves related to reinforcement discussed earlier in this chapter include many moves that are also effective for state management. Consider the effects of such moves as partner recaps, turn to your neighbor, creating a quick content diagram, doing a SSDR, summary reviews, or fast forwards. Each of these moves is also an effective state management move.

We have just explored a list of moves related to learning state management. Consider looking over the list frequently to pick a move or two you can add to your repertoire. When these moves become a regular part of what you do, come back and search out another couple of moves. This is about making small steady changes. It is about staying green and growing.

We will now consider a powerful model for encoding memory from expository reading. Some students lose their motivation with classes in which they are required to use expository reading to learn portions of the content. This problem has become so significant that teaching an effective strategy for learning from reading is essential for maintaining durable motivation in many educational organizations. If students were taught an excellent expository reading strategy starting in elementary school, this situation could be avoided in most cases. Many educators will need to introduce students to this strategy at the middle school or high school level.

PAGES

Many teachers in middle schools and high schools think that their students are not successful with texts, and many students are unable to gain much from their use. This situation is not necessary. Students must be taught how to handle the expository reading of textbooks to ensure their success as they continue their education.

Many students approach expository reading the same way they would approach literature or general reading. This is a big mistake. This breakdown occurs because the students have not been trained in effective expository reading strategy. The reading strategy called PAGES is powerful. It has helped students at all levels from middle elementary to graduate school. It is easy to apply and fun to use. It allows students to learn information in alignment with the way the brain is designed to operate and to tag information into long-term memory for excellent recall. If taught in the elementary grades, PAGES becomes automatic by middle school, high school, and college.

This strategy also breaks down the barrier of fear that many students experience with expository reading, and it allows teachers to use expository reading as another successful strategy for student learning. Because it is very effective for helping students understand the relationship of main points and supporting detail, PAGES can help not only with student memory tasks but also with student comprehension. Learners should be taught to see priorities and to know what is important. They should practice the art of understanding how pieces connect and develop skill in knowing what content should receive the greatest attention (Wiggins & McTighe, 2006). PAGES is a very effective model for enhancing these skills in students. This strategy also allows teachers to increase their own effectiveness with expository reading, saving time and improving recall.

PAGES is an acronym representing the five steps in the expository reading process. These steps stand for preview, ask, gather, expand, and study. Students are trained in the method so that it becomes automatic.

When I taught this process to Heather, she was upset. Heather was a student in an alternative high school who had been kicked out of a regular high school. She had failed most of her classes in the regular school arena. Heather was upset that she had not been taught this strategy before. She had excellent success once she started using PAGES and felt she would have been successful in her regular high school had she been taught the process earlier.

I have taught this process to fifth graders and to doctoral study groups. I have a friend who graduated from Oxford University who informed me that it was PAGES that got him through successfully. It is a powerful process.

PAGES is explained in a lesson plan format in the resources section. Please go through this description carefully, and try PAGES with some of the material you are teaching or need to learn for a college class. Doing this will allow you to experience its power. In the resources section, there is also a template for use in teaching the process to students. You have permission to make as many copies of this template as you need for your teaching of the PAGES process.

IMPLEMENTATION OF MOVES

We began our journey by focusing on leadership and its relationship to administration. We defined leadership as actions that result in the improvement of organizations through positive modeling, positive motivation, and the implementation of specific initiatives. We discovered that leadership would ideally occur at all levels of the organization. We explored motivation and examined the factors that influence it.

In Chapter 2, we began our exploration of the context connection by looking at context for teachers. In order for students to be resourceful, the teacher must be resourceful first. We explored the idea of systems thinking and the importance of systemic and personal victories. We were reminded of the importance of our profession and examined the "law of source and resource." We learned about educational charity, educational grace, and the power of positive self-coaching. This chapter ended with a catalog of moves. Review of this list will quickly remind us of a number of moves that we can make to support ourselves in our profession.

In Chapter 3, we turned our attention to the cognitive connection. This chapter contains valuable information about the brain and the process of learning, information that is valuable to us as educators and for our students. Teaching students about the brain and about how they learn pays significant dividends in motivation and participation and is an important move for upgrading durable motivation.

In Chapter 4, we returned our attention to the context connection, but with a focus on student context. We learned that setting proper context for students is a critical move for accelerating learning and increasing motivation. The principal sets the context for the school, and the classroom teacher sets powerful context for the classroom. The chapter ends with an extensive list of educational moves that can function as review and also as a valuable resource for implementation. It contains such suggestions as create a focus on effort, use inclusive language, maintain equal value relationships, establish a "home court advantage," use music and color to support student focus, and have a blue light special.

In Chapter 5, we explored the character connection. We began by learning about "the line" and how it functions as a powerful cognitive anchor for students. We learned about the gold coin of respect and the four gems of excellence. We then returned to the topic of positive self-coaching, but this time with a focus on teaching students to use this strategy.

We ended our journey with the classroom connection in this chapter. Here we discovered the "connected quartet" with its four ingredients of enroll, chunk, diversify, and reinforce. We explored a model called ALERT, which can be used with students to help them take responsibility for their own learning. We examined the issue of learning state management and developed an extensive list of possible moves. We ended our exploration with a focus on an expository reading strategy called PAGES.

Following this chapter is a section entitled "Resources." In it, you will find diagrams of the brain and many of the teaching and learning tools outlined in this chapter, including the Brain Preferences Survey for measuring modality, style, and brain dominance. Included are instructions for using the instrument. Also in the resources section is a template for teaching PAGES along with detailed instructions for teaching this strategy to students.

As you have witnessed, there is a large repertoire of educational moves suggested in this book. Selecting moves to orchestrate powerful context and effective teaching will result in increases in durable motivation throughout the educational organization. We start by selecting a few moves and implementing them. Once these moves are comfortably part of our personal repertoire, we come back to the material and select a few new moves to work on. This is the key to implementation: small steady steps forward. It is important to stay balanced in our approach to implementation. An educator could easily get overwhelmed by trying to do too much too fast. For many of us, coming to the end of this book will bring us to an exciting new beginning as we journey on toward greater personal and professional growth. May we all stay green and growing, and may the hundreds or thousand of students we teach reap rich rewards.

Catalogue of Educational Moves: The Classroom Connection

1. Adopt the connected quartet as a model for classroom instruction.

2. Show students the "why" behind their learning as an engagement step.

3. Use your own energy and enthusiasm as tools for engaging students.

4. Use enrolling questions to help engage students in the content of a lesson.

5. Connect to your students' own experience to help engage them.

6. Involve students in an activity or demonstration to engage them.

7. Continue to engage students throughout a lesson.

8. Use props to engage students.

9. Break content into chunks to avoid having students initiate a stress response and to promote better encoding of memory.

10. Diversify your instruction to accommodate student preferences for modality.

11. Diversify your instruction to accommodate student preferences for style.

12. Measure your own modality and style preferences. Use this knowledge to help with diversification of instruction.

13. Use the Brain Preferences Survey to measure the brain dynamics of your students, and help them discover their areas of strength and areas of challenge.

14. Use the Brain Preferences Survey with students to teach them tolerance for differences in people. Help them understand that it takes all modalities and styles to make the world work. Help them get excited about their own modality and style balances.

15. Use the Brain Preferences Survey with school staff to enhance the power of the educational team.

16. Use 10–24–7 as a reinforcement protocol to ensure consolidation of long-term memory.

(Continued)

(Continued)

17. In a block schedule, use a 10–48–7 protocol for reinforcement and assign homefun in two parts to maximize reinforcement and memory consolidation.

18. Use a variety of reinforcement moves including some of the following:
    - Teacher Recaps
    - Partner Recaps
    - Random Recaps
    - Summary Reviews
    - Turn to Your Neighbor
    - SSDRs (See-Say-Do Reviews)
    - Content Diagrams
    - Homefun
    - Content Mapping
    - Circuit Learning
    - Fast Forward
    - Gallery Walks
    - Gallery Scans
    - Content Map Reviews
    - Theta Scans
    - Teacher Reteach
    - Student Reteach
    - Reflect
    - Standing Down Strolls
    - Game Reviews

19. Teach students they are responsible for their learning by using ALERT.

20. Train students to use proper physiology in your classroom and help them understand the connection between physiology and attention.

21. Train students to adjust their attention.

22. Train students to look and listen.

23. Train students to encourage themselves in their learning.

24. Train students to encourage the teacher as part of their responsibility as a student. Teach them how to use the nod and encourage its frequent use.

25. Teach students that the bare minimum requirement in a classroom is to at least pretend to learn. Do this in a humorous way.

26. Help students use reframing to encode memory.

27. Use analogy to help students with picturing and reframing.

28. Train students to take ownership for their learning. Teach them that quality work respects themselves and the teacher.

29. Maintain a strong focus on learning state management and change learning states effectively to keep students resourceful.

30. Use a variety of learning state management moves to maintain resourcefulness and attention, including some of the following:
    - VAK Teaching
    - Pause and Look
    - Name Dropping
    - Touch
    - Proximity
    - Future Pacing
    - Unison
    - Callbacks
    - Incomplete Sentences
    - Random Response
    - Shifting Instructional Position
    - Eye Contact
    - Voice Variety
    - Silence
    - Gesture
    - Challenges
    - Time Targets
    - Props
    - Acknowledgements
        Applause
        Round of Applause
        Finger Snaps
        Microwaves
        Sitting Ovation
        Power Woosh
        Public Posters
        Private Notes
        Classroom Conspiracies
        High Fives
        Pat Yourself on the Back
        Teacher Acknowledgements
        Creative Acknowledgements

(Continued)

(Continued)

- Encouragement
- Teacher Enthusiasm
- Humor
- Sound Effects
- Music
- Dramatizing
- Frequent State Changes
- Storytelling
- This Is Important
- Big Picture
- Enrolling Questions
- Enrolling Statements
- Connecting to Experience
- Color
- Spotlighting
- Drum Rolls
- Natural Signing
- Graphic Organizers
- Timed Instruction
- Checking Questions
- Choice Talk
- Clap It Shut
- Celebrations
- Talk to Your Brain
- Talk to Your Neighbor's Brain
- Partner Shares
- Student Movement
- Shifting Student Location
- Elbow Disease
- Echo Claps
- Instant Replay
- Adjust Physiology
- Nods
- Reframing
- Thinking Aloud
- Early Finisher Routines
- Classroom Maps
- Tiebacks
  Payoff Tiebacks
  Objective Tiebacks
  Prior Learning Tiebacks
  Student Setting Tiebacks

- Signal Phrases
- Mnemonics

31. Teach students the powerful PAGES strategy. Use this strategy for your own learning in college and graduate classes.

32. Use the catalogue of moves located at the end of each chapter to assist with implementation. Remember not to attempt to run faster than you are able. There is great demand on us as educators. Stay balanced. Work with a few moves, and once they are a comfortable part of your repertoire, select a few more for implementation. There are enough moves in this book for several years of implementation.

LEADERSHIP NOTES

High quality teaching is an essential ingredient for upgrading the level of durable motivation in a learning community. Its importance cannot be overstated. The moves described here help with attention and the successful encoding of memory. They allow the students to stay more engaged in their learning. They make teaching more enjoyable and tend to motivate us as educators.

The classroom leader can show leadership by being bold about improvement. Trying new strategies and moves and embracing the idea of continuous improvement are important leadership initiatives. A teacher leader can learn about her or his own modality preferences and style and be willing to adapt to accommodate the needs of students. A teacher leader can learn to better celebrate the diversity among students and other staff members and act to strengthen tolerance. Teacher leaders can work to bring out the best in their colleagues and students.

A school leader can support continuous improvement in teaching by encouraging the implementation of moves suggested in this chapter. School leaders might work to help a teacher select moves to begin incorporating into his or her repertoire. They can establish a school climate where teachers feel safe taking the risks necessary for improvement. The school leader can use the Brain Preferences Survey to help establish a stronger school team. They can establish a climate where brain compatible instruction and methodology are a priority.

The school leader should look at the catalog of moves carefully and select moves for leadership initiatives. These moves will become a standard for instruction in the educational organization. Examples might include a strong focus on the connected quartet and on learning state management, the use of ALERT, the teaching of PAGES, or the implementation of acknowledgements, 10–24–7, or VAK teaching. Once these are adopted through the organization, they become a hallmark of how excellent instruction is accomplished in every classroom of the school.

RESOURCES

DePorter, B., Reardon, M., & Singer-Nourie, S. (1999). *Quantum teaching: Orchestrating student success*. Needham Heights, MA: Allyn & Bacon.

Jensen, E. (2000). *Brain-based learning: The new science of teaching and training* (Rev. ed.). Thousand Oaks, CA: Corwin Press.

Jones, S. (2003). *Blueprint for student success: A guide to research-based teaching practices K–12*. Thousand Oaks, CA: Corwin Press.

Marzano, R., Norford, J., Paynter, D., Pickering, D., & Gaddy, B. (2001). *A handbook for classroom instruction that works*. Alexandria, VA: Association for Supervision and Curriculum Development.

Saphier, J., & Gower, R. (1997). *The skillful teacher: Building your teaching skills* (5th ed.). Acton, MA: Research for Better Teaching, Inc.

Sprenger, M. (2002). *Becoming a "wiz" at brain-based teaching: How to make every year your best year*. Thousand Oaks, CA: Corwin Press.

Resources

Useful Diagrams of the Brain

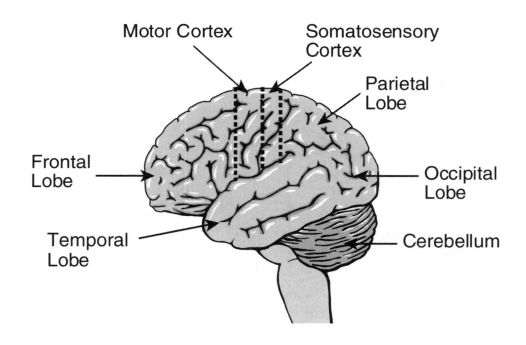

SOURCE: Reprinted with permission from Sousa, D. (2006). *How the brain learns* (3rd ed.). Thousand Oaks, CA: Corwin Press.

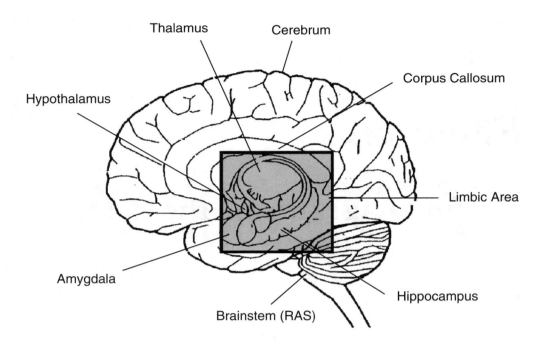

Thalamus   Cerebrum

Corpus Callosum

Hypothalamus

Limbic Area

Amygdala

Brainstem (RAS)

Hippocampus

LEFT SIDE   RIGHT SIDE

Analysis   Holistic

Sequence   Patterns

Time   Spatial

Speech   Context of language

Recognizes: Recognizes:

   words   faces

   letters   places

   numbers   objects

Processes external stimuli   Processes internal messages

SOURCE: Reprinted with permission from Sousa, D. (2006). *How the brain learns* (3rd ed.). Thousand Oaks, CA: Corwin Press.

Teaching Resources for Chapter Six

The Classroom Connection

BRAIN PREFERENCES SURVEY: TEACHER NOTES

The first page of the survey is an introduction page. Following this, you will find the Modality Indicator page. Follow the directions, and then graph the data on the bottom portion of the Brain Preferences Profile page. You will see a place to graph totals one, two, and three. These are followed by the words visual, auditory, and kinesthetic. Notice that there is a box following these words. This is for writing your totals from the Modality Data Sheet. Graph your scores to create a bar graph using markers. It is helpful to use three different colors, one for each modality. Notice that there is a place for name and date at the bottom of the profile page.

The Style Indicator follows the Modality Indicator. Follow the directions, and then graph your results on the top of the Brain Preferences Profile page. Write each of your scores in the box located next to the large bold line down the center of the profile. Notice the words "left" and "right" located on the profile. There is a separate place right below the style graphs to graph left and right brain dominance. To accomplish this, add the two scores for "structured" and "analytical" and graph the sum on the left side. Add the totals for "affective" and "original" and graph this sum on the right side. For both style and brain dominance, graph from the center out.

Following the Brain Preferences Profile page are some resource pages. The first one provides the teacher with a list of preference descriptors. A page designed for use with students follows. The teacher reads the descriptors and the students write them down. A discussion can then follow about how well the descriptors describe personal style.

The last four pages are resource pages to be used by the teacher or shared with students. One use of these pages for teachers is to review periodically the style areas that are the least dominant. This helps us evaluate our diversification. We have a tendency to teach to our dominant style, and reviewing characteristics that are not dominant may work well to suggest possible diversification moves.

BRAIN PREFERENCES SURVEY

"If a man does not keep pace with his companions, perhaps it is because he hears a different drummer. Let him step to the music which he hears, however measured or far away."

—Henry David Thoreau

Introduction

The study of brain preferences is the study of the differences and similarities in people resulting from their preference for sensory input, or modality, and how they process and store information, which is called "style." This information reveals valuable insights for understanding our own behavior and the behavior of those around us. This new knowledge helps promote self-acceptance, which leads to higher levels of self-esteem and confidence. It also fosters a greater respect for diversity in others, which can result in improved group effectiveness. Armed with these new insights, we can work to improve relationships, become more productive, and motivate ourselves toward greater self-improvement. This provides an important step forward in the journey to reach our fullest potential.

The Brain Preferences Survey consists of two parts: the Modality Indicator and the Style Indicator. The data for both indicators are graphed on the Brain Preferences Profile. This instrument is not meant to be a diagnostic tool, but it is an indicator of brain preferences.

Brain Preferences Survey: Modality Indicator

John Parks Le Tellier

Directions: Select A, B, or C based on the word group or sentence you like the best. Circle the letter of your selection. Then transfer your selections to the Modality Data Sheet. Add the number of selections in each column and multiply by 4. Graph your results on the Brain Preferences Profile.

	A	B	C
1.	**A.** Rustling–Hear–Tempo	**B.** Texture–Feel–Soft	**C.** Illustration–Snapshot–Picture
2.	**A.** I get it.	**B.** I see.	**C.** I hear you.
3.	**A.** I heard the train whistle.	**B.** I saw the rows of flowers.	**C.** I felt the breeze on my back.
4.	**A.** Focus–Color–Inspect	**B.** Chat–Stillness–Tune	**C.** Race–Latch–Loosen
5.	**A.** Bird's-eye view	**B.** Rings true	**C.** Hang in there
6.	**A.** Nod–Glide–Signal	**B.** Shiny–Reflection–Attractive	**C.** Call–Whisper–Bell
7.	**A.** This sounds good to me.	**B.** This feels good to me.	**C.** This looks good to me.
8.	**A.** Vision–Clear–Glimpse	**B.** Melody–Quiet–Hear	**C.** Touch–Smooth–Movement
9.	**A.** I sense how you feel.	**B.** I hear what you're saying.	**C.** I see what you mean.
10.	**A.** Peek–Sight–View	**B.** Scoot–Gallop–Skip	**C.** Describe–Song–Chime
11.	**A.** Get in touch with	**B.** Appears to me	**C.** Loud and clear
12.	**A.** Lend me an ear.	**B.** Keep an eye out.	**C.** Give him a hand.
13.	**A.** The sport was fun.	**B.** The sunset was beautiful.	**C.** It was music to my ears.
14.	**A.** Grip–Support–Relax	**B.** Mention–Tone–Rhyme	**C.** Show–Notice–Dream
15.	**A.** It sounded good.	**B.** It felt good.	**C.** It looked good.
16.	**A.** Look at this.	**B.** Catch this.	**C.** Listen up.
17.	**A.** Purring–Listen–Talk	**B.** Glow–Appear–See	**C.** Hold–Trot–Catch
18.	**A.** Clear as a bell	**B.** Smooth as silk	**C.** Bright as day
19.	**A.** The feel of the sand	**B.** The view of the ocean	**C.** The sound of the waves
20.	**A.** Look–Color–Glance	**B.** Upbeat–Speak–Sound	**C.** Motion–Lukewarm–Sprint
21.	**A.** Let me hear this.	**B.** Let me do this.	**C.** Let me see this.
22.	**A.** The sight on the stage	**B.** The sound of the instruments	**C.** The vibration in the air
23.	**A.** Discuss–Silence–Say	**B.** Watch–Shine–Observe	**C.** Run–Throw–Snap
24.	**A.** The sound had an interesting melody.	**B.** The cloth had a smooth feel.	**C.** The painting had bright colors.
25.	**A.** A glimpse of	**B.** Hear the sound	**C.** In touch with

Brain Preferences Survey: Modality Data Sheet

John Parks Le Tellier

Directions: Transfer your responses to this data sheet by placing a circle around the letter of each of your selections. Count the number of letters circled in each column, and enter the total for each column at the bottom in the box for total 1, 2, and 3. Multiply by 4, and then graph your results on the Brain Preferences Profile.

	Column 1	Column 2	Column 3
1.	C	A	B
2.	B	C	A
3.	B	A	C
4.	A	B	C
5.	A	B	C
6.	B	C	A
7.	C	A	B
8.	A	B	C
9.	C	B	A
10.	A	C	B
11.	B	C	A
12.	B	A	C
13.	B	C	A
14.	C	B	A
15.	C	A	B
16.	A	C	B
17.	B	A	C
18.	C	A	B
19.	B	C	A
20.	A	B	C
21.	C	A	B
22.	A	B	C
23.	B	A	C
24.	C	A	B
25.	A	B	C

Total Column 1		Total Column 2		Total Column 3	
	x4 =		x4 =		x4 =

Brain Preferences Survey: Style Indicator

John Parks Le Tellier

Directions: Select two items from each group that describe you best or that best finish the sentence. It is essential that you select two items from each group for the data to work properly. Once you have made your selections, transfer your selections to the Style Indicator Data Sheet by circling the letters you chose. Count the number of selections in each column to get your total for each column. Multiply this number by 4 to get your graphing score. Use these numbers to graph your results on the top of the Brain Preferences Profile.

1. A. Seeing Possibilities
   B. Completing Work
   C. Gaining Ideas
   D. Cooperation

2. A. Sharing
   B. Orderly
   C. Logical
   D. Innovative

3. A. Doing
   B. Feeling
   C. Thinking
   D. Experimenting

4. A. Theory and research
   B. Investigating and exploring
   C. Intuition and insight
   D. Consistency and order

5. A. Memorize
   B. Personalize
   C. Originate
   D. Think through

6. A. I enjoy working closely with others
   B. I can easily remember facts and details
   C. I like to figure out how things work
   D. I learn well through reading and lectures

7. I like . . .
   A. brainstorming and discovery
   B. listening to an expert and taking notes
   C. working on group projects
   D. practical learning with clear directions

8. In a group I am good at . . .
   A. seeing possibilities
   B. gathering information
   C. keeping the group on task
   D. helping group members work together

9. A. Communicating
   B. Discovering
   C. Cautious
   D. Reasoning

10. A. Conceptual
    B. Inventive
    C. Precise
    D. Flexible

11. A. Problem-solver
    B. People-person
    C. Non-fiction reader
    D. Planner

12. A. Discussing
    B. Getting to the point
    C. Creating
    D. Relating to others

13. A. Well planned
    B. Studious
    C. Understanding
    D. Curious

14. A. I like creative writing
    B. I like discussing concepts
    C. I like making timelines
    D. I like trying new things

15. A. Organized
    B. Caring
    C. Questioning
    D. Academic

Brain Preferences Survey: Style Data Sheet

John Parks Le Tellier

Directions: Transfer your selections from the Style Indicator to the data box below by circling the letters you chose. Count the number of selections in each column to get your total for each column. Multiply this number by 4 to get your score. Use these numbers to graph your results on the Brain Preferences Profile.

	Column 1	*Column 2*	*Column 3*	*Column 4*
1.	B	C	D	A
2.	B	C	A	D
3.	A	C	B	D
4.	D	A	C	B
5.	A	D	B	C
6.	B	D	A	C
7.	D	B	C	A
8.	C	B	D	A
9.	C	D	A	B
10.	C	A	D	B
11.	D	C	B	A
12.	B	A	D	C
13.	A	B	C	D
14.	C	B	A	D
15.	A	D	B	C

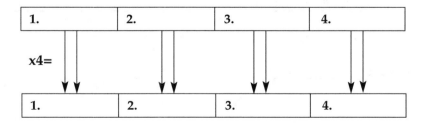

Brain Preferences Survey: Brain Preferences Profile

John Parks Le Tellier

Structured ☐							☐					**Affective**
1												**3**
	60	50	40	30	20	10	10	20	30	40	50	60
Analytical ☐							☐					**Original**
2												**4**
	60	50	40	30	20	10	10	20	30	40	50	60

LEFT   *RIGHT*

120	100	80	60	40	20	20	40	60	80	100	120

Modality Indicator

1 Visual
10 20 30 40 50 60 70 80 90

2 *Auditory*
10 20 30 40 50 60 70 80 90

3 *Kinesthetic*
10 20 30 40 50 60 70 80 90

Name: ——————————————— Date ———————————

Brain Preferences Survey: Preference Descriptors

Structured	**A**ffective
ORGANIZED	CARING
PRACTICAL	COOPERATIVE
SYSTEMATIC	CREATIVE
PRECISE	SOCIAL
CAUTIOUS	FLEXIBLE
REALISTIC	SHARING
EFFICIENT	INTUITIVE

LEFT   RIGHT

Analytical	**O**riginal
CONCEPTUAL	DIVERGENT
LOGICAL	INDEPENDENT
REASONING	RISK TAKING
ACADEMIC	PROBLEM SOLVING
EXAMINING	INVENTIVE
RATIONAL	INVESTIGATING
STUDIOUS	ADVENTUROUS

Brain Preferences Survey: Preference Descriptors

S
t
r
u
c
t
u
r
e
d

_____

_____

_____

_____

_____

A
f
f
e
c
t
i
v
e

_____

_____

_____

_____

_____

LEFT   RIGHT

A
n
a
l
y
t
i
c
a
l

_____

_____

_____

_____

_____

O
r
i
g
i
n
a
l

_____

_____

_____

_____

_____

Brain Preferences Survey: Student Preferences

| **S**
t
r
u
c
t
u
r
e
d | Likes clear time limits

Values order and structure in work and environment

Likes to create real products in hands-on ways

Likes to do worksheets

Likes exact directions

Likes realistic problems

Likes real and specific activities | Works best in shared learning time with others

Likes to give interpretations

Likes to create from personal understanding

Enjoys interpretative writing

Likes group discussion and cooperative learning

Likes role-play and drama | **A**
f
f
e
c
t
i
v
e |

LEFT   RIGHT

| **A**
n
a
l
y
t
i
c
a
l | Likes to gather much information

Values analysis

Likes to weigh and create new ideas

Likes to read and research

Likes to take notes

Likes to explain and debate

Likes to question ideas | Interested in many possibilities

Likes to investigate and discover

Likes brainstorming and divergent thinking

Values trial and error

Enjoys experiments

Enjoys finding alternatives

Enjoys simulations | **O**
r
i
g
i
n
a
l |

Brain Preferences Survey: Teacher Preferences

S t r u c t u r e d — LEFT

- Focus on practical learning
- Sticks to prepared lesson plan
- Structured assignments
- Use of outlines and checklists
- Detailed work
- Encourages perfection, wants good-looking product
- Orderly classroom
- Hands-on materials
- Creativity through prototypes and replicas
- Use of outlines and student work contracts

A f f e c t i v e — RIGHT

- Focus on positive self-concept and growth
- Develops content through cultural, artistic, aesthetic media
- Focus on personalization
- Emphasis on high morale, cooperative learning
- High value on creativity, imagination, and humor
- Promotes a sharing attitude
- Unstructured classroom includes plants, furniture, and artwork

LEFT

RIGHT

A n a l y t i c a l — LEFT

- Focus on ideas, concepts, and theories
- Expects students to analyze and evaluate
- Logical reasoning, develop and prove theories
- Consistent and reliable rules and procedures
- Likes libraries and traditional classrooms
- Challenges students intellectually
- Wants students to be curious about "why"
- Encourages students to learn by reading

O r i g i n a l — RIGHT

- Emphasis on investigation and exploration of possibilities
- Plays role of guide or facilitator
- Many varied and unusual activities
- Challenges students to move beyond given knowledge
- Encourages independent study
- Interested in futuristic and discovery learning
- Promotes original creations
- Wants students to think for themselves

Brain Preferences Survey: Parent Preferences

S t r u c t u r e d

- Loving but true disciplinarian
- Homework taken seriously
- Household by roster on refrigerator
- Immediate "thank-yous" within 24 hours
- Expects neat appearance
- Likes homework done first thing—effective use of time
- Likes to be on time and pays attention to child's schedule and deadlines
- Encourages orderly location for doing homework and study
- Wants to organize child's backpack and school materials

LEFT

A f f e c t i v e

- Involved in child's activities
- Tends to be soft with bottom lines and deadlines
- Likes to volunteer for activities related to child
- Strong supporter of child
- Sensitive to child's feelings
- Protects child's feelings
- Enjoys helping with creative tasks
- Encourages involvement in music, drama, dance, and art

RIGHT

A n a l y t i c a l

- High standards and goals
- Strong emphasis on social and academic success
- Proper manners important
- Reputation of family name important
- Exposes child to every opportunity for growth and development
- High value on grades as a measure of excellence
- Tends to encourage non-fiction reading
- Encourages quiet study environment

O r i g i n a l

- Gives options, not strict rules
- Not a strict disciplinarian
- Tends to be a "friend" parent
- Child expected to pick themselves up and try again
- Learn by trial and error
- Tends to give child much freedom
- Likes involvement with innovative school projects
- "Give it a try" attitude
- "It will all work out" attitude

Brain Preferences Survey: Learning Methods Preferences

Structured

LEFT

Using texts
Making models
Practical reading
Charts
Diagramming
Collecting facts
How-to-books
Worksheets
Flowcharting
Computer instruction
Making timelines
Maps and mapping
How-to discussions
Demonstrations
Outlines and outlining
Classifying
Summaries
Practical problems

Affective

Journal writing
Creative writing
Using metaphor
Personalized examples
Humor
Team games
Cooperative groups
Working with a partner
Mapping and webbing
Discussing feelings
Arts
Role-play
Reading about people
Group projects
Interviewing
Music
Drama
Drawing

Analytical

Using texts
Lecture
Note taking
Library work
Reading
Outlining
Making plans
Writing essays and reports
Using logic
Book reporting
Quiz bowl
Discussing concepts
Panel discussions
Doing research
Debating
Guided independent study
Questioning experts
Considering cause and effect

RIGHT

Original

Brainstorming
Inventing
Games
Experimenting
Investigating
Webbing and mapping
Independent study
Having options
Creating the unusual
Simulations
Open-ended activities
Designing
Problem solving
Optional reading
Doing case studies
Learning games
Making games
Hand-on learning

PAGES

Teacher Notes

If students use a text in your class, you can use it to teach PAGES. If you do not use a text but are teaching your students this strategy, they will need a text from another class, or they can use some pages you have copied from a text to learn the process. PAGES is easier to teach if all students are using the same material.

Be sure your students know the difference between expository reading and other kinds of reading. Sell PAGES to your students to help enroll them. Let them know they will be able to use the strategy now and for the rest of their lives. You might ask them how they feel when they get a reading assignment from a textbook. If they express concerns, let them know that those days are over. Tell them you are going to teach them the most powerful method in the world for taking information from a textbook and getting it encoded into long-term memory. Help them understand how important expository reading will be as they continue their education. Maybe share some of the textbooks you learned from in your college experience.

Teaching PAGES

Below are some suggestions for teaching PAGES to students. The material in italics represents notes to the teacher. The material in regular type is suggested wording to use with students.

Introduce Template

It is called PAGES. What's it called? *(Response.)* Please spell it. *(Spell it with your students.)*

Hand out the PAGES template to your students. This template is located behind these teacher notes. You will need one reproduction of the page that you can display from the front of the room using an overhead projector, flip chart, or other electronic media. We will refer to this as the master template.

Please write the letters P-A-G-E-S in the five circles at the top of the page. Please go over them a couple of times to make them bold. *(If your students have colored pens, it is beneficial for them to use color to organize this content. Each letter could represent a color going across the top and down the side. In this case, they will fill in everything related to the "P" or Preview step in the same color.)*

Notice that you also have five circles going down on the left of your sheet. Please fill these circles in with the letters P-A-G-E-S as well. Remember to make them bold. *(Fill these in on your master template.)*

If you are teaching this powerful strategy but do not use a text in your own classroom, it might be helpful to set up a school scenario for your students using a text from another class. A sample scenario follows just to show how this might be done. If you have copied pages from a text, create a scenario from that material. The notes and examples below are a high school example. The notes assume that students have been introduced to such terms as brain compatible and schema. The material should be adapted for different grade levels.

School Scenario

Let's set up a scenario so you can experience how PAGES works. Suppose you are a student trained in PAGES. You do not use this strategy except when it is needed. For example, suppose a teacher assigns you some reading that is not very demanding. You feel you could read it through one time and learn what you need to know. This would not be a time to use PAGES. The method is too powerful for this situation. It would be like killing a housefly with a 12-gauge shotgun! It's not necessary to use that much power to get the job done. PAGES is used when the content is challenging or when the volume of the content is high.

You walk into your world history class on Monday morning, and your teacher lets you know she is starting a unit on Japan. You will be having a guest speaker on Thursday and will also be responsible for taking notes on a video later in the week. Each student will be writing a short paper on various topics related to Japan. In addition, you are responsible for learning what is in Chapter 5 of your text. You will be tested on Chapter 5, notes from class, the video, and possibly content presented by the guest speaker.

Your teacher launches into an introduction about Japan, giving some interesting information and making some cultural comparisons. She finishes with 12 minutes left in the class period. She points this out and recommends that everyone get started on the reading for the remainder of the class period.

You have had experience with this text before. You know it is not an easy read, and you also know that your teacher is serious when she says you are responsible to know what is in this chapter. You only want to go through the material one time, and you want to tag it into your long-term memory. You decide to use PAGES.

Unfortunately, you are the only student in your class who is trained in PAGES. The other students have no clue how to approach this material. They will start with the first paragraph and just start reading the material the way you would a novel. This is the most ineffective way to learn the material. It won't be more than just a few minutes before their brains are saying, "I wonder how much of this stuff I have to know." Or they might begin asking, "How much of this is going to be on the test?" They are approaching the material using a method called "brain dump." What's it called? *(Response.)* This means they are dumping the information into their brains without giving their brains the tools necessary to put the material away so recall can occur. Brain dump should only be used when the material is easy and the demand for recall is low.

Perhaps these students will read through the entire chapter, hoping that the important information will stay in their brains and pop back out during the test. The night before the test, many of them will go to their room to study. What do you think many of them will do? *(Response.)* That is correct, many of them will read it again. This is very ineffective. But we do not approach our learning this way. We have been trained in PAGES. Let's take a look at what we will do. Without even thinking about it, we launch into the first step before we even leave the classroom.

Preview

The "P" stands for "Preview." Please write this in the rectangle following the letter "P." *(Write the word "Preview" on your master template at location #1 using the same color as you used for the letter "P.")*

Preview has two main parts. These include "Pre-scan" and "Content Map." Please write these in the remaining two large rectangles. *(Write these on your master template at boxes #2 and #3.)*

Pre-scan. Pre-scan has five steps. This is where we start. *(Boxes #4 through #8 represent the five steps of Pre-scan. Have students trace over the outline of box #2 and of boxes #4 through #8 all in the same color.)*

Graphics. We begin by looking at the graphics. We look at the what? *(Response.)* That's right, we always begin by looking at the graphics, including pictures, illustrations, charts, and graphs. These graphics are worth at least a thousand words each. Please write "graphics" in the first rectangle on the left. *(Write "Graphics" on your master template in box #4.)*

If we have a responsible author, the pictures, illustrations, and other graphics have been carefully selected to enhance main ideas in the text. The reason these graphics are worth so many words is that, as we look at them, the brain is scanning existing schemata related to the images. The brain is being primed for learning. We also read any captions connected to the graphics. Let's think of this in another way.

Imagine an eagle flying high above a forest. The eagle is going to enter the forest, but begins by flying high to get the big picture. *(Make motions showing the eagle flying over the forest with one of your hands.)* This is similar to what we are doing with the content in our text. We swoop over the content by looking at the graphics.

Have your students scan the graphics in the text and have them read the captions. Discuss with them what they learned from the process and let them express how they feel about starting this way. Ask them why this is the best way to start.

If you use a text that has a very long chapter, you can use two or three sections to teach the PAGES process.

Before we take the next pass over the content, let's explore one more thing about starting with the graphics. Looking at the graphics primes not only the schema pump but also the motivational pump because graphics are frequently designed to help connect to your interests, which increases motivation. This increase in motivation or interest is an extra important dividend, and starting with graphics is an easy way to begin something you may not be all that excited to do. With many of us, just getting started is the most challenging step. Having an easy and enjoyable first step can be very helpful.

Titles and Subtitles. The eagle now swoops over the forest getting a closer look. Step two in the pre-scan process is called "titles and subtitles." *(Write this on your master template in box # 5.)* This means we go back to the beginning of the chapter and read all the titles and subtitles, as well as any key words that are in boldface type or underlined in the text. We are getting closer to the content but have not yet entered the forest.

Please take an opportunity to quickly read the titles, subtitles, and key words. *(Students are using the text or material you have provided. Give them time to finish and then continue. Encourage them to move quickly.)*

Introduction. The eagle has made two passes over the forest and now comes back for another one getting even closer to the trees. *(Demonstrate with your hand each time getting closer to the floor.)* The next thing we do is read the introduction. *(Write "introduction" on your master template in box #6.)* If you have a responsible author, the introduction is designed to hook your attention and give general, global themes about the topic.

Summary. On our next pass over the content, we read the summary. *(Write "summary" on your master template in box #7.)* This is a very important step. It is like going up to the author and saying, "Hey, could you help me with something? I have to read this text you wrote, and I was wondering, could you just tell me what is important in this chapter before I read it?" Students should learn to always, always, always read the summary first.

Superscan. On the eagle's final swoop, he is almost touching the trees. The last step in pre-scan is called "superscan." What's it called? *(Response.)* Please write this in the last box. *(Write this on your master template in box #8.)*

Superscan means we attempt to see everything. We attempt to what? *(Response.)* This is not reading, it is just seeing. It means we ski down through the material by moving our hand and letting our eyes follow. Skiing looks like this. *Demonstrate this for your students using a text or the material you have provided. This is done very quickly. You will scan an entire page of text in about 5 seconds. Demonstrate the skiing motion by moving your finger down the page in a skiing pattern. Emphasize to your students that they are not reading, but just seeing everything they can.*

Let's superscan our material. I will do it with you so you can get an idea of how quickly it happens. Please do not worry about what you are getting. You are just trying to see things. You are not trying to learn anything. You are trying to see. You are trying to what? *(Response.)*

Superscan with your students, letting them know when you finish each page. They will have a tendency to move too slowly. Have them practice staying with you.

How many had a few things pop up at them as they were skiing through the content? *(Responses.)* Some of you may be thinking, "I really didn't get anything from that." What you mean is, you did not get much you can recall from conscious memory.

We know the brain takes in much more information than we can consciously recall. You might be surprised how much of this material is really there.

In a research setting, it is easy to show that superscan works. All you need are two groups of students in a controlled setting. Have them read the same material. Have one group read without superscan and have the other group use superscan. You will discover that the group using superscan will have higher comprehension of the material. Perhaps it is because when they read the material, their brain is seeing it for the second time.

You have now finished the final step in the pre-scan process. Of course, this process is automatic and very quick. There you are sitting in class. The other students open to the chapter and begin reading one paragraph at a time. But not you! You begin by looking at the graphics. You then start again and zip through the titles and subtitles. You next read the introduction and then skip clear to the end and read the summary. You launch into the final step and superscan the material. How long might this take on an average sized chapter? *(Take some guesses.)*

Content Map. Preview has two parts. One of them is called "Pre-scan." What is the other part called? *(Response—Content Map.)* That's right. But wait a minute. Do you think I am suggesting we construct a content map before we read? Of course! This is an essential step. We map the content from the titles and subtitles. Let's try this.

Demonstrate using a blank overhead transparency, flipchart, whiteboard, or other electronic media. The divisions are found by looking at the largest headings first and then breaking these into smaller categories using the smaller headings and key words in boldface type or underlined. You can use color to separate major divisions on your content map. This process is done with your students as they create their own content maps. When the maps are finished, continue with your lesson.

Congratulations. You just finished the "Preview" step of PAGES. You created a content map using the titles and subtitles. There must be a reason for this. What advantage do you now have over the other students in your class who are still reading through the chapter? *(Response and discussion.)*

This map gives the brain the necessary structure to bring in the details and tie them to something. The content map acts like an umbrella over the content. It provides the framework for adding schemata to a structure. You now have in your mind the same structure the author had in mind when he or she wrote the chapter.

Visit Your Neighbor when I say "recap," please explain to a neighbor what you have done since you started with the PAGES process. *Wear a recap if you use one.*

Ask

We are now ready to move to the next step. The "A" stands for "Ask." Please write this in the box right after the "A." *(Write this on your master template in box #9.)* It stands for what? *(Response.)* It means we move the brain to inquiry. We ask our self questions about the content. There are two kinds of questions. These include author's questions and your questions. *(Write these on your master template. Write "author's questions" in box #10 and write "my questions" in box #11.)*

Author's Questions. If the author of the text you are using included questions for the students, then have the students read these questions. They are not looking for answers, but just introducing the author's questions to their brain. It is a quick process and involves reading the questions and wondering what the answer might be.

My Questions. Next we consider your questions. You may say you can't think of any, but you are well positioned to ask a question or two about the material. You have looked at the graphics, read the titles and subtitles, read the introduction, read the summary, and done a superscan. You created a content map to act as a framework for the content. You should easily be able to form a quick question or two in your mind.

At this point, share a couple of questions that come to your own mind related to the material. If there is something in the material that brings a question to mind that is related to some past experience, share this with your students. Look over the content map and make the connection.

This "Ask" step is a quick operation. Remember, you are not looking for the answers but just letting your brain have the questions.

Gather and Expand

We are now ready to investigate the next two categories. These are done together. The "G" stands for gather, and the "E" stands for expand. *(Write these on your master template as your students write them on their templates. Write "Gather" in box #12, and write "Expand" in box #14.)*

Reading. We gather by reading. Please write "read" after the word "gather." What do we expand? We expand our content map. *(Write "Read" in box #13 on your master template, and write "Content Map" in box #15.)*

Before we experience how this works, let's pause and look at an important idea. It is called chunking. Chunking means breaking what we are learning into small logical chunks. Your content map acts as a framework for your content. It can allow you to chunk your content and learn it in a logical way, so the brain can organize it properly. You can also time manage your learning. Suppose you have several days before you must have the material in this chapter learned. You could make decisions about how you might break the material up to complete this homefun.

At this point, show students some options for learning the material. Look at the major categories. Perhaps they will do the first one on Monday night for homefun. Then complete another major chunk on Tuesday night. Help students understand that their content map can help them chunk their material for time and task management.

Next, show your students how the content map will give them the smaller chunks for learning under each of the major categories. For example, look at the major section they are going to do on Monday night, and show them how it is broken into smaller chunks based on smaller subtitles and words in boldface or italics. This represents the logical way to learn the material. Each time they are finished with one of these small chunks of learning students should do something to indicate a clean ending. Perhaps they will stand up and stretch and then move to the next chunk. Maybe they will take a one-song break after completing larger chunks. As soon as the break is finished, they can put on their personal focus music and begin another chunk. This process is a very powerful way for students to learn material at home.

Expanding Your Content Map. As you focus on each of these chunks, you will gather and expand. You read the content and expand your content map as you go. You must decide what is important and put it on your content map.

Work with your students to expand their content maps. Help them see what is important and how to represent the concept using only one or two words. Show them how to connect the concept into the proper category on their content maps. When they finish a chunk, have them change state and continue with the next chunk. A chunk might be everything under one subtitle. It is necessary for you to model everything for them the first time. You should continue to expand your content map as your students continue expanding their maps. Encourage them to be creative, using color and personalizing their maps.

Study

We now move to the final step in the PAGES process. The "S" stands for the most mysterious word in the English language. Almost nobody knows what this word means. Anyone want to guess what the "S" stands for? (*Responses.*)

The "S" stands for study. Please write this on your template. (*Write this on your master template in box #16.*) To the right of this box, we have a place to write two very important techniques for study. Please write "SSDRs" in box 17 and "Circuit Learning" in box 18. (*Write "SSDRs" on your master template in box #17, and write "Circuit Learning" in box #18.*) If your students are not already familiar with these strategies, take time to teach and demonstrate them.

SSDRs (See-Say-Do Reviews). This is a powerful method of review because it involves all three educational channels. These reviews are done by the student and should become a standard study method. The students see something that has a strong graphic component to it, for example, a content diagram, content map, picture, or some other graphic. They look at the item and say the concept it represents out loud. They do not just think it, but actually say it or whisper it. They also must do a kinesthetic motion that helps express the concept. (See Chapter 6 for a complete description of this excellent method of review.)

Circuit Learning. Circuit learning is a pattern students follow for the rein-forcement of learning. It involves reviewing what they know and then adding a chunk. They then review what they know including the new chunk and then add another new chunk. (See Chapter 6 for a detailed description of circuit learning.) Explain to your students that all the mate-rial gathered under one subtitle of their content map is a chunk and should be involved in the circuit learning process as a complete chunk. This means that, when they finish with their first subtitle on Monday night, they review it before they go to the next chunk. They review using an SSDR. They then proceed with their next chunk. When this is finished, they do an SSDR on both the first and second chunks before they move to the third chunk on their content map.

When they come back on Tuesday, they also use circuit learning by reviewing using SSDRs on Monday's material before they start the material for Tuesday. After they have done this one time, they do not continue to review Monday's material again, but just use circuit learning with the smaller chunks for Tuesday's material. This method is very different from the strategy called cramming. You might have your students wave goodbye to an old friend: CRAMMING!

Once you have completed this lesson on PAGES, it should be reinforced immediately. Have your students explain the entire process to a neighbor. Following this, have them work with a partner and reproduce the entire template from memory. You might want to assign some home-fun. Perhaps have them complete another portion of their content map.

If you are using a text for your own content in your class, continue to use PAGES and require that students use this process until it becomes natural and automatic. This will prove to be one of their most valuable learning assets as they continue their education.

Template

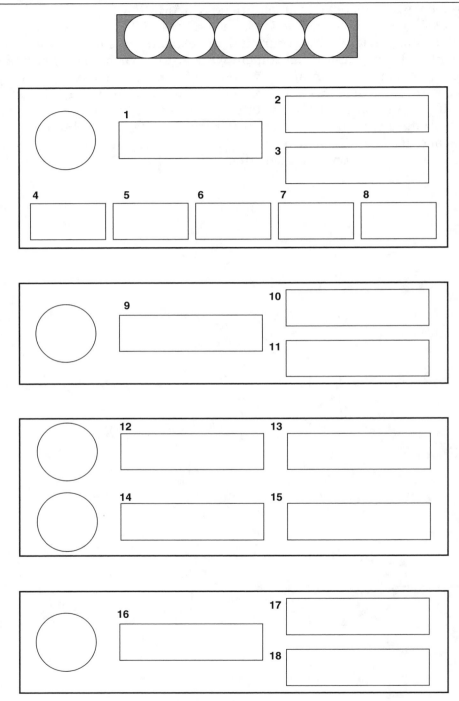

References

Brophy, J. (2004). *Motivating students to learn.* Mahwah, NJ: Lawrence Erlbaum Associates, Inc.

Caine, R., & Caine, G. (1997). *Unleashing the power of perceptual change: The potential of brain-based teaching.* Alexandria, VA: Association for Supervision and Curriculum Development.

Carter, R. (1998). *Mapping the mind.* Los Angeles: University of California Press.

Carter, R. (2002). *Exploring consciousness.* Los Angeles: University of California Press.

Cohen, N., & Eichenbaum, H. (1993). *Memory, amnesia, and the hippocampal system.* Cambridge: MIT Press.

Collins, J., & Porras, J. (1994). *Built to last.* New York: HarperCollins Publishers.

Daniels, M. (2001). *Dancing with words: Signing for hearing children's literacy.* Westport, CT: Greenwood Publishing.

Dennis, K., & Azpiri, T. (2005). *Sign to learn: American Sign Language in the early childhood classroom.* St. Paul, MN: Redleaf Press.

DePorter, B., Reardon, M., & Singer-Nourie, S. (1999). *Quantum learning: Orchestrating student success.* Needham Heights, MA: Allyn & Bacon.

Diamond, M., & Hopson, J. (1998). *Magic trees of the mind: How to nurture your child's intelligence, creativity, and healthy emotions from birth through adolescence.* New York: Dutton.

Gazzaniga, M., Ivry, R., & Mangun, G. (2002). *Cognitive neuroscience: The biology of the mind* (2nd ed.). New York: Norton.

Ginsberg, M., & Wlodkowski, R. (2000). *Creating highly motivating classrooms for all students: A schoolwide approach to powerful teaching with diverse learners.* San Francisco: Jossey-Bass.

Given, B. (2002). *Teaching to the brain's natural learning systems.* Alexandria, VA: Association for Supervision and Curriculum Development.

Glanzman, D., Kandal, E., & Schacher, S. (1990). Target-dependent structural changes accompanying long-term synaptic facilitation in Aplysia neurons. *Science, 249,* 799–802.

Greenfield, S. (1997). *The human brain: A guided tour.* New York: Basic Books.

Guenther, R. (1998). *Human cognition.* Englewood Cliffs, NJ: Prentice Hall.

Hargreaves, A., & Fink, D. (2006). *Sustainable leadership.* San Francisco: Jossey-Bass.

Healy, J. (1990). *Endangered minds: Why children don't think–and what we can do about it.* New York: Touchstone.

Hebb, D. (1949). *The organization of behavior.* New York: John Wiley & Sons.

Hirst, W., Spelke, E., Reaves, C., Charack, G., & Neisser, U. (1980). Dividing attention without alteration or automaticity. *Journal of Experimental Psychology, 109,* 98–117.

Hunter, M. (2004). *Mastery learning.* Thousand Oaks, CA: Corwin Press.

Jensen, E. (2000). *Brain-based learning: The new science of teaching and training* (rev. ed.). Thousand Oaks, CA: Corwin Press.

Jones, S. (2003). *Blueprint for student success: A guide to research-based teaching practices K–12.* Thousand Oaks, CA: Corwin Press.

Kotulak, R. (1996). *Inside the brain: Revolutionary discoveries of how the mind works.* Kansas City, MO: Andrews McMeel.

Lambert, L. (1998). *Building leadership capacity in schools.* Alexandria, VA: Association for Supervision and Curriculum Development.

LeDoux, J. (1996). *The emotional brain: The mysterious underpinnings of emotional life.* New York: Simon & Schuster.

LeDoux, J. (2002). *Synaptic self: How our brains become who we are.* New York: Viking Penguin.

Lerner, R., & Hood, K. (1986). Plasticity in development: Concepts and issues for intervention. *Journal of Applied Developmental Psychology, 7,* 139–52.

Levine, M. (2002). *A mind at a time: America's top learning expert shows how every child can succeed.* New York: Simon & Schuster.

Martin, K., & Kandal, R. (1996). Cell adhesion molecules, CREB, and the formation of new synaptic connections. *Neuron, 17,* 567–70.

Marzano, R., Norford, J., Paynter, D., Pickering, D., & Gaddy, B. (2001). *A handbook for classroom instruction that works.* Alexandria, VA: Association for Supervision and Curriculum Development.

National Research Council. (2000). *How people learn: Brain, mind, experience, and school.* Washington, DC: National Academy Press.

National Storytelling Association. (1994). *Tales as tools.* Jonesborough, TN: National Storytelling Press.

Restack, R. (2000). *Mysteries of the mind.* Washington, DC: National Geographic Society.

Restack, R. (2001). *The secret life of the brain.* Washington, DC: Joseph Henry Press.

Saphier, J., & Gower, R. (1997). *The skillful teacher: Building your teaching skills.* Acton, MA: Research for Better Teaching, Inc.

Schacter, D. (2001). *The seven sins of memory.* Boston: Houghton Mifflin.

Sousa, D. (2006). *How the brain learns* (3rd ed.). Thousand Oaks, CA: Corwin Press.

Sprenger, M. (2002). *Becoming a "wiz" at brain-based teaching: How to make every year your best year.* Thousand Oaks, CA: Corwin Press.

Stiegler, J., & Hiebert, J. (1999). *The teaching gap: Best ideas from the world's teachers for improving education in the classroom.* New York: The Free Press.

Sylwester, R. (1995). *Celebration of neurons: An educator's guide to the human brain.* Alexandria, VA: Association for Supervision and Curriculum Development.

Wiggins, G., & McTighe, J. (2006). *Understanding by design* (2nd ed.). Upper Saddle River, NJ: Pearson Education, Inc.

Wolfe, P. (2001). *Brain matters: Translating research into classroom practice.* Alexandria, VA: Association for Supervision and Curriculum Development.

Index

CORWIN PRESS

The Corwin Press logo—a raven striding across an open book—represents the union of courage and learning. Corwin Press is committed to improving education for all learners by publishing books and other professional development resources for those serving the field of PreK–12 education. By providing practical, hands-on materials, Corwin Press continues to carry out the promise of its motto: **"Helping Educators Do Their Work Better."**